27 C0 ABH 455

PROJECT MANAGEMENT FOR PROFIT

ELLIS HORWOOD SERIES IN MECHANICAL ENGINEERING

Series Editor: J. M. ALEXANDER, formerly Stocker Visiting Professor of Engineering and Technology, Ohio University, Athens, USA, and Professor of Applied Mechanics, Imperial College of Science and Technology, University of London

The series has two objectives: of satisfying the requirements of postgraduate and mid-career engineers, and of providing clear and modern texts for more basic undergraduate topics. It is also the intention to include English translations of outstanding texts from other languages, introducing works of international merit. Ideas for enlarging the series are always welcomed.

Alexander, J.M.	**Strength of Materials: Vol. 1: Fundamentals; Vol. 2: Applications**
Alexander, J.M., Brewer, R.C. & Rowe, G.	**Manufacturing Technology Volume 1: Engineering Materials**
Alexander, J.M., Brewer, R.C. & Rowe, G.	**Manufacturing Technology Volume 2: Engineering Processes**
Atkins A.G. & Mai, Y.W.	**Elastic and Plastic Fracture**
Beards, C.F.	**Vibration Analysis and Control System Dynamics**
Beards, C.F.	**Structural Vibration Analysis**
Beards, C.F.	**Noise Control**
Beards, C.F.	**Vibrations and Control Systems**
Borkowski, J. and Szymanski, A.	**Technology of Abrasives and Abrasive Tools**
Borkowski, J. and Szymanski, A.	**Uses of Abrasives and Abrasive Tools**
Brook, R. and Howard, I.C.	**Introductory Fracture Mechanics**
Cameron, A.	**Basic Lubrication Theory, 3rd Edition**
Collar, A.R. & Simpson, A.	**Matrices and Engineering Dynamics**
Cookson, R.A. & El-Zafrany, A.	**Finite Element Techniques for Engineering Analysis**
Cookson, R.A. & El-Zafrany, A.	**Techniques of the Boundary Element Method**
Edmunds, H.G.	**Mechanical Foundations of Engineering Science**
Fenner, D.N.	**Engineering Stress Analysis**
Fenner, R.T.	**Engineering Elasticity**
Ford, Sir Hugh, FRS, & Alexander, J.M.	**Advanced Mechanics of Materials, 2nd Edition**
Gallagher, C.C. & Knight, W.A.	**Group Technology Production Methods in Manufacture**
Gohar, R.	**Elastohydrodynamics**
Haddad, S.D. & Watson, N.	**Principles and Performance in Diesel Engineering**
Haddad, S.D. & Watson, N.	**Design and Applications in Diesel Engineering**
Haddad, S.D.	**Advanced Diesel Engineering and Operation**
Hunt, S.E.	**Nuclear Physics for Engineers and Scientists**
Irons, B.M. & Ahmad, S.	**Techniques of Finite Elements**
Irons, B.M. & Shrive, N.G.	**Finite Element Primer**
Johnson, W. & Mellor, P.B.	**Engineering Plasticity**
Kleiber, M.	**Incremental Finite Element Modelling in Non-linear Solid Mechanics**
Kleiber, M. & Breitkopf, P.	**Finite Element Methods in Structural Engineering: Turbo Pascal Programs for Microcomputers**
Leech, D.J. & Turner, B.T.	**Engineering Design for Profit**
Leech, D.J. & Turner, B.T.	**Project Management for Profit**
Lewins, J.D.	**Engineering Thermodynamics**
Malkin, S.	**Materials Grinding: Theory and Applications of Machining with Abrasives**
Maltbaek, J.C.	**Dynamics in Engineering**
McCloy, D. & Martin, H.R.	**Control of Fluid Power: Analysis and Design, 2nd (Revised) Edition**
Osyczka, A.	**Multicriterion Optimisation in Engineering**
Oxley, P.L.B.	**The Mechanics of Machining**
Piszcek, K. and Niziol, J.	**Random Vibration of Mechanical Systems**
Polanski, S.	**Bulk Containers: Design and Engineering of Surfaces and Shapes**
Prentis, J.M.	**Dynamics of Mechanical Systems, 2nd Edition**
Renton, J.D.	**Applied Elasticity**
Richards, T.H.	**Energy Methods in Vibration Analysis**
Ross, C.T.F.	**Computational Methods in Structural and Continuum Mechanics**
Ross, C.T.F.	**Finite Element Programs for Axisymmetric Problems in Engineering**
Ross, C.T.F.	**Finite Element Methods in Structural Mechanics**
Ross, C.T.F.	**Applied Stress Analysis**
Ross, C.T.F.	**Advanced Applied Stress Analysis**
Ross, C.T.F.	**Finite Element Methods in Engineering Science**
Roy, D. N.	**Applied Fluid Mechanics**
Roznowski, T.	**Moving Heat Sources in Thermoelasticity**
Sawczuk, A.	**Mechanics and Plasticity of Structures**
Sherwin, K.	**Engineering Design for Performance**
Stupnicki, J.	**Stress Measurement by Photoelastic Coating**
Szczepinski, W. & Szlagowski, J.	**Plastic Design of Complex Shape Structured Elements**
Thring, M.W.	**Robots and Telechirs**
Walshaw, A.C.	**Mechanical Vibrations with Applications**
Williams, J.G.	**Fracture Mechanics of Polymers**
Williams, J.G.	**Stress Analysis of Polymers 2nd (Revised) Edition**

ELLIS HORWOOD SERIES IN AUTOMATED MANUFACTURING

Series Editor: COLIN BESANT, Professor of Computer-Aided Manufacture, Imperial College of Science and Technology, London University

Besant, C.B. & Lui, C.W.K.	**Computer-aided Design and Manufacture, 3rd Edition**
Ding, Q.L. & Davies, B.J.	**Surface Engineering Geometry for Computer-aided Design and Manufacture**
Gosman, B.E., Launder, A.D. & Reece, G.	**Computer-aided Engineering: Heat Transfer and Fluid Flow**
Gunasekera, J.S.	**CAD/CAM of Dies**
Vickers, G.W., Ly, M. & Oetter, R.G.	**Numerically Controlled Machine Tools**

PROJECT MANAGEMENT FOR PROFIT

D. J. LEECH
B. T. TURNER
Department of Management Science and Statistics
University College of Swansea

ELLIS HORWOOD
NEW YORK   LONDON   TORONTO   SYDNEY   TOKYO   SINGAPORE

658.404
L 483

First published in 1990 by
ELLIS HORWOOD LIMITED
Market Cross House, Cooper Street,
Chichester, West Sussex, PO19 1EB, England

A division of
Simon & Schuster International Group
A Paramount Communications Company

© Ellis Horwood Limited, 1990

All rights reserved. No part of this publication may be reproduced, stored in a retrieval
system, or transmitted, in any form, or by any means, electronic, mechanical, photocopying,
recording or otherwise, without the prior permission, in writing, of the publisher

Printed and bound in Great Britain
by Bookcraft (Bath) Limited, Midsomer Norton, Avon

British Library Cataloguing in Publication Data

Leech, D. J.
Project management for profit.
1. Project management
I. Title. II. Turner, B. T.
658.404
ISBN 0–13–721887–7

Library of Congress Cataloging-in-Publication Data available

Table of contents

Acknowledgements

Turner and Leech are not the only authors of this book. Cliff Jones contributed to Chapter 2, Rhys Williams wrote Chapter 11 and Bob Harris wrote Chapter 12. The programs used in Chapters 4 and 12 were developed from the work of many people. Farhad Etemad wrote the program to determine the net present value and rate of return of a cash flow stream; Bob Harris wrote the critical path programs, using as a basis earlier work by Kathy Marklew.

The Ministry of Defence Procurement Executive provided much information in discussions, particularly for Chapter 5.

And Nicola typed from an almost illegible manuscript.

But Turner and Leech were the editors, as well as authors, and any faults are theirs.

1

Introduction—the nature of project management

When a major engineering project fails, it is not usually because the technical problems that it poses are thought to be insoluble. It is much more likely that the technical problems are not expected to be solved within the money that the customer is prepared to pay or the time that he is prepared to allow. As technology progresses, we must accept more exacting standards of management as well as more exacting standards of engineering.

Not only are today's engineering projects becoming more complex, expensive and time consuming but also each project impinges on others. Infrastructure projects in road or rail transport or in telecommunications can greatly affect the way that people live while an electronic data-processing project may completely change the way that a company operates. Change, too, produces a seemingly endless confrontation in which continuous improvement and replacement are required in a climate of ever-developing technology. This is particularly the case with defence projects where research and development, as much as manufacture, must be mobilized to ensure that equipment is up to date and in a state of readiness.

The process of bringing new projects on stream and into the market imposes special demands on established organizations and requires very different management techniques from those needed to maintain day-to-day operations. Projects call for more and faster decisions than normal routine work does, and clear precedents are usually absent.

In general, any engineering business can carry on its conventional marketing, research and development, and design and production activities with reasonable effectiveness and with each of these functional groups looking after itself. In such circumstances each group typically is concerned with the maintenance and improvement of its specialized competence, but the development of new ideas into commercially viable projects demands a different outlook and behaviour. The very nature of project management cuts across the established organization structure of a company, requiring contributions from personnel at various levels in many functions of the business. The duty of a project manager is to ensure that the overall objectives of the project are met, on time and within the allowed cost. To do this he must coordinate the efforts of many people who work in more specialist disciplines. Traditionally, information flows vertically in an organization: from the draughtsman to the designer, from the designer to the chief designer, from the chief designer to the technical director, from the fitter to the charge hand, from the charge hand to the foreman, from the foreman to the production manager, etc., and perhaps the directing of effort flows downwards. However, if a project is to be managed successfully, information must flow laterally in the organization: from the salesman to the designer, from the draughtsman to the fitter, and from the service engineer to the draughtsman. If project messages (whether information or directives) have to be sent up the hierarchical tree and down another branch to be transmitted from one functional area to another, the performance of those who manage the project is inevitably throttled back. Clearly, project management requires the introduction of new organizational forms to complement or replace the traditional pyramid structure.

To be successful, project management must embrace three major qualities.

- Firstly, a 'systems approach' that considers the market (customer or client), engineering (research and development, production or construction, commissioning), post-start-up feedback of information and product support.
- Secondly an organization that is appropriately staffed and structured to enable the necessary skills and resources to be mobilized to bring about the timely execution of the project.
- Thirdly a management style which ensures the optimum use of resources and deployment of personnel.

No one formula can offer success because there are uncertainties in the realization of any project and because each organization is unique and works in a unique environment, but new thinking about project work and the innovative process and experience gained from the management of earlier projects can point to preferred ways of dealing with problems.

Projects come and go within an organization and are of different sizes and complexities. In general a project may be defined as a new unit of industrial investment which has some distinct or unique features. At one end of the spectrum there is the large capital project such as a new power station, a water conservation project, or a new transport system, which is characterized by high-cost large-size complex technology, some innovation, some unique qualities and a limited time scale within which design, development and manufacture (or construction) has to take place. There is generally a high degree of interdependence between the activities of the project and this is often aggravated by the participation of many subcontractors. Reliability and safety are usually of concern, and since only one or two pieces of equipment may be produced, proof of integrity, as with all development, is difficult. Such projects can represent substantial proportions of the national economy, and failure may have grave consequences.

At the other end of the spectrum a project may be of comparatively small size but, nevertheless, have unique technological features. Small projects are likely to exist in a multiproject situation, competing with other projects for resources and effort. This situation will almost certainly demand as much management as technological skill.

It is rare that a company will exist for the management of only one project. If this is the case, that project is likely to be so large that activities within the project will require individual management and will compete for resources. More generally, however, a company will have many projects alive at any one time and these projects will compete for attention and resources. It will be argued in Chapter 2 that the management of any company can be resolved into the management of a portfolio of projects and that the planning and management of these projects are a major pert of the development and operation of the company's corporate plan. Each project must be budgeted for and must contribute to the company's well-being. Each project competes with every other for finance, manpower and equipment and each project must be an essential part of an optimal plan. Broadly, a plan is optimal if it is such that, were any project dropped, the company would be less profitable. Senior project managers must know the place of their projects in the corporate plan because they cannot properly manage them if they do not understand their interdependence and also because they will be required to contribute to the formulation of the plan.

Traditionally, innovation and invention have been the most admired qualities of an engineer, but a new idea is the easiest and cheapest part of a project to provide. At its simplest, a manufacturing project proceeds from idea to scheme, from scheme to drawings, from drawings to planning, from planning to tooling, from tooling to manufacture, from manufacture to development, from manufacture to sale, from sale to product support, from sale to eventual obsolescence and decommissioning. All these stages (and usually many more) are essential in the life of a project and most of them are more expensive than scheming and drawing. However, these stages are interrelated—bad design can mean expensive manufacture or poor reliability (leading to expensive product support); bad tooling can mean expensive manufacture; bad product support can lead to expensive operation and downtime. Chapter 3 discusses, briefly, the stages in the life cycle of a project because these define the milestones in its life and against which its management must be monitored.

Most companies are in business to make money, and profit is the yardstick by which they judge success or failure. Even a social project—within the National Health Service, say—must be controlled in its spending if it is to be run efficiently. Each activity in a project generates a cash flow—a few pounds worth of design hours to scheme the product, several hundred million pounds to build the tooling, a trickle of revenue from the customer, etc.—and ultimately, the significance of any project to a company is that it is a stream of cash flows. Early cash flows are usually negative as design, development and manufacture are paid for and these must be repaid, with interest, by the positive cash flows that sales will eventually generate. Whatever his technical achievements, the project manager will have succeeded if the net effect of the cash flow stream that his project generates is a competitive use of his company's capital. He must predict the cash flows and manage his project by monitoring performance against predictions. Chapter 4 discusses projects as cash flow streams. In the course of this chapter, discounted cash flow calculations are described and computer programs used to demonstrate these calculations.

A project must be generated, evaluated and selected by considering the contribution that it will make to the company. Usually this means that a project will be generated and valued for the profit that it is expected to make in the context of the company's existing business, but some projects are not profitable by themselves—they make other profitable projects possible. In the end, the cash flows generated by the company's portfolio of projects must make a profitable company. We cannot always be deterministic or even accurate in our prediction of the cash flows that a project will generate and many of our judgements must be subjective. However subjective our decision-making process, it must be controlled. It must be controlled because the decision-making process is, itself, expensive and any expensive operation must be controlled but also because control can improve the chances that this expensive decision-making process will, more often, make the correct judgements. Chapter 5 discusses the generation, evaluation and selection of projects, using commonly available procedures as a basis for this management process.

The objectives of project management are to supply the required goods or services for an agreed cost and within an agreed time and these objectives will be the bases of a contract between the project manager's company and the client (or customer). There is plenty of good advice on the form that a contract should take (from the major engineering institutions, for example) but skill, experience and effort are still required if the project manager is to commit himself to the scope, timing and price of the work that he is to do. A major problem is the apportioning of risk and incentive. There is no doubt that a 'fixed price contract' provides the project manager with considerable incentive because his company will lose money if he does not do the work within his budget but, if the work is innovative, the project manager may feel that there is too much risk for him to accept a 'fixed price'. Sometimes it may be necessary for the contract to be for 'costs plus' in which the contractor receives a profit, however much the work over-runs time and cost targets. Generally, of course, both risk and profit (or loss) will be shared by the contractor and the client. Chapter 6 discusses the skills that are required to formulate a contract and the forms of contract which provide incentives to good management.

'Brochuremanship' was often used as a term of abuse in the 1960s, by potential customers who believed that suppliers were better at making proposals than at delivering hardware. The implication was that a company that had produced good hardware in the past would not need to be eloquent in describing what it would do in the future. However, when a customer specifies, in a detailed way, what he requires, when the means of meeting the specification has some novelty, when the project is expensive, when it is known that circumstances will modify the requirements, and, above all, when the proposal will form the basis of a contract between supplier and customer, serious consideration must be given to its preparation. The proposal is the prospective supplier's response to an invitation to tender, but it is not merely an advertisement; it is a demonstration that the proposer has understood the customer's needs, that he can produce a system that will meet those needs and that the system will be shown to meet those needs and will be supported when it is in service. The proposal is also a document which will demonstrate the technical and managerial capabilities of the company to meet the product requirements. This may necessitate spending 10% or 15% of the total project costs before a decision is taken to buy the system or not. Chapter 7 discusses the form that proposals might take and the disciplines of preparing them.

A proposal may be rejected in favour of one from a competitor or it may be accepted, but it is unlikely to be accepted without question or modification. The proposal is the basis of the contract but it is not, itself, the contract, and between the proposal and the commitment to a contract there will be long hard negotiation. Chapter 8 discusses this process.

Conventional groupings of men and procedures do not cope well with project work. It is difficult, having divided the workforce into sharply differentiated units with specialized duties, to diffuse responsibility for cost and performance in a rapidly changing situation. The specialized units strive to perpetuate their own interests and privileges rather than to give and take men, time and budgets. The pursuit of the project objectives requires a more single-minded attitude than can be provided by the co-operation, however willing, of several men with departmental responsibilities. The speed at which decisions must be taken leads to the establishment of a separate network of reporting and control which cuts across existing functional boundaries. Competence in departmental procedures is no recommendation to meet the demands of a project where tactics and criteria may be modified from week to week. Reference has already been made to the fact that project work demands a different outlook and behaviour to the normal modes established by a conventional structure of a company. The situation is confused by the fact that the project manager is not always assigned complete responsibility for resources. Generally he has to share these with the rest of the organization. The main characteristic of a project organization is the exceptionally strong lateral working relationships demanded, necessitating close co-ordination between many individuals in differing functions. This inevitably produces conflict which the project manager has to handle carefully. Chapter 9 sets out alternative project structures which may be used. While there is no ideal organization for executing projects, some do work better than others in particular situations, and the advantages and disadvantages are listed.

Before a project may be managed, it must be broken down into a series of essential elements. The objective of each element will be defined and the effort and cost required to meet the objective must be evaluated. These objectives and time and cost budgets provide the basis of the management plan which is usually summarized as a bar chart or activity network. The plan and its reference points obviously permit us to monitor actual progress against required progress but they also provide the framework for dynamic management in the sense that the inevitable changes (to requirements and achievements) will be detected and means of bringing the overall project back on course will be demonstrated. Chapter 10 discusses the nature of the project plan, its formulation and operation.

Planning involves prediction. If we are to set milestones on the route of project management, we must know what it should cost us, in time and money, to reach each of these milestones. Predicting the cost (or duration) of an activity is difficult and there have been many well-publicized cases of our underestimating the difficulty and cost of major projects. We shall never be able to predict the future accurately, but disciplines have been developed which make us less likely to make mistakes. Chapter 11 discusses the problems of predicting costs and some of the techniques which go some way towards reducing those problems.

At the heart of project management are critical path methods. They provide the basis of any proposals and the programme against which the achievements are monitored. Chapter 12 summarizes these methods of time analysis and resource management. In addition to the manual methods, computer programs are discussed and an example provided of a simple computer program that will offer time and resource management.

When a project has been broken down into its activities and when times and costs have been budgeted, we have the milestones against which the project will be managed. Usually, the activity managers will meet regularly, under the chairmanship of the project manager, to monitor progress against the milestones and to determine any action that is needed if times and costs are slipping. The reporting methods and the procedures for project meetings are discussed in Chapter 13

The project manager is concerned with achieving adequate technical performance within agreed time and cost budgets, as specified in the contract, while making effective use of company resources. But what kind of person makes an ideal project manager? A cursory glance at the current advertisements for project managers shows that a wide range of qualities which include high engineering qualifications, ability at languages, expert knowledge of management techniques, organizational ability and financial acumen are asked for. A successful candidate is also required to have the strength of personality to motivate and control highly qualified teams of people. The ideal project manager is a superman—on the one hand he has to be an advocate and on the other a diplomat for he acts as a mediator between his company and the customer, subcontractors and other agencies.

It has been said, in the aerospace industry, that the project manager stands at the point where technical and managerial aspects intersect. If he does not know how to handle his project both technically and financially, no amount of argument and no amount of money will make a success of the programme. Chapter 14 discusses the skills and qualities demanded of a project manager.

However he is selected, the project manager must be responsible for the following.

— **Project definition**, so that he may properly serve the interests of his client.
— **Work definition**. Not only the final objectives but the intermediate accomplishments which lay down the route by which the final objectives are to be achieved.
— **Money**. The payment of which is monitored against the budget he has set for the project.
— **Placing work and ordering material.**
— **The programme.**
— **Control**. Monitoring progress, identifying problems and taking action.
— **Sweeping-up operations**. Ensuring a smooth handover to the customer, monitoring performance after commissioning and finally writing a project audit.

Note that computer programs are referred to in Chapters 4 and 12. Much use can be made of commercially available spreadsheet packages and project management packages. Nevertheless, the authors can make available simple (basic) programs for making discounted-cash-flow calculations of cash flow streams and for making time and resource analyses of simple project networks.

2

Project management within a corporate strategy

2.1 KNOWING THE MARKET

Manufacturing companies are becoming increasingly aware that their policies must be market led. The Engineering Council recommend technical reviews [1] which encourage the company to '... develop new products which properly anticipate market opportunities at home and abroad. ...' and assess '... markets, their development, and ... competition', while their guide to managing design [2] suggests that design must start with a clarification of the true market need. Many manufacturing companies—probably most that are successful— build organizational structures that are intended to ensure that there is close liason between marketing and engineering and that marketing will provide a major contribution to the determination of any corporate plan.

Common sense should dictate that a project cannot reasonably be started until its objectives have been defined but common sense does not always prevail. Military projects usually start with a broad statement of the requirement of the Ministry of Defence and the opportunity to spend time and money to create a more detailed specification of needs. If a military project is generated by the company that intends to make and sell the system (say a weapon system), then the company itself must budget for the expenditure of money to determine and define the requirements of that system. Generally, of course, both the potential customer and the supplier know what business the supplier is in and so both the invitation to tender and the response are made in the context of past achievements in a known field and in the knowledge that the innovative content of the project will be a comparatively small part of whatever system is eventually offered.

The procedure is not significantly different when the projects are civil. If there is a difference, it is probably that neither the supplier nor the customer is as careful as the Ministry of Defence in defining the objectives of a project nor as formal in their methods of achieving them.

Specifying, designing, developing and building hardware (or a service) for sale are not the only forms of project. Research to keep abreast of technology, the installation of new manufacturing machinery, new test equipment or new management systems, the recruitment and training of staff in new skills are all examples of projects which are not directly profitable but which are necessary if profitable projects are to be undertaken. Most companies have many projects alive at any one time and no project may be treated in isolation. Different projects will use common resources—men, skills, money, capital equipment and time—and although each project may be generated, directly or indirectly, by market forces its management must be dovetailed into the management of all the other projects in the company. It takes more than marketing skills to do this and an overall company plan must be developed by all the disciplines that will be required to operate it—financial, marketing, engineering and production.

2.2 COMPANY PLANNING

There are usually two plans: a long-range plan and a short-range plan. The short-range plan, which may be for a year, will be fairly precise because it must determine what will be sold, what will be made, what capital investment will be necessary, how many workers must be employed and what their skills need to be, and what materials must be bought.

The long-range plan, which may be for 5 (or even 10) years, will be less precise because it is not possible to say what the future will bring. Nevertheless, the managers must know where they expect the company to be in 5 or 10 years' time and the short-range plan must be consistent with the longer-term prediction. It would be silly, for example, if the long-range plan envisaged a major change in manufacturing technology while the short-term plan required a large investment in the currently available manufacturing plant.

2.2.1 The long-range plan

The long-range plan may be for 5 years or, in some businesses, as much as 10 years. The horizon chosen depends on the technology with which the company is involved, the size of the investment and the nature of the market. Obviously, the longer the horizon, the less accurate any prediction will be.

Changing technology creates a need for long-range planning and an example of this was given by a company making cheap watches. The change from clockwork mechanisms to electronic battery-powered watches required new designs, new manufacturing methods and new skills, all of which required more lead time than could be provided within the horizon of a detailed short-range plan. In the event, the new technology was forecast and design work commissioned but the new designs were developed too late by the consultants and the company lost its market to competitors.

Other examples could be the change from propeller-driven to jet-driven aeroplanes and its effect on aircraft manufacturers, the development of carbon fibre and its use in aeroplane engines, the change from black-and-white to colour television, and the reduction in the cost of computers which makes them available for use in the management of small businesses; there are many more situations in which failure to predict and take account of technological changes will spell death to a company.

Changes in future markets must also be predicted and it is possible to think of many projects which have been generated by predicted market changes or which have failed because market changes were not predicted.

Examples could be the effect of the publication of the relationship between ill health and smoking which has led tobacco companies into diversification, the increase in legislation about permissible car exhaust emissions which requires a design response from motor car manufacturers, current argument by members of the European Economic Community about generating projects to cut the emissions from coal-fired power stations, which contribute to acid rain, and the expected European legislation on beverage containers [3], which requires a response from tinplate manufacturers; there are many other examples from history of the need for a sufficiently long-range prediction of markets to permit response from the engineering department of the company. Ansoff [4] has described this as looking for a weak signal.

Much of long-range planning involves technological forecasting. It is necessary to forecast what technology will be used in manufacture, what technology will be expected by the customer and how the reduced prices brought about by improved technology will change the demand for and the role of the product sold. Superimposed on the effects of technological changes will be demographic and social changes.

The point about long-range planning is that it provides constraints on the short-range plan. Equipping a factory with new machines will be planned in the short term but this cannot ignore the likelihood of obsolescence and the possible need to replace the plant by more advanced machinery before it is worn out. Similarly, a belief that technology will change must generate projects which recruit and train new staff or which buy the new knowledge from more forward-looking companies.

The senior managers of a company must determine the long-range plan and must be responsible for its effect on the short-range plan. The detailed results of the long-range plan will, in fact, be such parts of the short-range plan as

— the amount of money to invest in research,
— the objectives of the research,
— the time over which new investments must pay for themselves,
— the amount of money to invest in new buildings,
— the likely changes needed in labour skills,
— etc.

The long-range planning must be initiated from the top and eventually published from the top, although managers lower in the hierarchy will be asked to contribute their ideas and information.

The need for long-range planning diminishes if the company can respond quickly to environmental changes. Changes in skirt length demanded by fashion can be catered for very quickly; changes in turbine blade material may be made several times within the life of an engine, to improve its efficiency; small design changes suggested by value engineering exercises may be accomplished without long lead times. What distinguishes long-range from short-range planning is as much the time needed to respond to a perceived need to change as the ability to look far into the future.

Usually both sorts of planning are necessary. While a fashion house may survive for generations by making small changes with short lead times, a major engine company will, from time to time, have to make large changes with lead times of many years as well as continuous small changes within each engine. A company making motor cars will have to make major model and tooling changes every 10 years or so as well as continuous small changes within each model.

Every company must ask itself the following questions.

— How often should a long-range plan be formulated?
— What procedure should be adopted for formulating a long-range plan?
— What costs are involved in the formulation of a long-range plan?
— What costs might be generated by failure to formulate a long-range plan?
— How should the long-range plan be published?
— Why not let the company die?

2.2.2 The short-range plan

The short-range plan will probably have a horizon of a year against the long-range plan's 5 or 10 years but of much more significance is that the short-range plan provides the detailed programme against which each departmental manager must manage, while the long-range plan provides constraints against which the short-range plan is formulated. The short-range plan more obviously provides targets and budgets for the manager and for simplicity it will be referred to as the plan.

Deriving the plan is an iterative process which may be described by Fig. 2.1.

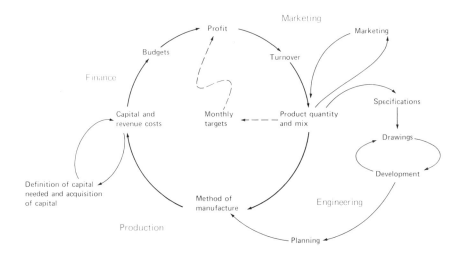

Fig. 2.1 — Stages in corporate planning.

We may start at any point on the circle to commence the iteration.

Assume that the managing director starts by specifying an acceptable profit.

The financial director and the marketing director will know, at least approximately, what value of goods must be sold to generate this profit. Further, the marketing director must be able to say what goods may be sold, at what price, to generate the required turnover.

When the product mix (and product value) has been specified, the technical director must be able to say what drawings (or other specifications of goods to be made) must be issued and when they will be issued.

When the product mix has been specified and descriptions provided of the goods yet to be designed, the production planners will be able to derive a manufacturing programme for the year. This programme will specify the labour required, the materials required and any capital investment necessary for the manufacture of the goods.

When the necessary capital investment has been specified, the financial director must believe that it can be raised and paid for.

The costs of manufacture and the return from sales determine the profit. This profit must be acceptable, although necessary compromise may mean that it is not the value that was originally specified.

Initially, it is unlikely that the marketing director will be able to specify a product mix that he is sure the customer will buy in sufficient quantity and at a high enough price to generate the profit that is required. Even when he can determine a saleable and adequate product mix, it is unlikely to be one that the production director will be able to make in the time or with the resources that can be made available. When a product mix has been determined that will be adequate, saleable and makeable, it is likely that some of the goods specified cannot be developed in time or that more capital will be required than can be raised.

At each stage in the iteration, the following **gaps** will become apparent.

— Gaps between what is needed to generate the profit and what the customer will buy.
— Gaps between what has to be made and what can be developed.
— Gaps between predicted manufacturing costs and acceptable manufacturing costs.
— Gaps between the required capital investment and the capital available.

Methods of closing these gaps must be devised. At each iteration the gaps become fewer and smaller until a plan is derived which satisfies everybody, as follows.

— The marketing director agrees that he can sell what must be sold at a price that the customer will pay and which gives an acceptable profit.
— The production director agrees that he can make what is to be sold, when it is required and at a cost which gives an acceptable profit.
— The technical director agrees that he can develop what has to be developed, when it is required and at a cost that gives an acceptable profit.
— The financial director agrees that he can raise any money needed by the plan at costs which are acceptable and that cash flow problems will not arise.

The role of marketing (in formulating the plan)
The marketing department must determine for next year (or for the plan's horizon) the following.

(1)   What products (or service) the customer will buy.
(2)   How many of each product the customer will buy (or how much of each service).
(3)   How much the customer will pay (the price will, of course be related to the quantity sold).
(4)   When the product must be available.
(5)   For how long the customer will buy the product.
(6)   What the competition is.
(7)   What related services will be required (e.g. spares, customer training and after-sales service).

Subsidiary problems for the marketing director are as follows.

(8) How much he needs to spend to get the information.
(9) How much he needs to spend to provide continuing service.

The marketing director must know the sort of ratio of **profit to turnover** to expect. This varies from one type of business to another. A typical figure is 7%.

The marketing director and the gap
The market changes; technology changes. If the first guess at the product mix and product quantity does not satisfy the plan, there will be a gap. The marketing director must modify the product mix by adding new products, modifying old products, changing selling tactics, identifying new markets and modifying prices until the gap is closed.

The role of production (in formulating the plan)
Assuming that the marketing director provides a first estimate of next year's product mix, the production director must determine the following.

(1) What mix of labour skills will be required to make the products.
(2) What the cost of labour will be.
(3) What raw materials and bought-out parts will be required and what they will cost.
(4) What elapsed time will be required to manufacture the products.
(5) What investment in plant and building will be required to manufacture the products.

The production manager and the gap
If the required product mix (as first estimated) cannot be made by the required time at the required cost, there will be a gap. Checking this will mean relating the required selling price to the required quantity and the acceptable profit-to-turnover ratio. If there is a gap, it may be necessary to re-estimate the product mix but it may be better

(6) to look again at the manufacturing efficiency,
(7) to look again at the manufacturing technology and
(8) to look again at the capital investment.

When the gap is zero, the production director will believe that he can make the goods required in each accounting period of the plan's horizon (an accounting period will probably be a month but will differ from company to company), that he will spend no more in an accounting period on labour and material than has been allowed by the plan and that he will spend no more on capital equipment than the plan allows.

The role of engineering (in formulating the plan)
If the estimate of next year's product mix requires that new products be designed or old products be modified, the technical director must determine the following.

(1) What labour and materials are required to design and develop the new products or the modifications.

(2)   What equipment is required to design and develop the new products or the modifications.

(3)   What elapsed time will be required to design and develop the new products or the modifications.

The Technical director and the gap

If the first estimate of the required product mix cannot be designed in the required time and within the required budget, there will be a gap. If there is a gap, it may be necessary to re-estimate the product mix but it may be better to reconsider the design schemes, the methods of design or the methods of development.

When the gap is zero, the technical director will believe that he can produce the drawings of the developed products by the time that they are needed, that he can produce the drawings of the developed products within his budget and that he can produce the required drawings with the capital equipment for which he has budgeted.

Every department is involved in the long-term plan as well as the plan for next year. The work of the marketing, production and commercial departments must dovetail into the long-range plan and their programme of work must allow for this, but the engineering department will inevitably be spending a very high percentage of its resources on projects which will extend well beyond the period defined by precise total planning. The more distant future affects the engineering department in two major ways.

(1)   It will be working on projects that will not be successful. For example, it will be responding to invitations to tender and a proportion of the tenders made will not be accepted by the customers. The budget for engineering work must accept the need to spend man hours and money on work which will not, invariably, lead directly to profitable projects.

(2)   It will be working on projects with lives of many years. Given a project with a life of many years (such as a large civil aeroplane, a power station, or a suite of management programs), any payments by the customer may come after the horizon of the immediate plan. This must be allowed for when budgeting for the man hours and money needed within the immediate plan's horizon but, more than this, targets must be defined within the plan, which are not immediately defined by payments by the customer. Examples of such targets will be the issue of drawings, the manufacture of prototypes, the solutions of the various specified development problems, environmental testing, life proving and the design of service and spares support systems. Most of these targets will mark stages in a project which must be achieved before payments are made by the customer and which must therefore be defined by something other than money. Sometimes, it will be necessary to break down major objectives into smaller objectives for the sake of good planning and management; thus the issue of drawings may be subdivided into several targets and prototypes may be built to various standards.

The plan must clearly allow for work within the engineering department which does not derive from the design and development of products that are sold within its horizon. Unless this work is allowed for, the many projects that are alive at any one time cannot be co-ordinated and the company's management will be constantly robbing future projects to pay for present embarrassments.

The role of the finance department (in formulating the plan)
Assuming that the marketing, production and technical directors have agreed on a product mix, then the financial director must determine the following.

(1)   Whether the plan will, in fact, be profitable.
(2)   Whether he can raise the capital required for the proposed development and production.
(3)   What working capital the plan will require.
(4)   What is the cost of the capital needed.

The financial director and the gap
If the first estimate of the required project mix demands more captial than can be obtained at any acceptable price, there will be a gap. If there is a gap, it may be necessary to re-estimate the product mix but it may be better to explore such other sources of capital as the European Community and government or local government grants. Sometimes assistance may be indirect, such as that which derives from accelerated plant write-down or benefits which are offered for relocation or job creation.

How do we estimate whether a plan is profitable?
Clearly all the cash flows out of the company must add up to no more than the sum of all the cash flows in. The problem is complicated by the fact that some of the cash flows are interest payments, dividends, taxes and allowances which require the use of discounting and made even more difficult by our inability to forecast cash flows accurately.

Where is capital raised?
Capital may be **equity**, which means that it is provided by the owners of the company or the shareholders. Equity may be raised directly through share issues or indirectly through retention of profits. The other main source of capital is **debt** which means that the capital is borrowed, probably from a bank and possibly at a known interest, but it may be an overdraft at an interest rate that can change from day to day. There is some significance in the proportion of capital which is debt (the capital structure) because this is seen to affect the risk that creditors are taking.

What is working capital?
Working capital is the amount by which current assets exceed current liabilities. Even in a healthy company, bills may come in before the money has been earned to pay them, and working capital may be regarded as a float to cope with this situation. The problem is often said to be one of liquidity and this is measured by the company's liquidity ratio, defined in Chapter 4. Broadly, however, the liquidity ratio is a measure of the company's ability to pay its bills or the float that it must maintain to be able to satisfy creditors before customers pay for the goods that they buy.

In today's financial climate a plan, or a project within a plan, is more likely to be killed by lack of working capital than by technical failure, and no project manager may permit himself the luxury of giving less consideration to the timing of cash flows than to the solution of technical problems. Sometimes, insufficient consideration is given to the balance between fixed and working assets; for example, more investment in plant may result in apparent underutilization but be rewarded by reductions in the stocks of raw materials, work in progress and finished goods required to keep pace with market demand.

How much will capital cost?

Whatever the source of capital, whether it is debt or equity, it will have a cost. Thus, when a shareholder invests money in the company, he will hope for a dividend and an increase in the value of his shares; when a bank lends money to a company, it will expect that money to be repaid with interest. For every pound that is invested in a company, more than a pound will have to be repaid. The providers of the capital are, in effect, selling it to the company at more than its face value; capital has a cost. Debt is generally less expensive than equity because it is assumed that, because creditors are paid before shareholders, they take less risk. Again, debt is cheaper than its nominal interest rate would imply because the interest payments are a tax-allowable expense.

The true cost of capital to a company (and hence to the project manager) will be the weighted average of the cost of capital from all the different sources, when adjustments have been made for tax allowances.

The significance of working capital and the cost of capital are discussed in more detail in Chapter 4.

The plan is a portfolio of projects

As soon as the plan is formulated, it is likely to become a casualty. If often becomes clear that the marketing director has overestimated the size of the market and the price that the customer will pay, that the marketing director has underestimated the market (although this provides an easier selling job the underestimate could lead to under-investing in tooling) or that prices have been forced down by competition and the production director has underestimated the cost of manufacturing the products. Costs rise above budgets, revenue falls and production targets are not met and it is almost always necessary to set up a cost reduction project.

However, the plan itself will be a portfolio of projects: new products will be designed, developed and built; existing products will be modified, developed and built; existing products will be enhanced in quality or reduced in cost; new environmental requirements will be specified; etc. The collection of all the projects is the plan. Executing the plan is a problem of project management as well as departmental management.

The project is a stream of cash flows

Almost all projects require investment early in their lives for market surveys, design, development and tooling and it is to be hoped that this investment will be repaid when the customer starts to pay for the goods or services that he has bought. Even when a profitable project has reached the stage in its life cycle when there is a net flow of cash inwards, this net flow will be the algebraic sum of positive cash flows from the customer and negative cash flows that pay for manufacture, distribution, servicing, etc. This is shown in Fig. 2.2. Nevertheless, it is to be hoped that, over the life of the project, the early net negative cash flows will be more than recovered by the later net positive cash flows.

We can consider that, when the project generates net negative cash flows, it is borrowing money from the company which the later net positive cash flows will repay.

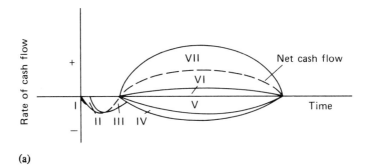

(a)

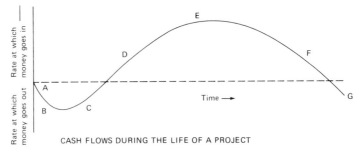

(b)

CASH FLOWS DURING THE LIFE OF A PROJECT

A at the start of the project the net cash flow is small but outwards. The cash flow is the cost of generating and appraising the project.

B all cash flows are negative and consist of the costs of design and development plus any appraisal that may still be going on.

C all cash flows are negative and consist of any continuing design and development costs and the cost of designing and building the manufacturing plant (or tooling).

D the net cash flow is the sum of positive and negative cash flows. Positive cash flows derive from selling the product and supplying any product support which may legitimately be charged to the customer (e.g. servicing; the supply of spares, repair, repair tools, etc. which have been contracted for; the supply of manuals; staff training; etc.).
Negative cash flows derive from modifications, product enhancement, cost reduction exercises and product support costs which cannot be charged to the customer (e.g. warranty costs; modifications which result in failure to meet the specification; etc.) and manufacturing costs.

E the causes of cash flows are approxiamtely the same as at d but sales will have increased, the cost of manufacture will have reduced (learning), develooment will have reduced support costs, etc.

F the **causes of** cash flows are approximately the same as at e but sales will be reducing (through obsolescence and competition) and the declining numbers of the product in service will reduce cash flows (both positive and negative).

G the causes of cash flows are approximately the same as at f but there may also be a large negative cash flow generated by the need to clear up after the projects

Fig. 2.2 — (a) Cash flows during the life of a manufacturing project: curve I, project generation and appraisal (cost); curve II, design and development (cost); curve III, design and building of plant and tooling (cost); curve IV, modification, product enhancement, cost reduction and product support not paid for by the customer (cost); curve V, manufacture (cost); curve VI, product support paid for by the customer (revenue); curve VII, sales to customers (revenue). However, these curves can look like the curve in (b) to the decision maker. (b) White-elephant curve.

The effective interest at which the project is borrowing money is the cost to the company of the capital that it is using.

The arithmetic of the cost of capital and the calculation of the value of a project using discounted-cash-flow (DCF) methods to determine net present values and internal rates of return will be discussed in Chapter 4 when computer aids will be introduced. Nevertheless, it is clear to anyone with a mortgage that, the longer it takes to pay back a loan and the greater the cost of capital (interest, in the case of a mortgage), the more money it takes. For example, if a project generates £1 in 5 years' time and if the cost of capital is 10%, that £1 will repay a debt (or has a present value) of only 62p. If the cost of capital is 20%, £1 generated in 5 years' time will repay a debt of only 40p. If a project generates £1 in 20 years' time, that £1 will repay a debt of only 3p if the cost of capital is 20%. What a future cash flow will repay (its present value) is shown in Fig. 2.3 for costs of capital of 10% and 20%.

One obvious lesson from this is that a project which does not start to earn money until it is several years old must generate huge positive cash flows when it does start to earn; another is that lateness in bringing a project to profitability is very expensive.

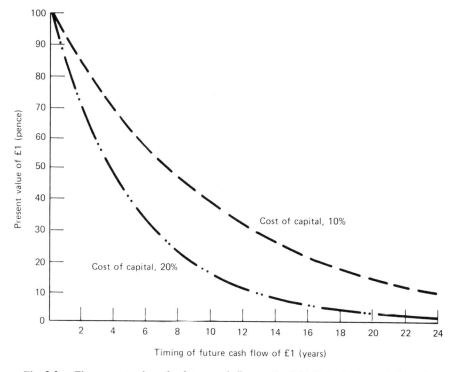

Fig. 2.3 – The present value of a future cash flow or the debt that a future cash flow of £1 will repay.

2.3 THE STRATEGY OF PLANNING

2.3.1 Discounted cash flow is not enough
Future cash flows cannot often be predicted with any great accuracy, and project appraisal and planning will have to make use of subjective methods as well as detailed

cost calculations. Again, we cannot usually plan on a project-by-project basis because we must consider the interaction between projects. While, in principle, we can use DCF methods to study portfolios of projects, there is considerable difficulty in practice and we often have to resort to subjective or heuristic methods. The use of DCF methods when they are inappropriate or the oversimplification of the problem so that DCF methods can be used has been blamed for wrong decisions in the past and even for wrong trends in management [5]. For example, the use (or, more realistically, the improper use) of DCF techniques has been blamed for the 'disinvestment spiral' that has been seen in the USA and for the preference for acquisition rather than internal investment (the take-over boom seen in Britain in the mid-1980s is, perhaps, further evidence of this). The problem is that acquisition is not an increase in investment (and it may even lead to a reduction in investment through rationalization) but only a change in ownership. This reluctance to invest in your own business really results from a misunderstanding of the assumptions about reinvestment that underpin DCF techniques—a misunderstanding which can make it appear more attractive to invest outside the business, in the shares of another company. It is really 'the technicians, not the techniques, (that) are the problem', and 'many DCF analyses of risky projects are overly simplistic and ignore three critical issues that managers and decision makers should consider: the effects of inflation, the different levels of uncertainty, and management's own ability to mitigate risk' [6].

The first of these issues derives from the fact that future cash flows are usually expressed in current values whereas the cost of capital implicitly includes an allowance for inflation. For example, a project manager may finance his project from money from the bank at an interest rate of 17% but, if inflation is at 8%, the true cost of his capital is 8.3%.

The second issue is that the change in risk with time is not understood. As DCF techniques are usually applied, it is assumed that risk increases with time but it can equally well be argued that risk decreases (or, at least, does not increase) because our knowledge of the project increases as we work on it. In BP, as a result of the work of the Post-Project Analysis Unit, it has been found that about 1% of the initially expected project budget is used to pay outside engineers and consultants to develop the case for the project [7] so that very little is being risked at the beginning. This compares with the Ministry of Defence recommendations [8] that about $\frac{1}{2}$% of the estimated cost of design and development of a product should be spent on a feasibility study.

The last, and perhaps most important, issue is that managers fail to realize that *the* investment project, the one at the centre of attention now, will, if accepted, be only a part of a company's overall business and it cannot be studied in isolation. While this problem is theoretically solvable (by a combination of linear programming and DCF techniques, say) the quantity and quality of the information that are needed to justify the computation involved is rarely, if ever, available. There is no virtue in making sophisticated calculations from information which is largely guessed and, if subjective reasoning is to be used, it may as well be used to provide decisions directly rather than to provide input information for a complex mathematical procedure which then generates the decisions. It is clear that a company will not generally put all its eggs into one basket so that risk will be spread over a number of projects. Apart from the inevitable inter-action between projects (calling on the same resources or complementing each other in the market, for example) a company will hope to 'diversify' risk and arguing that risk may be spread over a number of projects does not fully convey the problem. If the eggs are investment funds and the baskets the projects, then putting all the eggs into one basket means investing everything in one project and, if the project is a disaster, then everything is lost. However, if the available funds are spread over several projects and one fails or is not as successful as expected, then there are other projects to fall back on—not all is lost. Also, the reasons for the failure of one project may be exactly the reasons for the increased success of another. Carrying the analogy further, if we drop one basket, this will reduce the supply and increase the price of those that remain. One company with a long history in making metal containers has diversified into the manufacture of plastic containers. Some of its products are complementary but others are substitutes—a plastic container for a metal one. The cost advantage of one container over the other depends on the relative costs of the prime materials; tin and steel versus oil.

Again, projects should not be treated as 'doomsday projects' [5], i.e. projects with no successor, but overtly as part of 'going concerns' [9]. When investment alternatives are considered in the literature, the going concern is often equated with the case of no investment. What is forgotten is that, if all projects are rejected, the company will wither and die. Explicit consideration should be given to the question of corporate renewal and the accounting approach is in danger of ignoring these 'questions of corporate life and death until the time when insolvency becomes a pertinent issue' as well as using conservative predictions of future cash inflows and overinflated rates for the cost of capital that give pessimistic assessments of internal projects [9]. The strategic desirability of corporate renewal projects, other than replacement projects, must be considered as well as their financial desirability and, in practice, this means that, if the project does not yield the company's required return on investment, it could be worth calculating by how much the hurdle rate would have to be reduced to make the project appear acceptable—a strategic discount [9]. The reduction in the hurdle rate would then be balanced against the strategic case for the project. Here one is admitting that there may be limitations in the quantitative information and that there will, inevitably, be significant interdependencies between existing projects and the proposed new investment. In the language of strategy there will be synergy, the 2+2=5 effect [10].

The discussion of corporate renewal is relevant only at the business level and not the corporate level. 'Conceptually, the question of what set of businesses to be in is, and always has been, different from that of how to compete effectually in any given business, even though both are strategy questions' [11]. This relationship between the corporate level and the business level can be dangerous. In some organizations a corporation-wide hurdle rate is set and this rate is based on the overall cost of capital. 'To get projects approved, business-unit managers frequently juggle the numbers (usually boosting their sales estimates) in order to exceed the hurdle' [12]. The distribution of actual returns differs greatly from the distribution of desired returns, the former being much more dispersed than the latter, which tends to be centred just above the cost of capital. 'Corporate management needs to recognize the significance of this wide dispersion of likely incremental returns by business units. Knowing whether a particular business's return on incremental capital invested is likely to be 5% or 50% is critical to effective capital allocations' [12]. This is far more important than worrying about a couple of percentage points' difference in the cost of capital.

In general a business is a collection of investment projects, past, present and future. The past projects have made the business what it is today, the present projects will shape the business future and the future projects ensure the continued survival of the business.

This is the corporate renewal or more appropriately the **business renewal** process. Also, in general, a company is a collection of businesses or, to use a more helpful phrase, a collection of **strategic business units** (SBUs) [13]. Companies become diversified in this way because of the success of the original business. Enough cash has been generated, not merely to sustain the business but also to provide a surplus which requires investment in other areas.

We have already argued that any corporate plan is a portfolio of projects but the importance of projects in a plan is further demonstrated by the following 'old' definitions of Denning [14].

> **Corporate planning** is a formal systematic managerial process, organized by responsibility, time and information to ensure that operational planning, project planning and strategic planning are carried out regularly to enable top management to direct and control the future of the enterprise.
> **Operational planning** is the forward planning of existing operations in existing markets with existing facilities.
> **Project planning** is the generation and appraisal of, the commitment to and the working out of the detailed execution of an action outside the scope of present operations which is capable of separate analysis and control.
> **Strategic planning** is the determination of the future posture of the business with reference to its product-market posture, its profitability, its rate of innovation and its relationships with its executives, its employees, and certain external institutions.

Although Denning writes of 'outside the scope of present operations' and of 'separate analysis', he also states that 'the function of project planning is to assess new projects, to integrate new projects into the firm . . .' [15].

Projects cannot, then, be judged in isolation; they must fit into the strategy of the company since they help to shape its future. DCF techniques can assist with this judgement because they make investment decisions more rational. However, because of the way in which DCF techniques have been used—generally on a project-by-project basis—they have often turned investment decision making into an incremental process which ignores the interaction of projects. DCF may be combined with a technique such as linear programming in order to study project interaction. While we can learn much from such methods, DCF techniques are only useful if the numbers put into them are realistic—and this is rarely the case—and the users of the techniques fully appreciated the assumptions that are implicit in their use.

The past decade or more has seen the development of several 'tools and techniques for strategic management' [16] which have helped in this process. The rest of the chapter will describe some of these concepts.

2.3.2 Cost dynamics: experience and scale effects
The concept of the **experience curve** has been proposed by the Boston Consulting Group (BCG). The experience curve is an extension of the ubiquitous learning curve as applied to labour costs, discovered by a US Air Force officer in the 1920s [17]. The learning curve has shown that for many firms a reduction in unit labour cost of over 10% is achieved each time output is doubled. BCG have discovered that this phenomenon also applies to all other costs. 'After several years of study, and examination of countless

examples, it seems certain that this is a basic phenomenon. . . . it encompasses *all* costs (including capital, administrative, research and marketing) and traces them through technological displacement and product evolution . . . . After examining the costs, prices and market shares of hundreds of companies it seems clear that a large proportion of business success and failure can be explained simply in terms of experience effects' [18].

Typically, the total unit cost reduces by 15–30% for every doubling of experience, experience being usually measured by the total number of units produced. Cost must be measured in constant money terms, i.e. with inflation removed. Suppose the cost of producing the first unit is 100 and the unit cost is expected to follow an 80% experience improvement (i.e. costs are reduced by 20% for every doubling of output), then the experience curve will be as in Fig. 2.4.

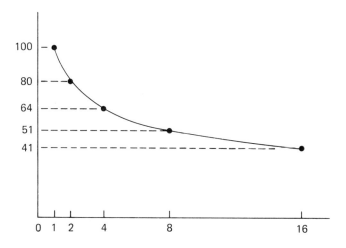

Fig. 2.4 – The experience curve.

The experience curve is discussed in more detail in Chapter 5 and it is sufficient here to remark that the reduction in cost as experience increases is not a natural law; it is the result of good management and, the better the management, the faster costs are reduced.

A business moves between revolutionary and evolutionary stages. The launch of a new product is one of those revolutionary stages. A new factory may be built, or an existing one changed. The layout will be changed, new technology implemented, etc., but it does not end there. There will, or should, be a war of attrition against costs. Work study officers, value engineers, production engineers, management scientists and production operators (often through suggestion schemes) will all play a part. There will be a continual evolution in all aspects of the business; shop floor working practices will be improved, metal parts will be replaced by plastic parts, fabricated parts will be replaced by single formed parts, quality will be improved, layouts will be modified, and selling and distribution methods will be changed.

The phenomenon is not new. The cost of a Boeing aeroplane is reduced and cost reductions are still being achieved in the thousandth aeroplane of a production run [19]. Maytag, the washing machine company, operate a continuous policy of product enhancement and cost reduction over the life of a product. The Volkswagen beetle had a reputation for continuous product enhancement and cost reduction, but cost reduction must not be taken for granted. 'Cumulative experience does not guarantee that costs will decline but simply presents management with an opportunity to exploit' [20].

However, adherence to the experience effect can have its dangers [21]. Ford found to their 'cost' that a blinkered approach to cost reduction can lead to a position where you are the cheapest producer of a product nobody wants to buy. The concept of the 'Model T' was great in the early days of motoring. A no-frills (and no-windows) black motor for the masses. In 1920, Ford dominated the motor industry. General Motors had become virtually bankrupt because of an opposite strategy (if one can call it that) of having a diverse collection of motor car manufacturers [22]. They competed against each other rather than against Ford. However, by 1927 the tables had been turned and Ford were in desperate straits. Production plants had to be closed for about a year for complete retooling. In those years, General Motors were revitalized through a simple (or so it seems today) segmented pricing strategy and the stubbornness of Henry Ford. The fundamental problem with the experience curve is that it focuses on process innovation at the expense of product innovation.

Cost reductions tend to be a bottom-up approach, i.e. it is work at the sharp end that creates these reductions. However, the pressure for cost reduction can have unintended consequences such as the narrowing of the product range. This process must be balanced by strong management at the top that ensures that attention is devoted to cutting the costs that need to be cut.

The concept of the experience curve is of importance both in strategic planning and in project management. In strategic planning, any plan must take account of the need continuously to attack costs and to achieve a balance between the unnecessary introduction of too many major projects and too great a reliance on the development of existing products. In project management, the same balance must be struck, i.e. the project manager must not desert the constant attack on costs, if his project is to be successful. He must allow for the effect of experience when predicting and monitoring costs and he must graft onto a major project many small projects of cost reduction and product enhancement.

2.3.3 The product life cycle

Another concept that helps us in our understanding of the importance and 'shape' of projects is the product life cycle which 'plays a fundamental role in strategic management' [16]. The product life cycle describes how a product passes through various phases. These are **development, growth, maturity** and **decline** [16] (Fig. 2.5).

Others have suggested other distinct phases. For example a phase is sometimes inserted between growth and maturity called '**shake-out**' [11] or '**competitive turbulence**' [20]. Both titles try to describe the increase in competition as growth diminishes. This sometimes comes about because of overambitious capacity expansions for the continued growth that does not materialize while competitors strive to keep utilization high. This is a particular problem for a high-fixed-cost industry such as petrochemicals.

The total sales in the life cycle can be translated into profit and cash flow (Fig. 2.6). As we can see, the cash flow curve is usually below the profit curve early in the life cycle and above it later. This is principally due to the normal accounting practice of depreciating long-term assets—mainly buildings and plant and equipment but sometimes research and marketing costs—and the build-up of working capital.

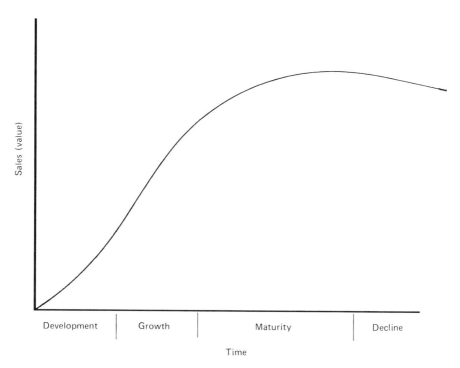

Fig. 2.5 – The product life cycle.

Of course, the product life cycle relates to the total market and not to an individual competitor in that market. The shape of the various curves for a particular competitor depends on how well it competes, and the same product may exist in different markets. For example a manufacturer of pneumatic hand tools, typically used on assembly lines, is seeing a decline in demand in the UK as a result of automation but growth in developing countries.

The precise shape of the product life cycle—length, height, rate of growth and rate of decline—will depend on the nature of the product, but it is clear that from inception a product, like you or me, will inevitably pass through the various phases and eventually die. Death is usually brought about by the relentless progress of technology; how many engineers still use their slide-rules today? The decline in thermionic valves is another example. The emergence of new technologies has greatly increased the power of computers [23]. Improvements in the use of valve technology resulted in an increase in the speed of early computers. However, this reached a threshold which could not be surpassed until the birth of transistors. The transistor was in turn beaten by integrated circuits. The next major stage, of course, was the microprocessor which has brought computing power to the fingertips of many of us. In this development the natural enemy was distance. All major developments have brought circuit elements closer together.

The foregoing suggests that the thresholds were reached and then the search for the next breakthrough began. Indeed, in many cases the breakthrough comes from a completely different source. This is the case of the transistor. All but one of the major valve manufacturers failed to make an impact in the new transistor industry. Another illustrative example is the substitution of tyre cord materials [23].

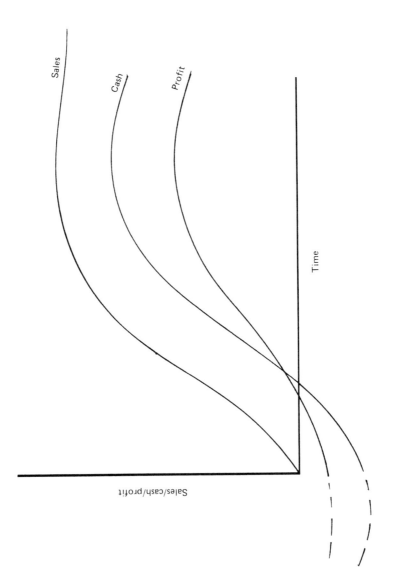

Fig. 2.6 – The product life cycle with profit and cash curves.

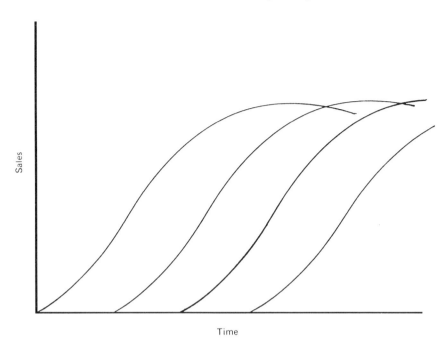

Sales

Time

Fig. 2.7 – A series of substitute products.

The death of a product, thus, is not usually due to 'natural causes' but murder by a substitute. Here we return to the idea of business renewal. The life of a company will not be determined by the life of a single product. There will (or should) be a succession or 'wave' [16] of products (Fig. 2.7).

The development of new products will be under way long before, and is the reason for, the demise of existing products. Many companies will consist of several products in several businesses, together forming a portfolio—just as a unit trust is a portfolio of shares. Products will be at different stages in the life cycle and together will add up to the total sales (and profit and cash) of the business. This is illustrated in Fig. 2.8.

2.3.4 The product–business portfolio matrix
Through the product life cycle and earlier discussion of diversifiable risk we have introduced the idea of the portfolio of products. It is difficult to think of a single statement of strategy that will be appropriate for all products. Each business will be, to put it at its simplest, in different stages of the life cycle. Thus, some will be net users of cash and others net generators of cash. The position on the life cycle is a simple view of the environment, or the attractiveness of the market, in which the product exists, a young and growing market being more attractive. This simple view of the environment is not shared by all. For example 'a market is neither inherently attractive nor unattractive because it promises rapid future growth' [20]. The company must also determine how well a particular product is competing. A simple measure of competitive position is market share dominance. These two ideas were brought together by the BCG to form the

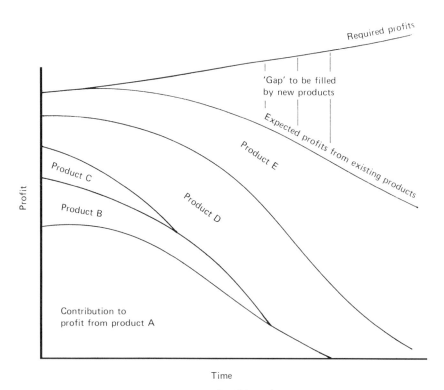

Fig. 2.8 – A 'portfolio' of life cycle curves.

four cell growth—share matrix shown in Fig. 2.9. Market share dominance is measured by 'relative market share' as defined by BCG. This is the ratio of one's own share to the market share of the largest competitor. Relative market share is used rather than absolute market share to emphasize the competitive position. For example, two companies in different industries each have a market share of 30% but, if the shares of their largest competitors are 50% and 15% respectively, then their competitive positions are significantly different. Thus, the boundary between high and low market share dominance is usually '1' and this axis is plotted on a logarithmic scale. The importance of relative market share is derived from the experience curve. The competitor with the largest market share is accumulating experience at the fastest rate and therefore gaining a cost advantage. The boundary between high and low market growth rate has been set at about 10%. A product is represented as a circle with the centre determined by its relative market share and market growth rate. The area of the circle is proportional to the sales revenue. Fig. 2.10 shows a portfolio of products—businesses on a matrix. Generally, the top half of the matrix referrs to the first half of the life cycle, the development and growth stages, and the bottom to the second half, the mature and decline stages. **Stars** are the most exciting. Growth is high and projects have dominant positions. They are roughly self-sufficient in cash. Cash generated from current sales is being used to fund growth. As growth slows net cash requirements will reduce and they will mature into **cash cows** which will generate large amounts of surplus cash, far more than can be profitably invested in their existing products and therefore can help new products to grow, i.e. they fund **question marks** which require large amounts of cash.

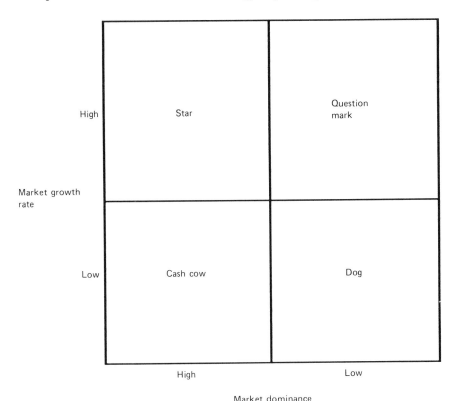

Fig. 2.9 – Growth-share matrix.

Fig. 2.11 summarizes the cash flows in the various quadrants and the results of successful and unsuccessful strategies.

Early in the life cycle, relative market share is less important and there is still time for a question mark to change its position. Question marks have also been referred to as 'problem children', 'wildcats' and 'dilemmas'. They are young and perhaps unruly, and the dilemma is whether to support them or not. A positive decision is required. Large amounts of cash will be needed not only to follow the market growth rate but also to surpass it in order to increase market share. According to BCG the only alternative is to sell off or abandon the product. There may be insufficient funds to support all question marks properly. The temptation is to support all, but because of the lack of funds support will be half-hearted, leading to **dogs**. The growth of dogs is low and so the market has stabilized. To increase market share will mean taking share from established superior competitors. Because of the lack of experience and lack of scale effect of dogs the profitability of dogs will be low. The cash needed by a dog will also be low because of its modest growth unless, of course, an attempt is made to improve its position.

There have been several criticisms of the use of the growth–share matrix. Firstly, cash flow has a dominant role in determining success. Return on investment (ROI) is more important as a basis for comparing the attractiveness of businesses for investment purposes. Secondly, the use of univariate models in which market attractiveness is equated with market growth rate, and competitive position is equated with relative

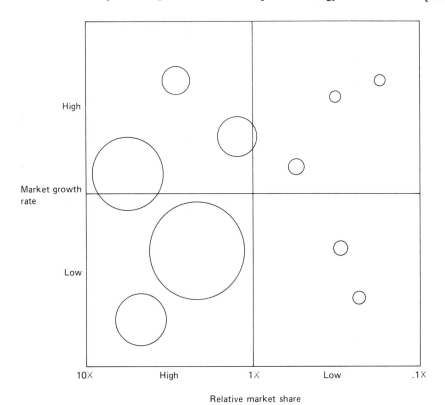

High

Market growth
rate

Low

10X   High   1X   Low   .1X

Relative market share

Fig. 2.10 − A portfolio of products−businesses.

market position, is too simplistic. Other factors will help to determine the attractiveness of the market, e.g. market size, competitive position or cost structure, and hence will influence cash flow.

The profit impact of market strategy (PIMS) program has focused on (accounting) ROI as the measure of 'success' [24]. PIMS is a large database from a large number of businesses (currently over 3000) and has been used to produce a regression model which has explained a substantial part of the variation in ROI. Other 'independent' variables have also been used: cash flow, relative price and relative direct cost. Relative market share (this time defined as the ratio of one's own share to the combined share of the three largest competitors) has been found to be an important factor (on average) in determining ROI success, but other factors have also been found to be important, e.g. investment intensity, quality, innovation and the degree of vertical integration.

The PIMS results are typically presented as cross-tabulations with a simple statement of their significance. One of the most 'famous' shows the relationship between relative quality and relative market share as shown in Fig. 2.12.

There are, of course, dangers in the use of ROI, at least as it is typically defined by accountants, for investment allocation. It is a static measure in that it states current return on the current level of investment. In BCG terminology it is the cash cow that has the large ROI but this is not the place to put your money. Question marks and to a lesser extent stars have low ROIs but are the products that require the investment. Large ROIs are the result of good decisions made in the past.

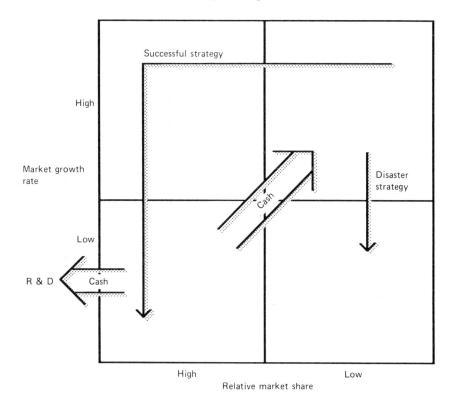

Fig. 2.11 – Cash flows between businesses.

Concern over these issues has led to the appearance of more general 'market attractiveness–competitive position' matrices. Market attractiveness is determined by several factors, one of which is likely to be related to market growth. Competitive position is determined by such factors as market share, production capacity and marketing capability.

Examples of this more general type of matrix are the direction policy matrix from Shell [25] and the General Electric business screen [11]. Other matrices relate to the product life cycle; the Hofer and Schendel product–market evolution matrix and the ADL (A.D. Little) Industry maturity–competitive position matrix [26].

SUMMARY OF CHAPTER 2

(1) Generally, projects must be market led although some will be only indirectly profitable in that they will be designed to create an environment in which profitable projects will flourish.

(2) Companies must know where they expect to be in 5 or 10 years or they will not be able to judge the merits of a project. A long-range company plan is essential to the environment within which projects are generated and managed.

(3) Within any one company, projects compete for resources. A detailed short-range company plan is essential to ensure that the different departments of a company (marketing, production, financial, etc.) work together and have related objectives.

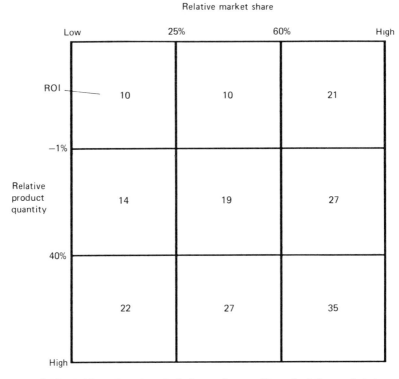

Relative market share

Fig. 2.12 – ROI as a function of relative product quality and relative market share.

(4) Within the corporate plan, each department will have budgets and objectives against which project management can be monitored.
(5) The corporate plan is a portfolio of projects.
(6) A project is a stream of cash flows. The project manager's task is to ensure that the positive cash flows generated by a project more than pay back the money invested in it.
(7) Simple cash calculations of the merits of a project are inadequate because they ignore risk and the fact that the project is essentially related to all the other projects which add up to the activity of a company.
(8) The cost of a project will be related to the experience achieved in producing it. A project which builds on experience is more likely to be competitive in terms of cost than one which involves breaking into a market, but experience is not inevitable; the advantages of experience are obtained only with good management.
(9) The results of experience must be assumed in cost prediction and when setting targets against which a project will be monitored. If they are not, competition will kill the project.
(10) The product (or project) life cycle must be taken into account in establishing its place in the corporate plan and its status relative to other projects in the company.
(11) The product matrix describes the quality of a project in relation to other projects within the company.

REFERENCES

[1] Industry Standing Committee of the Engineering Council (1983) *Technical reviews for manufacturing, process and construction companies*. Engineering Council, London.

[2] The Design Council and the Engineering Council (1986) *Managing design for competitive advantage*. Engineering Council, London.

[3] (1985) *EC directive on containers of liquids for human consumption*, 85/339/EEC. Council of European Communities, Brussels.

[4] H.I. Ansoff (1979) *Strategic management*. Macmillan, London.

[5] R.H. Hayes and D.A. Garvin (1982), 'Managing as if tomorrow mattered'. *Harvard Business Review,* **60** (May–June), 70–79.

[6] J.E. Hodder and H.E. Riggs (1985) 'Pitfalls in evaluating risky projects' *Harvard Business Review,* **63** (Jan–Feb), 128–135.

[7] F.R. Gulliver (1987) 'Post-project appraisals pay'. *Harvard Business Review,* **65** (March–April), 128–132.

[8] W.G. Downey (1969) *Development cost estimating*, Report of Steering Group for the Ministry of Aviation. HMSO, London.

[9] G. Pearson (1986) 'The strategic discount—protecting new business projects against DCF'. *Long Range Planning,* **19**, 18–24.

[10] H.I. Ansoff (1965) *Corporate strategy*. Penguin, Harmondsworth, Middlesex.

[11] C.W. Hofer and D. Schendel (1978) *Strategy formulation: analytical concepts*. West Publishing, St. Paul.

[12] B.T. Gale and B. Branch (1984) Beating the cost of capital. *PIMSLETTER*, No. 32. Strategic Planning Institute.

[13] W.K. Hall (1978) 'SBU's: hot, new topic in the management of diversification'. *Business Horizons,* **21**, 19–27.

[14] B. Denning (ed.) (1971) Introduction. *Corporate planning: selected concepts*. McGraw-Hill, New York.

[15] B. Denning (ed.) (1971) Top management and long-range planning. *Corporate planning: selected concepts*. McGraw-Hill, New York.

[16] P.B. Mcnamee (1985) *Tools and techniques for strategic management*. Pergamon, Oxford.

[17] A.A. Thompson, Jr., and A.J. Strickland III (1983) *Strategy formulation and implementation: tasks for the general manager*, revised edn. Business Publications.

[18] Boston Consulting Group (1972) Preface. *Perspectives on experience*. Boston Consulting Group, Boston, Massachusetts.

[19] P. Jefferson (1979) Unpublished paper. *Symp. organized by the Manchester branch of the Royal Aeronautical Society*.

[20] G.S. Day (1986) *Analysis for strategic market decisions*. West Publishing, St. Paul.

[21] W.J. Abernethy and J.M. Wayne (1974) 'Limits of the learning curve'. *Harvard Business Review,* **52** (Sept–Oct), 109–119.

[22] A.P. Sloan *et al.* (1968) *My years with General Motors*. Sidgwick and Jackson, London.

[23] B.C. Twiss (1974) *Managing technological innovation*. Longmans, London.

[24] S. Schoeffler, R.D. Buzzell and D.F. Heany (1974) 'Impact of strategic planning on profit performance'. *Harvard Business Review,* **52** (March–April, 137–145.

[25] S.J.Q. Robinson, R.E. Hichens and D.P. Wade (1978) 'The directional policy matrix: tool for strategic planning'. *Long Range Planning,* **11**, 8–15.

[26] P. Patel and M. Younger (1978) 'A frame of reference for strategy development'. *Long Range Planning,* **11**, 6–12.

3

The life cycle of a project

3.1 THE LIFE OF A PRODUCT

When the customer buys an engineered product, he expects it to have life that is sufficiently long for the purchase to be profitable. In a simple purchase—say, the purchase of a car—the customer pays for the product and hopes that it will last a long time or that he can get a good price if he sells it before its useful life is over. Clearly, if all else is equal, a car that costs £10 000 is better if its useful life is 10 years rather than 5 years, but purchase cost and life are not necessarily the most important factors in determining the cost to the customer of his purchase.

As we shall see in Chapter 4, the fact that capital costs money increases the effective annual cost of a product and reduces the advantage of a long life. Fig. 3.1 shows how much per year is the equivalent annual cost of a product which costs £10 000 to buy. The cost of capital is assumed to be 3% above the current bank's minimum lending rate and the cost of capital clearly increases the amount of money that a product must earn in each year of its life. As we expect the costs of maintenance and operation of a product to increase with its age, we may also find little advantage in a product with a very long life.

More important than the cost of capital is the fact that the purchase price of a product is likely to be a small fraction of the total costs that the owner must find over the product's life. Taylor [1], writing for the Institute of Cost and Management Accountants, suggests that the construction costs of a school are less than a quarter of its life cycle costs and it is a matter of common experience that the owner of a car will spend three or four times as much as its purchase price on operation and maintenance. It is quite common for the first (purchase, installation and commissioning) costs of a product to be a quarter or a fifth of its life cycle costs.

There is, of course, a trade-off between first costs and operating or maintenance costs and the Department of Industry [2] give an example of an electric arc furnace which cost £20 000 and failed for a period of 18 h early in its life. During this period, the company

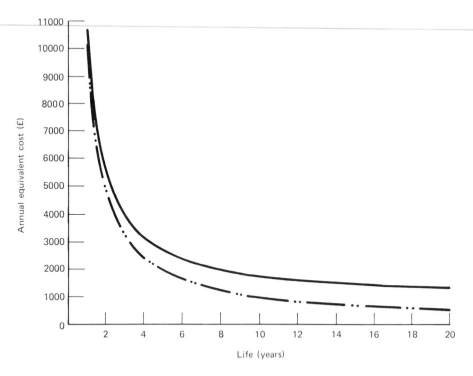

Fig. 3.1 – The annual equivalent cost of buying a product for £10 000: –, when the cost of
capital is 12%; – -- –, when there is no cost of capital (i.e. interest free).

lost £35 000 worth of production. There are many similar cases in which it is possible to
argue that low operating and maintenance costs and low down-time costs are more
important in the life of a product than low first (purchase and other non-recurring) costs.

It is important to consider life cycle costs from two main points of view, that of the
customer and that of the user of the product.

(1) The customer's project may derive from buying, operating and, finally,
    decommissioning a product. Examples are buying and running a car, buying and
    running a power station, and buying and running an aeroplane.

    In many cases the customer's project may derive from specifying, buying,
    operating and finally decommissioning a fleet, or sequence, of similar or related
    products. Examples are the army specifying and buying a fleet of armoured
    vehicles, which may remain in service for many years, during which time product-
    enhancing modifications and improvements to maintenance and operating manage-
    ment systems will be introduced, or an airline buying a fleet of similar aeroplanes.

(2) The supplier's project may derive from specifying, manufacturing, supplying and
    supporting a product. Examples are the design, supply and commissioning of a
    desalination plant for a foreign customer or the design, build and commissioning
    of a school.

    However, the supplier's project may derive from the specification, design,
    manufacture, sale and support of a continuous series of related products, modifying
    the products to improve them and providing supporting systems which are also

improved with time. An example could be the design and supply of a surface to air missile system for the army. The supplier will co-operate with the Ministry of Defence in formulating the concept of the project, establishing the specifications of the system and its component parts, manufacturing the products, training the users in operation and maintenance, designing the product support systems (spares logistics, fault-diagnosing equipment and procedures, testing equipment and procedures, special tools, etc.), co-operating with the user in determining and improving performance, availability in new environments and reliability, and eventually co-operating with the Ministry of Defence in the specification of the defence system that will replace the missile system that has become obsolete.

The Department of Industry [2] summarizes the elements of life cycle costs in Fig. 3.2 and we may derive much of the life cycle of a product from this.

(1)   The specification must be written before a product can be designed and generally a rational customer will evolve a specification of what he wants before he buys it. The specification of a product that is made in quantity, with no one customer in mind—a car or a washing machine—may be a simple description of performance that is nearer to an advertisement than a technical document but, when the product is expensive, one off, highly technical and required by a sophisticated customer, the specification not only will be a complex technical statement but also will take time and money to determine. The evolution of a specification not only will take time and money, in itself, but also will necessarily be preceded by some effort to establish a need for the product.

The completion of the specification to a level at which both the customer and the manufacturer agree that it may form the basis of a contract is an undoubted early milestone, against which the project may be managed. It may not be the first milestone because a specification will usually pass through several stages of development before it is complete and these stages may be definable.

(2)   Design and development may be among the most expensive operations early in the life of a product. Unless the product is very simple, it is unlikely to work when it is first built and, indeed, it is unlikely that it can even be built when the drawings are first issued. However, design and development are not merely the problem of producing drawings from which the product can be made and modifying the drawings until it works. A good specification will require more than performance; it will require life, availability, economic operation, economic maintenance and good support. Development is over when life cycle costs, as well as performance, have been demonstrated—usually by a certificate of design and performance or some such formal statement to the customer.

The completion of development to the level at which the contractual requirements of the specification have been demonstrated to have been met is also an early milestone against which the project will be managed. Again there may be earlier definable milestones within development (e.g. there may be many definable stages between the first building of an aeroplane and its obtaining a certificate of airworthiness).

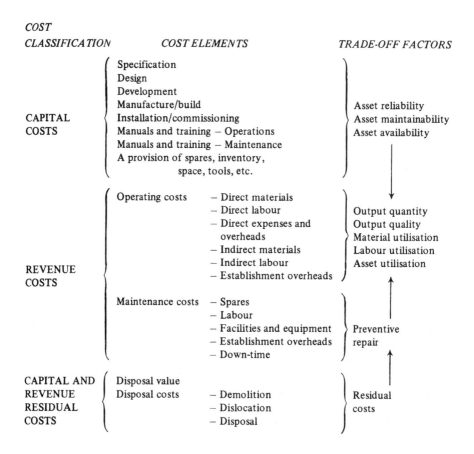

Fig. 3.2 – Physical asset cost elements and interactions.

(3)   Manufacture, in principle, follows design and development although, in almost all cases, the need to meet a delivery date for the product means that some manufacture will start before development is complete.

     Generally, several milestones will be defined for the period of manufacture. Manufacture may require large expenditure in tooling and it should be noticed that the commitment to this expenditure (as with the expenditure on development) is likely to be made before the product is bought, i.e. the manufacturer has involved himself in considerable expenditure, needing working capital, before he receives any money.

     Stage payments may be made and these will define milestones for project management.

(4)   Installation or commissioning will have different levels of significance in different fields, but their costs are rarely negligible. Installing a copying machine will require

several visits by the sales-and-service team before it operates to the satisfaction of the customer; the commissioning of a large plant before it is formally handed over to (and accepted by) a foreign customer may take months of expensive work.

The agreement by the customer that the product meets all his requirements and that he accepts it is clearly a milestone for the project's management but, again, there may be stages within installation or commissioning which can also be defined as milestones.

(5)   Training and the provision of manuals may be activities that are independent of design, development and manufacture, but they are essential, are usually a profitable part of the contract and must be planned.

Any milestones that are used to indicate the completion of these activities must stand before commissioning.

(6)   The provision of spares, tools and special test equipment is also an activity that is largely independent of the design, development and manufacture except that a plan must be evolved and some provision made before commissioning.

There will, therefore, be some early milestones for these activities, although support must be provided by the manufacturer through the life of the product.

Not only are the reliability, maintainability and availability of the product specified during the above activities, but also these qualities are determined by the quality of the work that is done.

(7)   Operating the product commences when it is commissioned and generally it must be assumed that this will generate positive cash flows for the owner.

However, the cash flows are the algebraic sum of the income which derives from the operation of the prcduct and the costs of that operation—the direct labour, the direct materials, the indirect labour, the indirect materials and the overheads.

Operation is part of the owner's project of buying and using the product, but it relies on support divided by the manufacturer. Operation and support must be activities in the manufacturer's project of designing, making and selling the product.

(8)   Maintenance is a budgeted expense for the owner of the product; it must be a planned activity within his project of buying and owning the product.

For the manufacturer of the product, maintenance is a saleable activity, commencing when the product is commissioned, although he is certain to be involved in repair as soon as it is built. For the owner, maintenance generates only negative cash flows but, for the supplier, the cash flows are a mixture of positive and negative: positive for contracted maintenance and the reasonable sale of spares and support, and negative for repairs during development, repairs during warranty and for loss of sales if maintenance has not been properly allowed for.

However, whether positive or negative, cash flows should be planned and the planning should provide milestones against which the project is managed.

(9)   The owner of a product must allow for decommissioning and disposal in his project planning. The cost of disposal has not always been considered and the twentieth century is having to spend a great deal of money cleaning up derelict nineteenth-century projects—derelict coal mines, poisoned land, derelict mills, etc. One of the unsolved problems of atomic power is how to deal with a power station that has reached the end of its useful life. On a smaller scale (and perhaps generating a positive cash flow) the owner of a car has to consider its disposal value when he buys it.

3.2 FACTORS IN A PROJECT'S LIFE CYCLE

When we consider the factors that affect the life cycle cost of a project, we may list the following.

3.2.1 Finance

(1) The cost and availability of capital.
(2) The effectiveness of cost-estimating methods.

3.2.2 Product performance

(3) Operation.
(4) Compatibility with operational environment.

3.2.3 Development and proving

(5) Development test schedules.
(6) Approval test schedules.

3.2.4 Manufacture

(7) Production quantity.
(8) Design of tooling.
(9) Effectiveness of tooling.

3.2.5 Installation and commissioning

(10) Installation.
(11) Contracted standard at handover.

3.2.6 Quality and reliability

(12) Life.
(13) Reliability.
(14) Cost of maintenance.
(15) Cost of malfunction.
(16) Warranty costs.
(17) Spares supply.
(18) Spares holding.
(19) Service.
(20) Modification procedures.
(21) Fault diagnosis.
(22) Test after repair.

(23) Special tools.
(24) Special test equipment.

3.2.7 Support literature

(25) Maintenance manuals.
(26) Operating manuals.

3.2.8 Training

(27) Training the customers' operators.
(28) Training the customers' service engineers.

3.2.9 Changes

(29) Changes to the specification.
(30) Modification procedure.
(31) Cost monitoring and control.

3.2.10 Disposal

(32) The cost of disposal.
(33) The gain from salvage.

These factors are not listed in the order in which they occur in the project's life cycle. This would not be possible because the activities in which they are significant are bound to overlap and, in any case, they would be of different significance in different projects and they would be of different significance to the supplier and user. Scrapping a motor car is a different sort of problem from decommissioning an open-cast coal project and regenerating the agricultural potential of the site. Warranty costs are of different significance to the supplier and customer (although high warranty costs for the supplier may well reflect customer dislike of a product and a reduction of sales).

3.3 THE LIFE CYCLE OF A PROJECT

The stages in a project life cycle will be of different significance in different projects and will be of different significance to supplier and user. Within any given project it is essential that all the stages in its life cycle be defined because it will be managed by monitoring the time and cost expended at the achievement of each stage and comparing those times and costs with what had been predicted.

If we consider the stages in the life cycle of a project, we may list the following.

3.3.1 Project definition
A project cannot be defined immediately that it is generated. Money and time must be spent to formulate a precise specification of what the project is intended to achieve. In addition to specifying the performance, costs and incomes have to be predicted. Project definition is achieved only after several stages of work.

(1) **Project generation** (or concept formulation in a military context). The project is specified imprecisely.
(2) **Feasibility study**. After the feasibility study, the project is specified more formally and a decision is made either to proceed with or to kill the project.
(3) **Project definition**. If the feasibility study does not show it to be undesirable, project definition is work to improve the precision of the specification of what is required by the project. A decision could be taken to kill the project at the completion of this work if the project is shown to be undesirable. In large projects, project definition may occupy two stages of work. At the end of each stage, the desirability of the project is reviewed. At the end of stage (2), the specification of requirements should be in its final form.

The definition of the requirements of the project must include

 — the required performance,
 — the operating environment,
 — the quantity required and
 — the product life, reliability, maintainability and availability.

The project definition stages of the project must include

 — project activity cost prediction and
 — analysis of the financial desirability of the project.

3.3.2 Contract determination

The determination of contractual arrangements between the supplier of a product and the customer will be an activity that is parallel to the project definition stages of the project. In a complex project, the customer may offer a series of contracts for a feasibility study; for the first stage of project definition (PD1); for the second stage of project definition (PD2); etc.

It is unlikely that a contract for the whole project will be agreed before the end of project definition because the project must be defined before it can be the subject of a contract.

3.3.3 Design and development

Design is assumed to be complete when the drawings have reached a standard at which manufacturing may be started with confidence that the product made will meet the specification. Design cannot, therefore, be separated completely from development and prototype manufacture.

Design is likely to be broken down into several activities for monitoring progress: the issue of drawings; the manufacture of prototypes; the development tests; proving (or type) tests. In some cases, allowance may be made for rework on the assumption that development will require drawing changes.

3.3.4 Product support

Product support must be designed just as the product is. Many of the activities related to product support will be parallel with design and development, but some product support cannot be useful until the product is in service. Activities must include the following.

(1)   The production of operating and maintenance manuals.
(2)   The design of fault-diagnosing equipment, test equipment and special tools for maintaining the products.
(3)   Training the customers' operatives and maintenance men.
(4)   Training the supplier's service men.
(5)   Supplying spares.
(6)   Supplying service engineers.

3.3.5 Manufacture

Manufacture must be planned and the requisite tools designed and built before the product itself can be built. The activities of manufacture must include the following.

(1)   Tool design.
(2)   Tool manufacture.
(3)   Manufacture of the product.

Tools may range from the simplest of drill jigs to a plant to assemble motor cars and costing several hundred million pounds. Ideally manufacture is planned when the prototypes have been proved and commenced when the tools (or plant) have been built. In fact, the need to meet delivery dates usually means that some manufacture is started before design and development are complete and tool design may continue until well into manufacture.

Usually we need to predict the market (or the number of products to be made) before we can design tooling.

3.3.6 Installation

A washing machine, a machine tool and a steam turbine are examples of products that must be installed before they are any use to the customer. They must be grouted in, wired up for power, piped into a supply of water, etc. The commitments of the supplier and customer to ensuring satisfactory installation of the product will probably be determined contractually.

3.3.7 Commissioning

When a product is delivered or installed, it is likely that there will be a commissioning period before the customer will accept it and agree that it meets his requirements. Commissioning will depend on the product, but it is likely to involve the following.

(1)   Adjustments to make the product work.
(2)   Ensuring that the customer's operatives have been trained to take over the use of the product.

3.3.8 The management of change

Throughout the life of the product it will be necessary to introduce changes as faults or opportunities for improvement are discovered. There must be an agreed procedure for the following.

(1)   Observing the need for changes.
(2)   Generating changes.
(3)   Costing the changes.
(4)   Managing the changes.

3.3.9 Decommissioning
At the end of a product's life it will be necessary firstly to demolish and dispose of any physical assets that remain by salvaging and selling if possible, and by scrapping cleanly if not, and secondly to reclaim the land, or anything else that has been spoilt by the project.

How the stages in the life cycle of a project will be converted to milestones in its management will differ from project to project, but clearly some such check-list as that above must provide the basis for defining the milestones in any given project.

SUMMARY OF CHAPTER 3

(1)   The purchase of a product (whether hardware or a service) is a project with a life cycle.
(2)   The supply of a product (whether hardware or a service) is a project with a life cycle.
(3)   The life cycle of the project extends from determining the needs that the product must meet—through design, development, manufacture, commissioning, writing operating and maintenance manuals, training operators and maintenance staff, the provision of spares, the operation and maintenance of the product, changing the product, product support and, eventually, disposal of the product.
(4)   The life cycle of the project determines the milestones against which the project will be managed.

REFERENCES

[1]   W.B. Taylor (1980) *The management of assets: technology in the pursuit of economic life cycle costs.* Institute of Cost and Management Accountants, London.
[2]   Department of Industry, Technology Education and Training Working Party (1981) Report. Available from Asset Management Group, British Institute of Management.

4

The cash flows generated by a project

4.1 THE FLOW OF FUNDS INTO AND OUT OF A COMPANY

One model of a company is shown in Fig. 4.1. Here money flows in and out of the company, to and from the projects in hand. If enough money flows in, the current projects will provide some of the investment that will be needed by new projects. If, over a long period, more cash flows out of the company than flows in, the company will die.

Much of Fig. 4.1 is self-explanatory, but it is worth commenting on some of its features.

(1)   The accountant uses the concept of **depreciation** to ensure that capital equipment is paid for by the company's projects. Every project must therefore make a contribution each year to the cost of the equipment that it uses and these contributions must eventually pay for the equipment to be replaced when it wears out. Because the depreciation is only a figure in the company's accounts, it is not a real cash outflow and it does not reduce the **funds available** to increase **working capital**. Again it may be thought that, because capital equipment must be paid for, its depreciation must be deducted from the funds available in order to determine whether the company has made a profit but, as we shall see, the discounted-cash-flow (DCF) approach to the evaluation and monitoring of projects does not require us to determine depreciation. We do need to calculate the tax which must be paid by the company, however, when we are determining cash flows and to do this we need to know by how much the Chancellor will allow us to **write down** capital equipment in each year of its life. Like depreciation, write-down is not a cash flow but, unlike depreciation, permissible write-down is defined by the Chancellor.

(2)   When **operating costs, interest on debt** and **tax** have been paid and when an allowance has been made for depreciation, what is left belongs to the shareholders. Some of this is actually distributed to the shareholders as **dividend**, but some is left

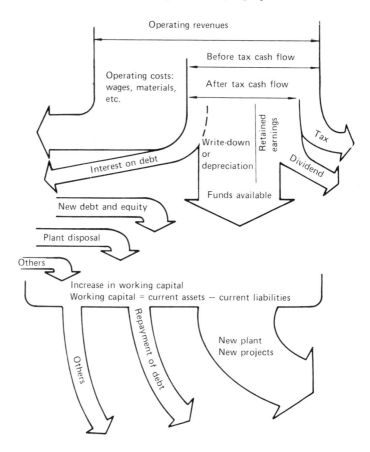

Fig. 4.1 – The flow of money into and out of the company.

in the company as **retained earnings** for further investment. Since retained earnings increase the value of the company, the shareholder will expect his shares to increase in value. The return to the shareholder (or the return on equity) will, therefore, be more than the dividend; it includes the increase in his share value (this is really a simplification because there are many reasons why shares increase in value and not all of them can be explained).

(3)   The major sources of funds are **operating revenues, equity** (shareholders', or owners', investment), **debt**, and receipts from the sale of old plant, but **others** include such government assistance as regional development grants (15% of capital equipment costs in some designated areas), a rate-free period (in an enterprise zone), contributions to marketing exercises, contributions to the costs of energy-saving demonstrators, etc.

(4)   Fig. 4.1 is a snapshot of the company's flow of funds in any year and it is not essential that positive funds available are generated every year. When we break down a company's business into projects, we certainly cannot expect each project to generate positive cash flows in every year of its life. Realistically, provided that a project more than pays for itself over its life, we do not care whether it sometimes generates negative cash flows. We must be careful, however, because an apparently

good project (i.e. one that will more than pay for itself over its life) can kill a company if it generates too many early negative cash flows, because creditors will not accept promises of future payments. Liquidity must be maintained, i.e. a company must not get itself into a position in which creditors can close it down by demanding their money before the company is in a position to repay it. A plan, or project within a plan, is more likely to be killed by shortage of working capital than by technical failure, and no project manager may permit himself the luxury of giving less consideration to the timing of cash flows than to the solution of technical problems.

There are several versions of the liquidity ratio, each related to the urgency with which money has to be found. One is the **current ratio** which is defined by

$$\text{current ratio} = \frac{\text{current assets}}{\text{current liabilities}}$$

where the current assets are stock, the amount due from debtors, and cash. The current liabilities are the amount owed to creditors, the currently payable taxation, short-term loans and overdrafts.

One could argue that there is some doubt about the value of stock, especially if that value had to be realized quickly and it may be desirable to use the **quick or acid test ratio** which is defined by

$$\text{quick ratio} = \frac{\text{current assets} - \text{stock in trade}}{\text{current liabilities}} .$$

Calculating the liquidity of a company requires some judgement because it is necessary to consider how long creditors will be prepared to wait for their money and how soon current assets can be realized.

Rule-of-thumb values for the current and quick ratios are 2.0 and 1.0 respectively.

4.2 THE PROJECT AS A SERIES OF CASH FLOWS

Early in the life of a project, cash flows will be negative or, in other words, early in its life a project will cost money. Money will be spent on market surveys, on design, on development, on tooling and on many other activities essential to the start of a new venture. Even a project which does not involve manufacture will cost money early in its life; putting a computer system into a shop would involve buying the computer and training staff; setting up a loan scheme in a bank involves the cost of study and advertizing; etc.

Later in the life of a project, it is to be hoped that positive cash flows will be generated; mostly this money will come from the customer who buys the products or the service, although there may be income from government grants, the sale of old plant, tax reduction and other sources. Often the project will still be making a loss when early sales are being made because methods of manufacture will be being developed, operators will be being trained, and managers are learning. Even when most of the manufacturing problems have been solved, sales are at a high level and positive cash flows are high, there will be costs associated with maintenance, after-sales service, spares holding, etc. Nevertheless, it is to be hoped that during the life of a project the early negative cash flows will gradually be replaced by positive cash flows and in the long run the project will be profitable. This description of a project as a cash flow stream may be pictured as the 'white-elephant curve' in Fig. 4.2.

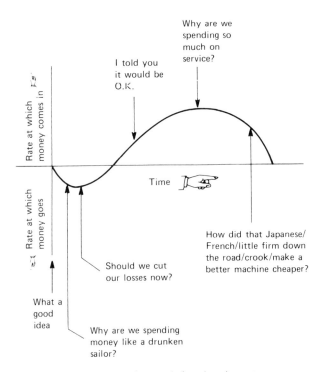

The inexorable increase in costs before there is a return:

20 min in the bath may yield an idea
80 man hours may develop the idea into a scheme
The first prototype cannot be made
The first protoptype will not work when it is made
Development may cost £200m
Tools may cost £300m
Recognizing a good idea may be a commitment to spend £1000m
What is the market?

Fig. 4.2 — White-elephant curve.

Not all projects will be profitable but there will be some projects which must be under-taken, whether they are profitable or not. These may be generated, for example, by the need to meet the requirements of the Health and Safety at Work Act. Such projects, if not profitable, must be paid for by the projects that are profitable.

One way of looking at a project is that, when it generates negative cash flows, it is borrowing money from the company; the positive cash flows that it generates must repay (or, preferably, more than repay) the loan.

4.3 THE PROJECT MANAGER AS A USER OF THE COMPANY'S (OR THE CLIENT'S) CAPITAL

One view of the project manager's job, then, is that he borrows money from the company to initiate and run the project; if he runs the project well, it will generate more than enough money to repay the loan. However, borrowed money must be repaid with interest and we have to ask what is the cost of the firm's capital that the project manager is using.

4.3.1 The cost of capital

There are two main classes of capital—debt and equity—but within each class there will be several divisions. Thus debt may be

- a cheap soft loan from a source intended to encourage projects which give employment,
- a long-term loan negotiated with debenture holders or a bank,
- a mortgage,
- an overdraft,
- etc.

Sometimes the interest on the loan will be fixed, sometimes the interest will vary with the bank's minimum lending rate, sometimes the loan repayment will be programmed and sometimes the debt will vary with the company's profitability.

Just as there is more than one source of debt, so there is usually more than one source of equity for a company's capital. Thus there are likely to be preference shares and ordinary shares with the preference shareholder expecting a smaller dividend than the ordinary shareholder, because he takes less risk.

The cost of capital is the weighted average of the costs which apply to the different sources. Interest on debt, however, is less than the nominal value would suggest because interest is a tax-allowable expense. Consider borrowing £100 at 12% interest. Nominally, the cost of using this £100 would be £12 a year. Suppose, however, that the company is paying tax at 30% on taxable profits. Because the £12 a year is a tax-allowable expense, the company will pay $0.30 \times £12$ less tax than had it not borrowed the money, and the true cost of using the £100 for a year will be $£12 \times (1 - 0.30) = £8.40$. This idea will be familiar to any man with a mortgage: the true interest on the loan will be reduced by the reduction in tax that the borrower pays.

Generally, if the interest on debt is $100I(d)$ and the tax rate is T, the after-tax cost of debt will be $(1 - T)I(d)$.

Consider £100 of shareholder's money. The shareholder might expect £10 a year as dividend, but he might also expect the value of his shares to rise by £10. The cost of this shareholder's capital is thus £20 a year because there must be sufficient earnings per share to pay the dividend and to retain enough money in the company to increase the company's value. As we have seen in Fig. 4.1, the cost of equity is not only the dividend.

The simple formula for the cost of capital is

$$I = [1 - R(d)] I(e) + R(d) (1 - T)I(d)$$

where $R(d)$ is the debt ratio (i.e. the debt divided by the sum of the debt plus the equity), $I(d)$ is the interest on the debt, $I(e)$ is the cost of the equity and T is the tax rate. This is a simplification because, as discussed above and as a glance at any company's accounts will show, there are likely to be several sources of debt (each with its own value of $I(d)$) and several sources of equity (each with its own value of $I(e)$). The tax rate T is also likely to be a variable, e.g. the tax rate is likely to increase with increased taxable profits, and it may also change from year to year with government policy. Nevertheless, the principle is clear; the cost of capital is calculable from the weighted average of the costs of all the sources with some reduction provided by tax relief on the interest on loans.

Even before we allow for tax, we would expect the cost of debt to be lower than the cost of equity because the creditor is taking less risk than the shareholder. This is because the interest on debt must be paid before the company can calculate the profit from which it must pay the shareholders. It might be to the company's advantage if as much of its capital as possible is debt, but the process of raising capital is self-regulating. Usually, creditors do not wish to see a high debt ratio because this will imply that they are beginning to take the risks that are rightly the shareholders'. Debt ratios tend to settle at around one third or one half.

4.3.2 Discounted cash flow and net present value

Although the calculation of the cost of capital requires more than a simple formula, a reasonable assessment may be made from the company's capital structure. Often, the finance department will estimate the cost of the company's capital from time to time and those who need to know it are informed. The project manager will thus know the cost of the capital that he is using to finance the project.

Consider that at the end of the year 0 (i.e. at the beginning of the project) a sum of £P is borrowed at a cost of capital of $100I\%$; consider that at the end of year n the debt is repaid by a single payment of £$F(n)$; at the end of year n, immediately before repayment, the sum owed is

$$£P(1 + I)^n$$

Therefore

$$F(n) = P(1 + I)^n$$

or

$$\frac{P}{F(n)} = \frac{1}{(1 + I)^n} \; .$$

P is called the **present value** of $F(n)$. In other words, the present value of $F(n)$ is $F(n)/(1 + i)^n$. Suppose the project generates the cash flow stream $F(0), F(1), \ldots, F(n), \ldots, F(N)$, where $F(n)$ is the cash flow generated at the end of year n and the project lasts N years. It is likely that the early cash flows, $F(0), F(1), \ldots,$ will be negative and will represent borrowing while the later cash flows will be repayments.

All loans will be cleared, however, if the **net present value** (NPV) of the project, which is the sum of the present values of all the cash flows $F(n)$ is zero. If the NPV of the project is less than zero, then the project will not pay back the investment made in it (the early negative cash flows). If the project has a NPV that is greater than zero, then it will repay more than it needed to borrow and the NPV represents the sum of money that the project contributes to the growth of the company.

The cost of debt is usually called interest and the word debt has a particular meaning in the capital structure of the company. When we say that the project manager 'borrows' the money to invest in the project, it can be confusing if we refer to the cost of capital as 'interest' and generally the expression 'discount rate' is used in calculations of present value.

There are many aids to the calculation of NPV. The simplest is Table 4.1 which shows us $1/(1+I)^n$ for different values of the discount rate I and for different periods n years. We can find the present value of any future cash flow by simply multiplying it by the appropriate tabulated figure, but note how little is the present value of sums in the future. If the discount rate is 10%, £1 generated in 10 years' time is worthy only 39p now; a pound generated in 20 years' time is worth 15p.

As an example of the calculation of the NPV of a cash flow stream, consider the following simple project.

The cash flows are −£6000, £700, £1500, £4200 and £2100 at the ends of years 0, 1, 2, 3 and 4 respectively. The discount rate is 10%. Hence we have the following.

Column	1	2	3	4
		Cash flow	$P/F(n)$	P
End of year	0	−6000	1.000	−6000
	1	700	0.909	636
	2	1500	0.826	1239
	3	4200	0.751	3154
	4	2100	0.683	1434
			NPV	463

The entry in column 3 is read from Table 4.1; the entry in column 4 is the product of the entry in column 2 and the entry in column 3.

The NPV of the project is £463 which is good. Therefore borrow £6463, invest £6000 in the project and spend £463 on a holiday (or use it to increase the value of the company).

Other short cuts to the calculations of present values are the use of more extensive formulae such as the following examples.

(1)   If all cash flows are identical, $F(n) = A$ for all n, and then

$$P = \frac{A}{1+I} + \frac{A}{(1+I)^2} + \dots + \frac{A}{(1+I)^N}$$

i.e.

$$P = \frac{A}{I} \frac{(1+I)^N - 1}{(1+I)^N}$$

and

$$\frac{P}{A} = \frac{1}{I} \frac{(1+I)^N - 1}{(1+I)^N}$$

may be found in Table 4.2.

Table 4.1 — The present value of a future cash flow. For a given discount rate (column) and a given period (row), read $(P/F)_{I,N}$ in the table. Then the present value is $(P/F)_{I,N} F(N)$, where $F(N)$ is the cash flow at the end of year N.

	1	2	4	5	6	8	10	12	14	15	16	18	20	25	30
1	0.9901	0.0000	0.9615	0.9524	0.9434	0.9259	0.9091	0.8929	0.8772	0.8696	0.861	0.8475	0.8333	0.8000	0.7692
2	0.9000	0.9612	0.9246	0.9070	0.8900	0.8573	0.8264	0.7972	0.7695	0.7561	0.7432	0.7182	0.6944	0.6400	0.5917
3	0.9706	0.9423	0.8890	0.8638	0.8396	0.7938	0.7513	0.7118	0.6750	0.6575	0.6407	0.6086	0.5787	0.5120	0.4552
4	0.9610	0.9238	0.8548	0.8227	0.7921	0.7350	0.6830	0.6355	0.5921	0.5718	0.5523	0.5158	0.4023	0.4096	0.3501
5	0.9310	0.9087	0.8219	0.7835	0.7473	0.6806	0.6209	0.5674	0.5194	0.4972	0.4761	0.4371	0.4019	0.3277	0.2693
6	0.9420	0.8880	0.7903	0.7462	0.7050	0.6302	0.5645	0.5066	0.4556	0.4323	0.4104	0.3704	0.3349	0.2621	0.2072
7	0.9327	0.8706	0.7099	0.7107	0.6651	0.5835	0.5132	0.4523	0.3996	0.3759	0.3538	0.3139	0.2791	0.2097	0.1594
8	0.9238	0.8038	0.7307	0.6768	0.6274	0.5403	0.4665	0.4039	0.3506	0.3269	0.3050	0.2660	0.2326	0.1678	0.1226
9	0.9143	0.8360	0.7024	0.6446	0.5919	0.5002	0.4241	0.3606	0.3075	0.2843	0.2630	0.2255	0.1938	0.1342	0.0943
10	0.9083	0.8203	0.6756	0.6139	0.5584	0.4632	0.3955	0.3220	0.2697	0.2472	0.2267	0.1911	0.1615	0.1074	0.0725
11	0.8963	0.8043	0.6496	0.5847	0.5268	0.4289	0.3505	0.275	0.2366	0.2149	0.1954	0.1619	0.1346	0.0859	0.0558
12	0.8674	0.7888	0.6246	0.5568	0.4970	0.3971	0.3186	0.2567	0.2076	0.1869	0.1685	0.1372	0.1122	0.0687	0.0429
13	0.8787	0.7730	0.6006	0.5303	0.4688	0.3677	0.2897	0.2292	0.1821	0.1625	0.1452	0.1163	0.0935	0.0550	0.0330
14	0.8700	0.7879	0.5775	0.5051	0.4423	0.3405	0.2633	0.2046	0.1597	0.1413	0.1252	0.0985	0.0779	0.0440	0.0254
15	0.8613	0.7430	0.5563	0.4810	0.4173	0.3152	0.2394	0.1827	0.1401	0.1229	0.1079	0.0835	0.0649	0.0352	0.0195
16	0.8528	0.7284	0.5339	0.4581	0.3936	0.2919	0.2176	0.1631	0.1229	0.1069	0.0930	0.0708	0.0541	0.0281	0.0150
17	0.8444	0.7142	0.5134	0.4363	0.3714	0.2703	0.1978	0.1456	0.1078	0.0929	0.0802	0.0600	0.0451	0.0225	0.0116
18	0.8360	0.7002	0.4936	0.4155	0.3503	0.2502	0.1799	0.1300	0.0946	0.0808	0.0691	0.0508	0.0376	0.0180	0.0089
19	0.8277	0.6064	0.4746	0.3957	0.3305	0.2317	0.1635	0.1161	0.0829	0.0703	0.0596	0.0431	0.0313	0.0144	0.0063
20	0.8195	0.0673	0.4564	0.3769	0.3118	0.2145	0.1486	0.1037	0.0728	0.0611	0.0514	0.0365	0.0261	0.0115	0.0053
21	0.8114	0.6098	0.4388	0.3589	0.2942	0.1987	0.1351	0.0926	0.0638	0.0531	0.0443	0.0309	0.0217	0.0092	0.0040
22	0.8034	0.6468	0.4220	0.3418	0.2775	0.1839	0.1228	0.0826	0.0560	0.0462	0.0382	0.0262	0.0181	0.0074	0.0031
23	0.7954	0.6342	0.4057	0.3256	0.2618	0.1703	0.1117	0.0738	0.491	0.0402	0.0329	0.0222	0.0151	0.0059	0.0024
24	0.7876	0.6217	0.3901	0.3101	0.2470	0.1577	0.1015	0.0659	0.0431	0.0349	0.0284	0.0188	0.0126	0.0047	0.0018
25	0.7798	0.6095	0.3781	0.2953	0.2330	0.1460	0.0923	0.0588	0.0378	0.0304	0.0245	0.0160	0.0105	0.0038	0.0014

Table 4.2 – The present value of a stream of equal cash flows. For a given discount rate (column) and a given number of periods (row) read $(P/A)_{I,N}$. The the present value is $(P/A)_{I,N}\,A$, where A is the cash flow at the end of each year of project life.

	1	2	4	5	6	8	10	12	14	15	16	18	20	25	30
1	0.990	0.980	0.962	0.952	0.943	0.926	0.909	0.893	0.877	0.870	0.862	0.847	0.833	0.800	0.769
2	1.970	1.942	1.886	1.859	1.833	1.783	1.736	1.690	1.647	1.626	1.605	1.566	1.528	1.440	1.261
3	2.941	2.884	2.775	2.723	2.673	2.577	2.487	2.402	2.322	2.283	2.246	2.172	2.106	1.952	1.816
4	3.902	3.808	3.630	3.546	3.465	3.312	3.170	3.037	2.914	2.855	2.798	2.690	2.589	2.362	2.166
5	4.863	4.713	4.482	4.329	4.212	3.993	3.791	3.605	3.433	3.352	3.274	3.127	2.991	2.689	2.436
6	5.795	5.601	5.242	5.076	4.917	4.623	4.355	4.111	3.889	3.784	3.685	3.490	3.326	2.951	2.643
7	6.728	6.472	6.002	5.786	5.582	5.206	4.868	4.564	4.288	4.160	4.039	3.812	3.605	3.161	2.802
8	7.682	7.328	6.733	6.463	6.210	5.747	5.335	4.968	4.639	4.487	4.344	4.078	3.837	3.329	2.925
9	8.866	8.162	7.400	7.108	6.802	6.247	5.759	5.328	4.946	4.772	4.607	4.303	4.031	3.463	3.019
10	9.471	8.963	8.111	7.722	7.360	6.710	6.145	5.650	5.216	5.019	4.833	4.494	4.192	3.571	3.092
11	10.368	9.787	8.760	8.306	7.887	7.139	6.495	5.938	5.453	5.234	5.029	4.656	4.327	3.656	3.147
12	11.255	10.875	9.385	8.863	8.384	7.536	6.814	6.194	5.660	5.421	5.197	4.793	4.439	3.725	3.190
13	12.134	11.340	9.986	9.394	8.853	7.904	7.103	6.424	5.842	5.583	5.342	4.910	4.533	3.780	3.223
14	13.004	12.106	10.563	9.899	9.295	8.244	7.367	6.628	6.002	5.724	5.468	5.008	4.611	3.824	3.249
15	13.865	12.849	11.110	10.380	9.712	8.559	7.606	6.811	6.142	5.847	5.575	5.092	4.675	3.859	3.268
16	14.718	13.578	11.682	10.838	10.106	8.851	7.824	6.974	6.265	5.954	5.668	5.162	4.730	3.887	3.283
17	15.562	14.292	12.166	11.274	10.477	9.122	8.022	7.120	6.373	6.047	5.749	5.222	4.775	3.910	3.295
18	16.398	14.992	12.689	11.690	10.828	9.372	8.201	7.250	6.467	6.128	5.818	5.273	4.812	3.928	3.304
19	17.226	15.678	13.134	12.085	11.158	9.604	8.365	7.366	6.550	6.198	5.877	5.316	4.843	3.942	3.311
20	18.046	16.361	13.590	12.462	11.470	9.818	8.514	7.469	6.623	6.259	5.929	5.353	4.870	3.954	3.316
21	18.857	17.011	14.029	12.821	11.764	10.017	8.649	7.562	6.687	6.312	5.973	5.384	4.891	3.963	3.320
22	19.660	17.650	14.451	13.163	12.042	10.201	8.772	7.645	6.743	6.359	6.011	5.410	4.909	3.970	3.323
23	20.456	18.292	14.857	13.489	12.303	10.371	8.883	7.718	6.792	6.399	6.044	5.432	4.925	3.976	3.325
24	21.243	18.914	15.247	13.799	12.550	10.529	8.985	7.784	6.835	6.434	6.073	5.451	4.937	3.981	3.327
25	22.023	19.823	15.622	14.094	12.783	10.675	9.077	7.843	6.873	6.464	6.097	5.467	4.948	3.985	3.329

The use of this formula will be familiar to any project engineer who has obtained a mortgage. For example, if you borrow £50 000 (*P*) for 25 years (*N*) at a building society interest rate of 12% (*I*), *P*/*A* may be seen from Table 4.2 to be 7.843 or $A = P/7.843 = £6371$ a year (this example assumes annual repayments; monthly repayments will add up to slightly less paid in a year).

(2)   If discounting is daily as for many loans and overdrafts, then

$$\frac{P}{F_n} = \exp(-in)$$

where *i* is the nominal annual discount rate and *n* is the year of cash flow F_n. An extension of this is that

$$\frac{P}{A} = \frac{1 - \exp(-in)}{i}.$$

These formulae may often be used as reasonable approximations to annual discounting.

However, nowadays, the most sensible short cut to the calculation of present values is to use a computer.[*] Lotus and Supercalc are commonly used spreadsheet packages which will immediately calculate the NPV of any cash flow stream that is typed in.

4.3.3 The cash flow stream defines the duties of the project manager

As we have seen, unless a project is mandatory, the cash flows that it generates must have a positive NPV. In theory a zero NPV is permissible because this would imply that all bills will be paid, all wages will be paid, creditors will be repaid with interest and the shareholders will be satisfied, although the project will not generate a surplus which allows the firm to grow. In practice, we cannot make such fine calculations and a project with a zero NPV is unlikely to commend itself.

DCF methods are clearly an important tool for assessing the desirability of undertaking a project, but the project manager cannot undertake DCF calculations until he has predicted the cash flows. Enthusiasm for a project is not enough to permit good management and the use of DCF methods goes some way to ensuring that the discipline of cash flow prediction will be taken seriously. For good project management it is necessary to have milestones that relate to engineering achievements as well as to cash flows but, as each cash flow is the algebraic sum of design costs, development costs, operating revenues, operating costs, interest, tax, maintenance costs, service costs, spares holding and many other costs, their estimation cannot be divorced from the engineering factors.

4.4 THE SHAREHOLDER'S CRITERION FOR A GOOD PROJECT

Most shareholders invest in a company to get a return on their investments. The higher the return, the better they like the company in which they are investing. As far as any

---

[*] The authors of this book can supply a computer disc which enables you to calculate the NPV of any cash flow stream. This disc may be used with any IBM PC computer and with most IBM PC 'look-alikes'. Appendix 4A shows some examples of the calculation of NPV, using the authors' program.

one project is concerned, the shareholder may consider that he is lending his money to that project and wants as high a return as he can get from it.

But what is the rate of return from a project? As we have seen, the negative cash flows generated by a project must be repaid, with interest, by the positive cash flows. If this is done precisely, then the NPV of the project is zero.

The project manager's problem is 'I know the cost of capital; how much more money will the project generate than is necessary to repay the company's capital invested in it?'

The shareholder's problem is 'I have some money to invest; will I get a better return by allowing my money to be invested in this project than by investing it elsewhere, perhaps even in another company?'

The shareholder's problem can be restated as 'What discount rate is earned when the net present value of the project is zero?' or, given the prediction of the cash flows that the project will generate in years 0 to N, as $F_0, F_1, F_2, \ldots, F_N$, for what value of I is

$$\text{NPV} = 0 = F_0 + \frac{F_1}{1+I} + \frac{F_2}{1+I} + \ldots + \frac{F_N}{(1+I)^N}?$$

This value of I is called the **internal rate of return** (IRR) of the project.

The IRR of a project is more difficult to calculate than the NPV and generally we have to resort to trial-and-error methods.

Consider a project with the following cash flow stream.

End of year	Cash flow £
0	−10 000
1	1 500
2	4 000
3	5 000
4	3 000
5	3 000

We can find the NPV of this cash flow stream for any given discount rate. In fact, at a discount rate of 20% the NPV is −£426 and at a discount rate of 15% the NPV is +£823.

Clearly, to obtain a NPV of zero, the discount rate must lie between 15% and 20% and will be nearer to 20% than to 15%. Further trial-and-error calculations show that at a discount rate of 18% the NPV is £46 which, in the circumstances, is a near enough approximation to zero for us to accept 18% as the IRR of the project.

The IRR of the project is not usually the shareholder's return on his investment for as we have seen, the cost of capital within the firm is

$$I = [1 - R(d)]\, I(e) + R(d)\,(1 - T)I(d).$$

Suppose that, in the above example, the debt ratio is 0.3, tax is at 30% and the cost of debt is 12%; then the IRR of the project is given by

$$I = 0.18 = 0.7I(e) + 0.3 \times 0.7 \times 0.12$$

and

$$I(e) = 0.221 = 22.1\%$$

and the shareholder benefits by the fact that some of the capital is raised, comparatively cheaply, as debt.

These calculations are, of course, much easier to carry out on a computer and most spreadsheet packages will determine the internal rate of return of any given cash flow stream.*

4.5 THE USE AND ABUSE OF DISCOUNTED-CASH-FLOW CALCULATIONS

The calculation of the IRR or the NPV of a project is a very approximate business.

— It is based on predictions of cash flows.
— It is based on predictions of interest rates.
— It is based on predictions of what will satisfy the shareholder.
— It assumes that all predictions are of deterministic quantities.

These rash predictions embrace even more doubtful information; thus the prediction of cash flows over the life of the project requires us to predict the life of the project, the market for the product (or service) over the life of the project, the selling price of the product, the cost of the raw materials and labour, the problems likely to be encountered during development, what will be the government's economic policy during the life of the project, and so on, almost indefinitely.

However, these are not reasons for refusing to make an assessment of the value of a project; they are indicators of the risks that must be considered in its management. Clearly deterministic project appraisal is not enough but even subjective methods must be based on predicted cash flows and the cost and availability of capital.

4.5.1 Raising capital
Almost any project must start with raising the necessary capital and we cannot normally convince either shareholders or creditors that they should invest until we supply the following.

(1)   A predicted balance sheet of the project over its life.
(2)   A predicted profit and loss statement for the project over its life. Normally this will be on a month-by-month basis over the first year (or two) of the project and on a year-by-year basis over the rest of its life.
(3)   A prediction of the cash flows generated by the project over its life. Normally these will be on a month-by-month basis over the first year (or two) and on a year-by-year basis over the rest of the project's life.

    The prospective creditor is looking particularly for the need for working capital during the early part of the project's life cycle for, as we have seen, a project which is profitable over its whole life may be killed by heavy needs for working capital before it makes any profit at all.

---

* Appendix 4B shows some examples of the calculation of the IRR, using the authors' program.

In some cases these predictions may be for a shorter period than the life of the project. For example, if the Welsh Development Agency provides equity, they want a demonstration that these funds can be withdrawn within 7 years.

(4)   An evaluation of the desirability of the project. Normally this will be a simple DCF calculation of NPV or IRR, once the cash flows are predicted but of course, although the calculation itself is simple, it requires further predictions of the cost of capital, how much the Chancellor will permit in the write-down of capital equipment, what the tax rates will be, and even the value of other projects, both in the firm and outside it (a good project in the firm may divert funds, and a bad project will influence taxation; a good external project will provide a yardstick against which internal projects will be judged).

Fig. 4.3 shows some extracts from a prediction of the balance sheet, profit-and-loss account, cash flows and DCF calculations that were submitted to possible providers of capital for a new manufacturing project.

4.5.2 Allowing for risk

DCF calculations are deterministic, i.e. they do not, of themselves, take account of risk. Chapter 11 is devoted to the assessment of risk and methods of prediction in an uncertain world but we can make some simple common-sense allowance for risk when using DCF methods.

(1)   We may simply be pessimistic about our cash flows. It seems to be a natural law that most of our positive cash flows will have been overestimated and most of our negative cash flows will have been underestimated. It is a fairly straightforward process to determine the effect of reducing the positive cash flows by some 'ignorance factor' and increasing the negative cash flows.

      If we wish to be slightly less subjective in allowing for risk, we may use what is known as **certainty-equivalent** cash flows. This is based on comparing the project in question with a risk-free project. There are, of course, no absolutely safe projects, but some, such as investing in a building society or keeping surplus cash in a bank's deposit account, may be considered risk free.

      When evaluating the project, the manager asks himself what return on a risk-free project he would find equivalent to the company's cost of capital (in the prevailing uncertainty of in-company projects). For example, the manager might be indifferent between project A and project B where project A is the cash flow generated by a typical company project (subject to the risk that the company normally takes), discounted at the company's cost $I(c)$ of capital and project B is a cash flow stream, discounted at the rate of return $I(rf)$ offered by a risk-free investment. Because of the risk involved, $I(c) > I(rf)$.

For example, a company's cost of capital is 12% and the rate of return of risk-free projects is believed to be 8%. A project is offered that generates the following cash flow stream.

Balance sheet

		End of year 0	End of year 1	
Fixed assets				
Building	0			
Plant (A)	350 000			
Plant (B)	65 000			
Installation cost	40 000			
Fixtures and fittings	8 500			
New plant		463 500	0	We allow for improving plant
New fixtures and fittings		0	1 848	
Total new plant		463 500	1 848	
Plant		0	463 500	
Undepreciated plant		463 500	465 348	We allow for depreciation although this is not used in cash flow calculations or in calculations of NPV or IRR
Less depreciation		0	46 350	
Total plant		463 500	418 998	
Total fixed assets		463 500	418 998	
Current assets				
Stocks and work in progress		0	0	The simplifying assumption that all purchases and sales are paid for immediately has been made. As the cash flows (below) demonstrate, delayed payments can turn a good project into a bad one
Debtors		0	30 560	
Pre-payments		0	0	
Cash carried forward		59 750	59 750	
Cash		59 750	30 560	

Current liabilities		
Creditors	0	0
Accruals	0	0
Bank balance	0	−20 313
	0	20 313
Net current assets	59 750	10 247
Total assets	523 250	429 245
Represented by		
Share capital HB & Co.	350 000	350 000
Share capital X	0	0
Loan 10%	75 000	75 000
Loan 18%	98 250	98 250
Assumulated profit	0	−94 005
Total assets	523 250	429 245

Fig. 4.3 (a)

The cash available in the opening balance (end of year 0) derives from Regional Selective Assistance

PROFIT FORECAST YEAR 1

	Month 6	Month 7	Month 8	Month 9
Rent				
Sales	50 933	50 933	50 933	50 933
	50 933	50 933	50 933	50 933
Cost of sales				
Raw material 1	17 520	17 520	17 520	17 520
Raw material 2	2 503	2 503	2 503	2 503
Tooling	857	857	857	857
Power	3 337	3 337	3 337	3 337
Maintenance	1 000	1 000	1 000	1 000
Clothing	150	150	150	150
Transport	964	964	964	964
Packaging	4 571	4 571	4 571	4 571
Fuel	71	71	71	71
	30 974	30 974	30 974	30 974
Gross profit or loss	19 959	19 959	19 959	19 959
(gross profit (%))				

Overheads

Salaries	4 250	4 250	4 250	4 250
Rent	1 875	1 875	1 875	1 875
Rates	1 000	500	500	500
Light and heat	2 500			2 500
Repairs	500			
Insurance				
Telephone	1 000			1 000
Vehicles and plant lease	3 145	3 145	3 145	3 145
Post	20	20	20	20
Stationery	500	500	500	500
Advertising				
General	100	100	100	100
Legal				
Finance costs	2 336	2 336	2 336	2 336
Depreciation	3 863	3 863	3 863	3 863
Hire purchase interest	1 110	1 100	1 100	1 100
HM Customs and Excise (recovered)	−3 150			−4 575
	19 048	17 698	17 698	16 623
Profit or loss	911	2 261	2 261	3 336

Fig. 4.3 (b)

CASH FLOW YEAR 1

	Month 6	Month 7	Month 8	Month 9
Inflow				
Payments (end ms)	50 933	50 933	50 933	50 933
Payments (1 ms cred)	0	50 933	50 933	50 933
Payments (2 ms cred)	0	0	50 933	50 933
Payments (3 ms cred)	0	0	0	50 933
Payments (4 ms cred)	0	0	0	0
Total (%) Maximum 100				
Payments total	30 560	40 747	50 933	50 933
Post-horizon cash flow				
Capital	0	0	0	0
	30 560	40 747	50 933	50 933
Outflow				
Staff costs	4 250	4 250	4 250	4 250
Purchases (subect to value-added tax)	12 859	11 359	11 359	12 359
Purchases (not subject to value-added tax)	28 755	25 755	25 755	28 255
Interest	2 336	2 336	2 336	2 336
Other finance charges	1 110	1 110	1 110	1 110
Capital expenditure	154	154	154	154
HM Customs and Excise (recovered)	−3 150			−4575
Net inflow	46 314	44 964	44 964	43 889
Net inflow	−15 754	−4 218	5 969	7 044
Balance brought forward	−31 403	−47 157	−51 375	−45 405
Balance carried forward	−47 157	−51 375	−45 405	−38 361

Fig. 4.3 (c)

Notice that more than £30 000 is needed at the end of month 5 for working capital. If we assume that customers are 2 months late in paying, this figure rises to £140 000

PROJECTED CASH FLOW

| | \
End of year						
	0	1	2	3	4	5	6	7
Inflow								
Payments	0	325 972	1 070 852	1 221 000	1 221 000	1 221 000	1 221 000	1 221 000
Post-horizon cash flow								60 114
Capital	523 250	0	0	0	0	0	0	0
	523 250	325 972	1 070 852	1 221 000	1 221 000	1 221 000	1 221 000	1 281 114
Outflow								
Staff costs	0	51 000	80 880	80 880	80 880	80 880	80 880	80 880
Purchases (subject to value-added tax)	0	121 990	199 045	210 620	210 620	210 620	210 620	210 620
Purchases (not subject to value-added tax)	0	205 760	547 360	602 240	602 240	602 240	602 240	602 240
Interest	0	28 029	25 182	25 185	25 185	25 185	25 185	25 185
Other finance charges	0	13 320	13 320	13 320	13 320	13 320	13 320	13 320
Capital expenditure	463 500	1 848	26 848	1 848	1 848	1 848	1 848	1 848
HM Customs and Exise (recovered)	0	−15 912	−25 962	−27 472	−27 472	−27 472	−27 472	−27 472
	463 500	406 035	868 676	906 621	906 621	906 621	906 621	906 621
Net inflow	59 750	−80 063	204 176	314 379	314 379	314 379	314 379	374 493
Balance brought forward	0	59 750	−20 313	183 863	498 242	812 621	1 127 001	1 441 360
Balance carried forward	59 750	−20 313	183 863	498 242	812 621	1 127 001	1 441 380	1 815 873

Capital write-down		115 875	116 337	123 049	123 511	8 098	8 098	1 848	The write-down of the capital for tax is not depreciation
Taxable profit		−163 530	145 177	193 178	192 716	308 129	308 129	314 379
Taxable loss carried forward		−163 530	−18 353	0	0	0	0	0
Profit before tax		0	0	174 825	192 716	308 129	308 129	314 379
Tax at 27%		0	0	27 000	27 000	27 000	27 000	27 000
Tax at 37%		0	0	27 685	34 305	77 008	77 008	79 320
Cash flow after tax	−463 500	−80 063	204 176	314 379	259 694	253 074	210 371	270 485

NPV (%)   0.2   166 386

IRR   0.2 895 703

(d)

Fig. 4.3 – Extracts from (a) the predicted balance sheet, (b) the first year's profit-and-loss account, (c) the first year's cash flow predictions and (d) the prediction of annual cash flows and the calculation of the IRR.

End of year	Cash flow (£)
0	−10 000
1	+ 3 000
2	+ 5 000
3	+ 4 000
4	+ 2 000

We can easily calculate that, at the company's cost of capital (12%), the NPV of the project is £783.

If the project were risk free (i.e. at a cost of capital of 8%), it would generate a NPV of £1710 but the decision maker is prepared to accept the NPV of £783 (calculated from the discount rate associated with the company's normal risk posture). It can be argued, then, that the decision maker is indifferent between a normal company project and a certain project with lower cash flows (in the ratio of 783 to 1710).

Normally we consider the cash flows year by year and we make the following annual calculations.

Whatever the discount rate, the present value of £10 000 at the end of year 0 is £10 000 so that this sum of £10 000 has a certainty equivalent of £10 000 and the certainty-equivalent coefficient (CEC) is 1.

The cash flow of £3000 at the end of year 1 has a NPV of £2679 at the firm's cost of capital. What sum would give the same NPV at the risk-free rate? Clearly this is £2679 × 1.08 = £2893. The certainty equivalent of £3000 at the end of year 1 is thus £2893 and the CEC is 2893/3000 = 0.9643.

The cash flow of £5000 at the end of year 2 has a NPV of £3986 at the firm's cost of capital and, to obtain this at the risk-free rate, we would need not £5000 but £3986 × $(1.08)^2$ = £4649 (i.e. a CEC of 4649/5000 = 0.9299).

The cash flow of £4000 at the end of year 3, by the same reasoning would have a certainty equivalent of $[4000/(1.12)^3] \times (1.08)^3$ = £3587 (i.e. a CEC of 0.8966).

The cash flow of £2000 at the end of year 4 would thus have a certainty equivalent of £1729 (i.e. a CEC of 0.8646).

As we can easily demonstrate the certainty-equivalent cash flows discounted at the risk-free rate yield the NPV that is expected from the project at the firm's cost of capital (and at whatever the risk that the company normally takes).

The cash flow stream −£10 000, £3000, £5000, £4000, £2000 has a NPV of £783 at the company's normal discount rate of 12% and the cash flow stream −£10 000, £2893, £4649, £3587, £1729 has a NPV of £783 at the risk-free cost of capital of 8%.

Whatever the company's risk posture, there will be some projects that are more risky than others. For the riskier project, the CEC will be lower and the decision maker will need to have good records from which he will be able to classify projects according to their risk. For any given risk, the CEC will also decrease with time. Clark et al. [1] suggest CECs, for the end of year 1, that range from 0.95 to 0.7. The high CEC is for replacing equipment by new equipment which introduces no new technology while the lower CEC applies to basic research. For the same range of project risk, CECs for the end of year 4 range from 0.85 to 0. A CEC of 0 for cash flows at the end of year 4 simply means that the company ignores the possibility that its research projects generate cash flows after 3 years.

If the company wishes to use certainty-equivalent cash flows and has the records that enable it to estimate CECs, then the NPV of a project will be calculated at the risk-free discount rate using certainty equivalent cash flows. If the NPV of a project is determined in this way to be positive, then that project is a candidate for acceptance.

(2)   We may be pessimistic about the cost of capital. If we raise the predicted cost of
capital, future cash flows will have less effect on overall project performance. This
applies to both positive and negative cash flows but it is to be assumed that any
reasonable project will generate mainly positive cash flows in the years ahead, when
the cost of capital has the greatest effect in reducing the present value.

The risk-adjusted discount rate (RAR) is given by

$$I(ra) = I(rf) + I(f) + I(a)$$

where $I(rf)$ is the risk-free discount rate, $I(f)$ is an adjustment to take account of the
company's normal risk posture and $I(a)$ is an adjustment to take account of the
difference between the perceived risk of the project under discussion and the
company's normal risk. Note that $I(c) = I(rf) + I(f)$ is the company's cost of capital
since it is appropriate over the normal range of the company's projects.

The decision maker must know the company's cost of capital and what is a
typical project within the company's risk posture for which the appropriate
discount rate would be the cost of capital.

He must then have an opinion about the value of $I(a)$ in the case of a project
under discussion. Clark *et al.* [1] suggest that $I(a)$ could be between 3% and 20%
for projects which range from replacing old equipment with new equipment that
has technological advances to projects which are basic research.

Consider the project with the following cash flow stream.

End of year	Cash flow (£)
0	−10 000
1	+ 3 000
2	+ 5 000
3	+ 4 000
4	+ 2 000

At the firm's cost of capital of 12%, we know that the NPV is £783.

If, however, we believe that the project falls into a risk category for which $I(a)$ is
6%, we must discount the cash flows at 18% $(I(c) + I(a))$. The NPV of the project
is then −£401 and it must be rejected.

It should be noted that certainty-equivalent calculations do not give the same
NPVs as RARs do. It is quite possible for a project which would be accepted if
CECs are used to be unacceptable using RARs.

The problem of both certainty-equivalent and risk-adjusted discounting is that
they need information of a quality that is not often available. We may use mainly
subjective judgement to suggest values for CECs and risk adjustments to discount
rates although this judgement will be tempered by the mathematics of their
definitions. However, to derive CECs and RARs analytically and objectively must
require a detailed knowledge of how future cash flows may vary in a probabilistic
way and, if we knew this, we could dispense with both certainty equivalence and
risk adjustment.

(3)   We may extend our pessimism over cash flow and cost-of-capital assumptions by
simply determining the sensitivity of the project's profitability to the variation in

any number of input parameters. Although such a sensitivity analysis is simple enough in conception and execution, it can be long winded. The sensitivity analysis simply asks 'What if?' What is the IRR of the project at the originally predicted value sof the parameters and how is this value decreased if positive cash flows are reduced or delayed, and if the negative cash flows are increased or accelerated?

A question that will certainly be asked by a prospective investor is 'How will the required working capital increase if payments by customers are delayed?' A 60 day period of grace in the payment of bills by the customer can turn an apparently successful project into a failure and this particular sensitivity analysis may well affect the design of contracts between the company and its customers. Fig. 4.4 gives one example of such an analysis.

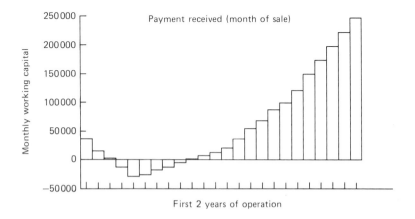

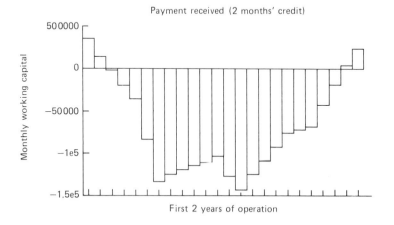

Fig. 4.4 – A histogram showing the effect on working capital of delayed payments by the customer.

(4)   One method of coping with risk is to use the pay-back period (PBP) as a criterion for judging a project. Here, having predicted the cash flows that the project will generate, we merely determine how long it will be before the positive cash flows cancel out the early negative cash flows. Thus, if we buy, for £1000, a machine

which generates positive cash flows of £250 a year, the PBP will be 4 years. Usually the cash flows are more complex than this but the calculations of the PBP is rarely difficult.

The problem is that the PBP as a criterion for judging projects is usually applied by companies who foresee liquidity problems and who do not wish to accept projects with PBPs of less than, say, 2 years (18 months in the case of at least one company). The benefit of such a method is that it does not require us to look far into the future and so we are likely to be reasonably accurate in our estimates of cash flows. If, therefore, the project pays for itself in a short PBP and we are reasonably confident that cash flows thereafter will mostly be positive, the project will involve little risk. The drawback of the method is that it will virtually eliminate all long-term projects, some of which will be of great benefit in the long run. Consider such projects as the Severn Bridge, an atomic power station or the building of a large civil aeroplane; all these projects would fail if judged by short PBP criteria, but any one could be very profitable in a long-term calculation.

As we have seen in Chapter 2, a company that establishes a corporate strategy will use subjective methods to consider the probabilistic nature of the projects within its plan. A more detailed account of methods of dealing with the appraisal and estimation of probabilistic parameters is given in Chapter 11 but a great deal can be achieved by using common sense on a basis of DCF calculations.

SUMMARY OF CHAPTER 4

(1)   Any project generates a sequence of cash flows. Early in the life of a project the cash flows are likely to be negative (outward); later positive cash flows must pay for the early negative cash flows. (One exception is the mandatory project which must be undertaken even if it is not profitable; a second exception is the project which is not in itself, profitable but without which other profitable projects cannot be undertaken.)

(2)   The 'time' value of money must be taken into account in any estimate of its profitability. DCF methods enable future cash flows to be assessed against present cash flows.

(3)   Predicting the cash flows that a project will generate is a discipline which reveals firstly engineering problems that will have to be overcome and secondly milestones against which the project may be managed.

(4)   Although DCF calculations are generally deterministic, the probabilistic nature of a project can, to some extent, be taken into account.

APPENDIX 4A

The use of the authors' program to calculate net present value of a project.

(1)   Boot up the machine. This generally means inserting a DOS disc into drive A of the machine, switching on and typing the date and time when prompted. The screen will show A> when ready for further commands.

(2)   Call up the BASIC workspace by typing BASIC A.*
(3)   Remove the DOS disc from drive A.
(4)   Insert the book disc in drive A.
(5)   Type LOAD "IRRNPV".
(6)   When the screen shows the OK prompt, type RUN.

The program is then self-explanatory but below is a print-out of two simple NPV calculations.

First we recalculate the exercise on p. 57.

```
NO. OF YEARS IN CASH FLOW, (MAX 100), NY=? 4

ENTER A VALUE FOR YEAR  0 ,              Y0=?   −6000

ENTER A VALUE FOR YEAR  1     CF( 1 )=?  700      (These are simply the cash flows:
ENTER A VALUE FOR YEAR  2     CF( 2 )=?  1500     −£6000,  £700,  £1500, £4200,
ENTER A VALUE FOR YEAR  3     CF( 3 )=?  4200     £2100 at the end of years 0, 1, 2,
ENTER A VALUE FOR YEAR  4     CF( 4 )=?  2100     3, 4.)

INTERNAL RATE OF RETURN,      TYPE   R
NET PRESENT VALUE        ,    TYPE   P   p        (p is typed to obtain the NPV of
                                                 the cash flow stream.)

ENTER DISCOUNT RATE,          IR=?  10           (10 is typed because the internal
                                                 rate is 10%.)

NET PRESENT VALUE IS,         NPV=   465.88       (This is a slightly more accurate
                                                 answer than the one obtained by
                                                 using tables.)

TRY AGAIN WITH SAME CASH FLOW,   TYPE A
TRY A NEW CASH FLOW          ,   TYPE N
END OF SESSION              ,    TYPE E  e       (e is typed to end the session.)
```

Next we do a simple check on the mortgage calculation on p. 60.

```
NO. OF YEARS IN CASH FLOW, (MAX 100), NY=? 25

ENTER A VALUE FOR YEAR 0,        Y0=? −50000

ENTER A VALUE FOR YEAR 1     CF(1)=? 6371
ENTER A VALUE FOR YEAR 2     CF(2)=? 6371
ENTER A VALUE FOR YEAR 3     CF(3)=? 6371
ENTER A VALUE FOR YEAR 4     CF(4)=? 6371
ENTER A VALUE FOR YEAR 5     CF(5)=? 6371
ENTER A VALUE FOR YEAR 6     CF(6)=? 6371
ENTER A VALUE FOR YEAR 7     CF(7)=? 6371
ENTER A VALUE FOR YEAR 8     CF(8)=? 6371
ENTER A VALUE FOR YEAR 9     CF(9)=? 6371
ENTER A VALUE FOR YEAR 10    CF(10)=? 6371
ENTER A VALUE FOR YEAR 11    CF(11)=? 6371
ENTER A VALUE FOR YEAR 12    CF(12)=? 6371
ENTER A VALUE FOR YEAR 13    CF(13)=? 6371
ENTER A VALUE FOR YEAR 14    CF(14)=? 6371
ENTER A VALUE FOR YEAR 15    CF(15)=? 6371
ENTER A VALUE FOR YEAR 16    CF(16)=? 6371
ENTER A VALUE FOR YEAR 17    CF(17)=? 6371
```

---

* An IBM-compatible machine will not use BASIC or BASICA. In such a case it will be necessary to call up the version of BASIC supplied with the machine (e.g. GWBASIC).

ENTER A VALUE FOR YEAR 18	CF(18)=? 6371
ENTER A VALUE FOR YEAR 19	CF(19)=? 6371
ENTER A VALUE FOR YEAR 20	CF(20)=? 6371
ENTER A VALUE FOR YEAR 21	CF(21)=? 6371
ENTER A VALUE FOR YEAR 22	CF(22)=? 6371
ENTER A VALUE FOR YEAR 23	CF(23)=? 6371
ENTER A VALUE FOR YEAR 24	CF(24)=? 6371
ENTER A VALUE FOR YEAR 25	CF(25)=? 6371

(Note that the NPV is −£31.36 and so the more accurate computer calculation shows that an annual repayment of £6371 will not quite repay the mortgage of £50 000.)

INTERNAL RATE OF RETURN,	TYPE R
NET PRESENT VALUE ,	TYPE P p
ENTER DISCOUNT RATE,	IR=? 12
NET PRESENT VALUE IS,	NPV= −31.36

(Note that this is a clumsy way of calculating the repayments since it involves typing 6371 25 times.)

TRY AGAIN WITH SAME CASH FLOW,	TYPE A
TRY A NEW CASH FLOW ,	TYPE N
END OF SESSION ,	TYPE E

APPENDIX 4B

The use of the authors' program to calculate the internal rate of return of a project.
    The calculation of the IRR may be done in two ways.

(1)   Trial and error. This means that we calculate the NPV of the project for a given the NPV is negative, we try again with a reduced discount rate. After a few trial-and-error calculations, we find the discount rate for which the NPV of the project is zero (or a reasonable approximation of it). This is the IRR of the project.
(2)   Direct calculation using a program which searches for an acceptable approximation. To do this, we use the book disc and set up to run the program IRRNPV as before (see Appendix 4A). From this point, the program is self-explanatory—we simply ask for the IRR of the cash flow stream instead of the NPV but below is a print-out of several simple IRR calculations.

The first calculation uses trial and error to determine the value of the discount rate which yields a NPV of 0.

NO. OF YEARS IN CASH FLOW, (MAX 100), NY=? 5

| ENTER A VALUE FOR YEAR 0, | Y0=? −10000 |

ENTER A VALUE FOR YEAR 1	CF(1)=? 1500
ENTER A VALUE FOR YEAR 2	CF(2)=? 4000
ENTER A VALUE FOR YEAR 3	CF(3)=? 5000
ENTER A VALUE FOR YEAR 4	CF(4)=? 3000
ENTER A VALUE FOR YEAR 5	CF(5)=? 3000

The cash flows −£10 000, £1500, £4000, £5000, £3000, £3000 at the ends of years 0, 1, 2, 3, 4 are entered.

INTERNAL RATE OF RETURN,	TYPE R
NET PRESENT VALUE ,	TYPE P p
ENTER DISCOUNT RATE,	IR=? 15

We guess an IRR of 15% at which we find the NPV is £823.

| NET PRESENT VALUE IS, | NPV= 823.29 |

TRY AGAIN WITH SAME CASH FLOW,	TYPE A
TRY A NEW CASH FLOW ,	TYPE N
END OF SESSION ,	TYPE E a

INTERNAL RATE OF RETURN,	TYPE R
NET PRESENT VALUE ,	TYPE P p

ENTER DISCOUNT RATE,	IR=? 20

We try a new guess of 20% at which we find the NPV is –£426.

NET PRESENT VALUE IS,	NPV= –426.31

TRY AGAIN WITH SAME CASH FLOW,	TYPE A
TRY A NEW CASH FLOW ,	TYPE N
END OF SESSION ,	TYPE E a

INTERNAL RATE OF RETURN,	TYPE R
NET PRESENT VALUE ,	TYPE P p

ENTER DISCOUNT RATE,	IR=? 18

We try a new guess of 18% at which we find the NPV is £46.

NET PRESENT VALUE IS,	NPV= 45.77

We could continue to improve our guess (the IRR is obviously between 18% and 20% but very close to 18%) but the current estimate is almost certainly near enough. The computer will do the guessing for us, however, with a considerable saving in effort.

NO. OF YEARS IN CASH FLOW, (MAX 100), NY=? 5	
ENTER A VALUE FOR YEAR 0,	YO=? –10000

ENTER A VALUE FOR YEAR 1	CF(1)=? 1500
ENTER A VALUE FOR YEAR 2	CF(2)=? 4000
ENTER A VALUE FOR YEAR 3	CF(3)=? 5000
ENTER A VALUE FOR YEAR 4	CF(4)=? 3000
ENTER A VALUE FOR YEAR 5	CF(5)=? 3000

INTERNAL RATE OF RETURN,	TYPE R
NET PRESENT VALUE ,	TYPE P r

To ask the computer for the IRR of the cash flow stream, we type r at this prompt.

INTERNAL RATE OF RETURN,	IRR= 18.19

TRY AGAIN WITH SAME CASH FLOW,	TYPE A
TRY A NEW CASH FLOW	,	TYPE N
END OF SESSION	,	TYPE E e

A further example calculates the IRR of the cash flow stream –£6000, £700, £1500, £4200, £2100.

NO. OF YEARS IN CASH FLOW, (MAX 100),	NY=? 4
ENTER A VALUE FOR YEAR 0,	YO=? –6000

ENTER A VALUE FOR YEAR 1	CF(1)=? 700
ENTER A VALUE FOR YEAR 2	CF(2)=? 1500
ENTER A VALUE FOR YEAR 3	CF(3)=? 4200
ENTER A VALUE FOR YEAR 4	CF(4)=? 2100

INTERNAL RATE OF RETURN,	TYPE R
NET PRESENT VALUE ,	TYPE P r

INTERNAL RATE OF RETURN,	IRR= 12.95

NO. OF YEARS IN CASH FLOW, (MAX 100), NY=? 25	
ENTER A VALUE FOR YEAR 0,	YO=? –50 000

ENTER A VALUE FOR YEAR 1	CF(1)=? 6371
ENTER A VALUE FOR YEAR 2	CF(2)=? 6371
ENTER A VALUE FOR YEAR 3	CF(3)=? 6371

```
ENTER A VALUE FOR YEAR 4        CF(4)=? 6371
ENTER A VALUE FOR YEAR 5        CF(5)=? 6371
ENTER A VALUE FOR YEAR 6        CF(6)=? 6371
ENTER A VALUE FOR YEAR 7        CF(7)=? 6371
ENTER A VALUE FOR YEAR 8        CF(8)=? 6371
ENTER A VALUE FOR YEAR 9        CF(9)=? 6371
ENTER A VALUE FOR YEAR 10      CF(10)=? 6371
ENTER A VALUE FOR YEAR 11      CF(11)=? 6371
ENTER A VALUE FOR YEAR 12      CF(12)=? 6371
ENTER A VALUE FOR YEAR 13      CF(13)=? 6371
ENTER A VALUE FOR YEAR 14      CF(14)=? 6371
ENTER A VALUE FOR YEAR 15      CF(15)=? 6371
ENTER A VALUE FOR YEAR 16      CF(16)=? 6371
ENTER A VALUE FOR YEAR 17      CF(17)=? 6371
ENTER A VALUE FOR YEAR 18      CF(18)=? 6371
ENTER A VALUE FOR YEAR 19      CF(19)=? 6371
ENTER A VALUE FOR YEAR 20      CF(20)=? 6371
ENTER A VALUE FOR YEAR 21      CF(21)=? 6371
ENTER A VALUE FOR YEAR 22      CF(22)=? 6371
ENTER A VALUE FOR YEAR 23      CF(23)=? 6371
ENTER A VALUE FOR YEAR 24      CF(24)=? 6371
ENTER A VALUE FOR YEAR 25      CF(25)=? 6371

INTERNAL RATE OF RETURN,        TYPE  R
NET PRESENT VALUE          ,    TYPE  P r

INTERNAL RATE OF RETURN,           IRR= 11.99

TRY AGAIN WITH SAME CASH FLOW,  TYPE  A
TRY A NEW CASH FLOW         ,    TYPE  N
END OF SESSION             ,     TYPE  E
```

Clearly this is a clumsy way of dealing with a mortgage because it involves typing in 6371 25 times.

We see that, when we calculated the annual repayments from tables, at 12%, we made a slight approximation. The annual repayment of £6371 will repay at 11.99%.

REFERENCES

[1]   J.J. Clark, T.J. Hindelang and R.E. Pritchard (1979) *Capital budgeting*. Prentice-Hall, Englewood Cliffs, New Jersey.

Useful further reading
[2]   D.J. Leech (1982) *Economics and financial studies for engineers*. Ellis Horwood, Chichester, West Sussex.
[3]   G.W. Smith (1979) *Engineering economy*. Iowa State University Press, Ames, Iowa.

5

The generation and evaluation of projects

5.1 PROJECT GENERATION

A project need not be large; making a modification to a washing machine so that it will be more reliable is as much a project and in need of a good management as designing a supersonic aeroplane. Every project will have to be conceived, born (possibly stillborn) and probably nurtured and protected through its early life, before it can become useful enough to repay the effort that has been invested in it. Like children, some projects never repay the care lavished on them and like children even the most rewarding projects will eventually cease to be useful and will die. In the joy of conception, the parents of the project cannot ignore the chain of events—some profitable, some expensive—to which their enthusiastic activities will give rise.

It is important that projects are generated which are likely to be profitable. Generally, limitation of resources will require that some of the generated projects will have to be rejected and, in any case, some of the projects which seemed good when generated will not survive early analysis.

Whether a project is civil or military does not really affect the way in which it should be managed. Nevertheless, the Ministry of Defence lays down procedures which should be followed in the generation, selection and management of military projects and the manager of civil projects can learn from them and adapt them to his own environment. But, in a general way, why and how should projects be generated and what procedures are available to increase the probability that those which we select will be worthwhile?

If we attempt to list the reasons for injecting new projects into a company, we may obtain Table 5.1.

The first thing to notice about this list is that the projects generated may range in size from the very large to the very small, but there is no reason to suppose that small projects are less important than large ones.

Table 5.1 — Reasons for new projects.

Reason for project	Possible origin of project
A new product or service is required to meet a customer need	Customer or manufacturer
A new product has been invented	Designer or manufacturer
Manufacturing costs are to be reduced	Operative or planner or quality control department
A product does not work and must be developed	Development engineer
The serviceability of a product must be improved	Service engineer
The life, reliability and maintainability of a product must be improved	Service engineer
The distribution of a product must be improved or reduced in cost	Almost any engineer
The design specification of a product has been changed	Customer

The reader will easily add to this list.

A large project may be very profitable but risky and could lose large sums of money [1]. Small projects are usually less risky than large projects so that a company with many small projects may generate as much profit as a company with a few large projects.

We must also consider small projects because their generation and management are essential to the success of large projects. Almost any large project will eventually generate positive cash flows that are smaller or later than have been predicted and negative cash flows that are larger or earlier than have been predicted. The good management of a large project will, therefore, generate cost reduction exercises to bring the project back into profitability. These cost reduction exercises become projects.

5.2 THE LEARNING CURVE

It has been known since before the Second World War [2] that in any well-run company, the contribution of labour to the cost of a product reduces as more products are produced. Two models are in common use: the first suggests that the average labour cost of manufacturing the first $2n$ products is $k\%$ of the average labour costs of manufacturing the first n products; the second suggests that the labour cost of the $2n$th product is $k\%$ of the nth. Each of these models is the result of observation. In neither case can predictions be more than approximations to actual costs because so many probabilistic factors are involved.

Typical values for k are 80% or 90%. If the labour cost of the first article to be made were £100 and if k were 80%, then the first model would predict that the average labour cost of the first two products is $0.8 \times £100 = £80$ (from this it can be reasoned that the total labour cost of the first two products is $2 \times £80 = £160$ and, as the first cost £100, the second cost £60), the average labour cost of the first four products is $0.8 \times £80 = £64$, the average labour cost of the first eight products is $0.8 \times £64 = £51.20$, etc. The second model would predict that the labour cost of the second product is $0.8 \times £100 = £80$, the labour cost of the fourth product is $0.8 \times £80 = £64$, the labour cost of the eighth product is $0.8 \times £64 = £51.20$, etc.

It is not enough to know the cost only at intervals of 1, 2, 4, 8, 16, etc., and we can calculate intermediate values using the expression

$$C(n) = n^{-b}. C(1)$$

where $C(n)$ is the average labour cost of the first n products or the labour cost of the nth product (according to the model used). $C(1)$ is the labour cost of the first product and $b = 0.322$ when $k = 80\%$, $b = 0.415$ when $k = 75\%$ and $b = 0.152$ when $k = 90\%$.

It is simpler, however, and probably sufficiently accurate to plot the learning curve. Fig. 5.1(a) shows the learning curve for $k = 80\%$ and, by using logarithmic scales for the axis, this curve may be drawn as a straight line, as shown in Fig. 5.1(b). By using graph paper with logarithmic scales, we need only two points to draw the learning curve. If, for example, $k = 90\%$, we have one point on the curve where $\alpha = 100\%$ and $n = 1$ and another point where $\alpha = 90\%$ and $n = 2$ and a straight line may be drawn though these two points.

For any given production quantity n, we may read α on the vertical scale and according to the model we choose either the average labour cost of the first n products $= \alpha \times$ (the labour cost of the first product) or the labour cost of the nth product $= \alpha \times$ (the labour cost of the first product). Students of the learning curve are able to weave many subtle variations into the theory. They will, for example, assume that k changes after some level of production has been reached and will find families of lines of best fit and variances of data about those lines. The important point in any discussion of project generation, however, is that good management will continue to reduce the cost of a product as more and more are made.

Engineers frequently assume that the process of learning, i.e. the reduction of labour costs in manufacture, derives from the operative's increased dexterity as he gains familiarity with the task that he has been set. This, however, is a small factor in the reduction in labour costs and the main contributions to learning derive from good management.

Typically, labour costs will be high

- if there is a shortage of components from which the operative will build the product,
- if there is poor tool support, so that the operative has to wait between activities or to take longer to perform a task than is necessary,
- if the ergonomics of the workplace have not been well designed,
- if the plant layout is poor,
- if the payment scheme discourages the operative from accepting change,
- etc.

All this means that, when it is necessary (as it always is) to reduce the cost of the product to conform with the project's cash flow predictions, a number of cost reduction projects must be generated.

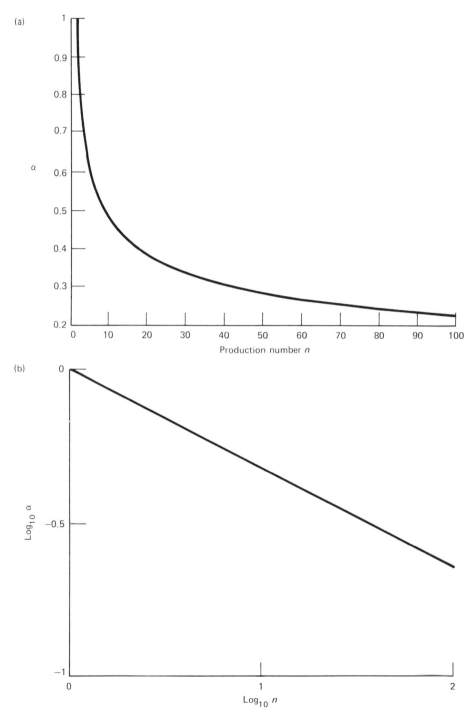

Fig. 5.1 – (a) The learning curve for $k = 80\%$. For the first model, the average labour cost of the first n products is $\alpha \times$ (the labour cost of the first product) and, for the second model, the labour cost of the nth product is $\alpha \times$ (the labour cost of the first product). (b) Same information as in (a) but with $\log \alpha$ plotted against $\log n$ to give a straight line.

The management problems listed above, for example, could lead us to consider such new projects as

- installing a good production and inventory control system,
- designing adequate tools or an adequate tool support system,
- designing a work place with good ergonomics,
- improving plant layout,
- abandoning payment by results (PBR),
- etc.

These cost reduction projects are all small compared with, say, designing and building an air-borne radar surveillance system, but they are important because the major project, on whose back they sit, would be a failure without them. They have a considerable pay-off and yet each small project is predictable and comparatively risk free.

A deeper study of this problem by British Aerospace [3] has shown that, when comparing the costs of a typical aeroplane, a US company is likely to produce the first at a higher cost than its British counterpart but, because of the effort devoted to cost reduction projects, costs are reduced much faster in the USA. Typically, by the time that 15 aeroplanes have been built, the US product is cheaper than the British. This cost reduction is believed to be faster and to continue over a longer production run in the USA than in Britain and it has been said that, while costs level out before a 100 aircraft have been built in a British company, a US company is still learning when it has built 1000 aeroplanes.

The effect of learning is shown on Fig. 5.2.

What work has been done on the management of learning clearly demonstrates that cost reduction projects must be generated, selected and managed and that the survival of major projects will depend on this being well done.

There must be a defined procedure for the generation of cost reduction projects and this will range through constant vigilance on the shop floor (not to demonstrate that the operatives are not working hard enough, but to find out why production management is failing to make the work easy), a constant review of manufacturing methods to ensure that newer cheaper methods are installed, the use of scrap meetings (not merely to find ways of salvaging scrapped components, but to find ways of avoiding scrap in the future), the use of quality control to point to ways of making higher-quality goods more easily, and a constant review of the costs (including quality costs) of bought-out materials, components and subassemblies. These observations and reviews will lead to the listing and then the appraisal of possible cost reduction projects, some of which may be regarded as projects in their own right but some of which may be essential to the successful management of major projects.

5.3 PRODUCT ENHANCEMENT

There are many examples, from washing machines to motor cars, in which the life of a project has been extended by product enhancement. One example is the continuous improvement of the reliability of a washing machine so that it has a longer working life and requires less maintenance and fewer repairs than its competitors. Such improvements

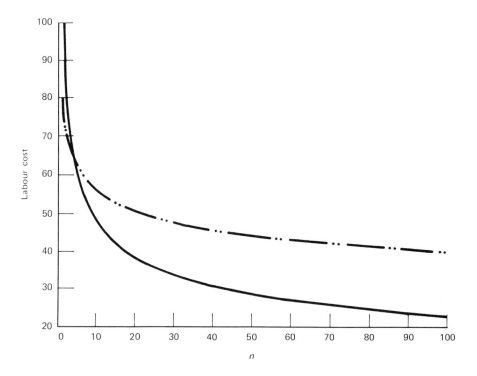

Fig. 5.2 – The effect of learning. Firm A builds the first unit at a labour cost of 100 cost units but by good management reduces labour costs by 20% every time the production doubles ($k = 80\%$). Firm B builds the first unit at a labour cost of 80 cost units but reduces labour costs by 10% every time that production doubles ($k = 90\%$). Firm B loses its competitiveness by the time that it has built about 5 units.

increase the life of the tooling, increase the popularity of the product with customers, reduce service and warranty costs and permit a higher price to be charged.

This approach has also been seen with motor car improvement, but here we may have more incorporation of new technology into existing models and modifications to meet environmental requirements.

Just as with cost reduction, product enhancement projects can extend the life of a major project or even turn failure into success.

5.4 METHODS OF GENERATING PROJECT

5.4.1 Small projects
If we are to generate useful cost reduction and product enhancement projects, we must have a system for doing so. There must be a formal system for examining problems and reporting so that the suggested solutions of the problems become, automatically, part of the agenda of new projects for consideration.

We must bring to a common centre

— reports from methods engineers,
— reports from value engineers,

— reports of shop floor suggestion schemes or quality control circles,
— reviews of standard times,
— reviews of allowances in standard times,
— reports from scrap meetings,
— reports from quality managers,
— reports of storage costs,
— reports of spares holding,
— reports of sales,
— reports from customers,
— etc.

Any of these reports or reviews may show that a change to the product, its manufacture, marketing, operation or servicing (or other support) will reduce the product's cost or enhance its profitability by design. It will be the function of the system to ensure that such changes are defined and their benefits assessed. One function of any formal project generation and assessment system will be to convert what seem to be good ideas into formal specifications of engineering problems.

5.4.2 Major projects

Much of what follows is derived from information supplied by the Procurement Executive of the Ministry of Defence and is published with their permission. Thanks are due to the Procurement Executive for their help in making such information available.

There are many ways in which a major project may be generated. In the military field, generating the project is called **concept formulation** and is defined as covering the period from the emergence of an idea for a project to the initial formal statement of an operational need. Factors which may lead to the generation of an idea for a military project include the following.

(1) The need to replace old or obsolescent equipment.
(2) A change in defence policy that requires a new capability.
(3) The identification of a new actual or potential threat.
(4) An output from a research programme which offers a new capability.
(5) An advance in technology.
(6) The need to meet a new concept or to overcome a deficiency which has been identified in operation, in training, in simulation exercises or by operational research.
(7) The existence of a foreign project in which Britain may wish to collaborate.
(8) Work on an existing project that stimulates the idea for its successor or a new use for existing technology.
(9) A proposal from industry (which may have been derived from commercial or export opportunities).

Ideas that are generated from the above (or any other) sources are expanded by discussion between the user, the various defence committees, the research and development establishments and industry, and this discussion is a necessary contribution to project development.

Civil projects are often generated in the same way as military projects, although there are some obvious differences in terminology and there is rarely a formally established mandatory procedure. It is reasonable to set up a procedure to generate projects that reflects military concept formulation, even where a company has no military market and firms which impose the discipline of a procedure on themselves are more likely to be successful than those which do not.

Just as in the weapons industry, new civil products may be generated for the following reasons.

(1)	Old or obsolescent products must be replaced. It is clear that any company that wants to stay in business must continue to review its products and to replace those that are failing to compete with more modern products. It is a function of the marketing department to ensure that there is a procedure to introduce the timely replacement of obsolescent products.

(2)	The company's long-range plans require a new capability. Any well-run company will plan its future (see Chapter 2). Plans are usually set both annually and for longer horizons (5 or 10 year horizons are commonly set) and these plans must map out strategies which will require the establishment of new capabilities. The most obvious need to establish new capabilities derives from extending the product range, often with new products that will complement and enhance sales in existing markets. It is a function of the marketing, technical and sales departments to generate such projects for consideration when the corporate plan is being formulated.

(3)	A threat to the company's existing market is identified. Again the formulation of the company's strategy must consider what to do to counter the threat of losing markets to competitors who offer better or cheaper products or services, and it is the function of the corporate plan, led by marketing, to generate projects which meet threats from the market. If we are looking for a civil analogy to the military threat, it is, perhaps, to be found in the perception of a customer need or an invitation from a customer to respond to his stated need, but this too will result from market-led engineering.

(4)	An output from a research programme offers a new means of meeting an existing customer requirement or offers a new capability. In some industries (the pharmaceutical industry, for example) future markets can only be determined by current research.

(5)	There is an advance in technology. The technical and production departments must continually look for new technology to exploit in their product designs or methods of manufacture. If they do not, their products will be poorer and dearer than those of their competitors. Clearly the corporate plan is only one method of introducing new technology and this must be reinforced by a procedure which will inject (particularly small) changes.

(6)	The need to meet a new requirement or a deficiency in the existing product that has been identified by technological forecasting or by the operations of groups within the company that have been asked to identify scenarios of the future.

(7)	An opportunity to collaborate in a project with another company.

(8)	Work on the development of an existing project which stimulates the idea for a successor or some new product.

It is usually necessary to set up a formal procedure to ensure that projects are generated. Many of the origins of concept formulation are in the market, deriving from customer needs, and it might be thought that a customer need would be made known by an invitation to tender, but a prospective supplier who knows nothing of a customer need until the invitation to tender arrives is unlikely to be a strong competitor for the job. The marketing department of any potential supplier must know what business they are in and should know of the requirement long before the customer formalizes it. Indeed, since the engineers of the tendering company would profess to be experts in the field, they would hope to obtain a position from which they can help the customer to formalize his requirement. Many market-led requirements will not derive directly from the customer's own perception of his needs but should be identified by the marketing department or by service engineers. Service engineers are particularly important in identifying faults in existing systems which provide an opportunity for offering enhanced or new systems.

However, market-led requirements are as likely to be small enhancements as major new concepts and the process for generating projects will not, initially, be concerned with (perhaps not even aware of) the size of the projects that are being generated.

One way of formalizing concept formulation is to set up a 'new projects committee', usually chaired by a senior member of the company—the technical director and the quality manager are examples of such chairmen in different companies. A procedure for generating projects for consideration will analyse reports from sales engineers, service engineers, scrap meetings, project managers, etc., as has been suggested in section 5.4.1, but the agenda will include invitations to tender or to respond to Ministry of Defence concept formulations. Reports on the development of existing projects will also be included in any agenda because they must be considered in a competition for resources; a project does not become immune from criticism when work starts on it. We shall be reviewing projects in hand while we look for projects which are new in conception as well as projects which reduce the cost of existing products or enhance their performance, life, reliability, maintainability or appearance. This procedure is shown diagrammatically in Fig. 5.3.

5.5 PROJECT APPRAISAL

The procedure in Fig. 5.3 is a simplification of what must occur because it implies that a committee will be able to review a suggested product and either accept or reject it. In fact, it will nearly always be necessary to spend time and money to study a proposed project and even then an acceptance of the project does not mean that it cannot be rejected later. The review of a suggested project is more likely to lead to the allocation of money (or man hours) to further study than to its outright rejection or acceptance and the company's budget must contain allowance for such study.

In the military context, if concept formulation generates a project which is not immediately rejected, the Defence Staff initiates the formulation of a first formal statement of the operational need, called the **staff target**. Once the decision is taken to formulate a staff target, a **feasibility study** is initiated and usually the Ministry of Defence will pay one or more companies for the work involved although they may undertake the study in a research and development establishment.

When the project is a civil one, there is still a need to study it before committing the company to the cost of the whole of the design, development and manufacture that will

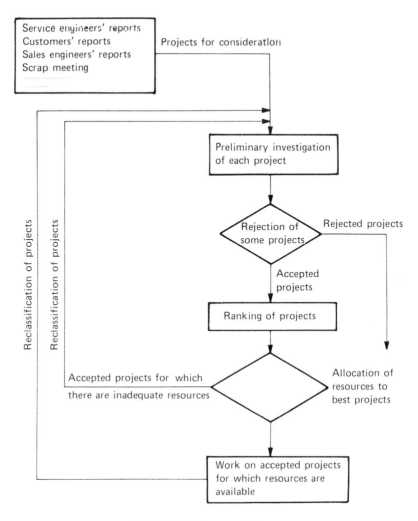

Fig. 5.3 – Project appraisal.

be required if the project is undertaken in its entirety. This problem does not arise in the case of projects which are clearly mandatory. There is no need for debate, for example, before installing a modification to a motor car that removes a danger but, if a project is not mandatory, the only reason for selecting it will be its profitability and the measure of profitability is likely to be the net present value (NPV) or the internal rate of return (IRR). If there is sufficient information to permit discounted-cash-flow (DCF) calculations, there need be no debate but generally much work has to be done to predict the cash flows that a project will generate before any such calculations are possible. When we attempt to predict cash flows, we find that they are uncertain and we need to study the risks inherent in a project as much as its nominal performance.

These difficulties have led to the development of heuristic methods of projects appraisal, particularly in companies which are involved in research and development. One such method that has been described (particularly in the literature of the 1960s) is the scoring model, although it may be that the procedure is more written about than formally used. Hart [4] devised a scheme in which the decision maker determines the merit of a project to the company from values that he has given to its different aspects. Fig. 5.4 is the chart that was suggested by Hart for evaluating projects. The logarithmic way in which the score for a project quality is derived means that the total score for the project is related to the product of the values (or the inverses of the values) awarded by the decision maker. Some aspects of the project require a more complex treatment than others, e.g. the life of the market must be related to the time to set up production in order to discount the positive cash flows over the project life. The chart in Fig. 5.4 was devised for a particular company some years ago and so it is likely that the relationship between factors would be different in another company and costs and values would be considerably greater in a modern application.

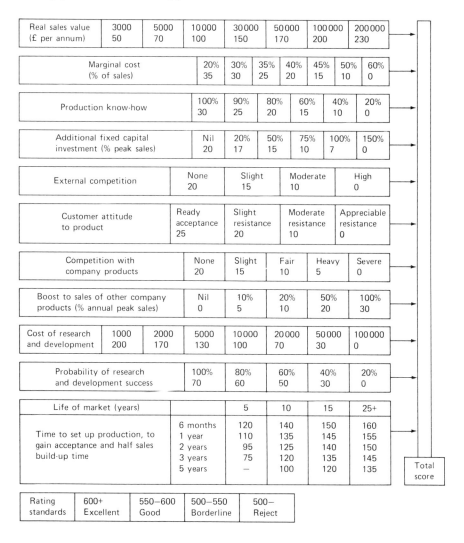

Fig. 5.4 – Hart's evaluation chart for research and development projects.

Another method of scoring a project was suggested by Pope [5]. This combines the following.

(1) The cost A of development.
(2) The gross profit B.
(3) Time sensitivity C. A measure of the variation in net return with marketing date.
(4) Competition D. A measure of the competitive activity in the same market.
(5) Chance E of success.
(6) Ultimate potential F. A measure of any further opportunities.

These factors are combined to give a project score:

$$ACE\left(\frac{B}{A} + D + F\right).$$

Although Pope's model has many factors in common with Hart's, the score is derived in a slightly more complicated way. Both models, however, force the decision maker to enumerate and evaluate those factors which could influence the success of a project, although in neither case is there any analytic justification for the way in which those factors are converted to a project score.

Two problems arise immediately that we try to use a scoring method of appraising projects: the heuristic nature of the method and the time that must be devoted to it. In a commercial context, we should undertake only projects which are mandatory or which are profitable.

If a project is mandatory, if for example, it is forced upon us by health and safety considerations, then we need not waste time assessing its value. We shall, of course, need to assess costs in order to determine milestones for the management of the project but this is not part of the selection procedure.

If a project is not mandatory, we should accept it only if it has a positive NPV at the company's cost of capital or if it has an IRR that is as attractive to the shareholder as any other project on offer. But the NPV or the IRR can rarely be calculated with any degree of certainty. To calculate either the NPV or the IRR of the project, we need to predict the cash flows that it will generate over its life and the likely cost of capital. To make these predictions we need to be able to forecast the government's financial policy and the economic state of the world. Clearly we cannot do this with any precision—risk is involved. We may find a product more or less difficult to develop than we thought (generally we find it more difficult and sometimes we even fail, for technical reasons, to bring a product to the level of development at which it is saleable—consider TSR2 and Nimrod). We may believe that the market for the product is much more or much less than we thought, we may find that a competitor produces a better product, we may find that changes in technology make our product redundant, etc.

The fact that we cannot make precise predictions of the behaviour of a project must not prevent us from attempting to do so. Backing horses and playing cards are games of chance but the chances of backing the right horse or making a good call at solo will be much improved if we study the factors that lead to success.

If we consider Pope's formula we see that the factors that must be determined by the decision maker are as follows.

(1)   The cost of development which, at best, is an educated guess since we cannot know, in advance, what we have designed wrongly and needs to be put right.
(2)   The gross profit which, again, is an educated guess. Estimates of development cost and profit are really both estimates of future cash flows.
(3)   Time sensitivity, which is simply a measure of the amount by which future positive net cash flows must be discounted.
(4) ⎰ Measures of competition and the chances of success which are a heuristic approach
(5) ⎱ to the consideration of certainty-equivalent cash flows.
(6)   Ultimate potential, which is a guess at further future cash flows that the project might generate.

Generally, scoring methods are heuristic attempts to allow for risk in DCF calculations but they should not be dismissed. Their heuristic nature may well provide short cuts to the evaluation of parameters which can be determined no more than approximately, whatever the sophistication of the techniques used.

However, a project cannot be evaluated without spending money, and the money that we spend is, itself, a risky investment that requires some care. If we spend money evaluating a project and show that the project is not, in fact, worth further investment, we have wasted the money already spent. We might have wasted more money still had we gone ahead with the project without properly evaluating it but in either case some money is spent that cannot be repaid by the project under investigation.

If the customer initiates the main project effort by inviting tenders, the purpose of his early evaluation will be to ensure that the product (system or service) that he wants to buy really will be valuable to him. The customer's invitation to tender is a decision to proceed with the project, taken after the expenditure of time and money. If a supplier is invited to tender for the provision of a product (system or service), the purpose of his project evaluation will be to ensure that he can predict cost and times well enough for his tender to be realistic. In this case, the supplier will be competing for the job and he may not get it. He will then have wasted the money already spent, but perhaps he should have spent more evaluating the project so that he could support his tender more effectively.

Evaluating a project requires a compromise between risking too much money so that good predictions of future cash flows are made at a cost that the company cannot afford to write off and spending too little money on prediction so that, although the company can afford to write off the money, it spends too little effort to make an adequate forecast of cash flows. It was certainly believed in the 1960s [6] that many expensive defence projects were started because their costs had been underestimated, only to be cancelled when actual costs were found to be too great for the country to afford.

How much we should spend on the early evaluation of a project before we commit ourselves to the whole cost of its design and development must vary from industry to industry. Pugh [7] suggests that spending 10% of the expected design and development costs leads to cost predictions of acceptable accuracy. Downey [6] suggested 15% or 16%. Fig. 5.5 shows the increase in accuracy of the forecasting as work proceeded in one project. This is unlikely to be representative but shows how much we may have to spend to achieve good forecasts. However, the whole cost of the evaluation need not be ventured before any decision is made and normally decision making is a step-by-step process.

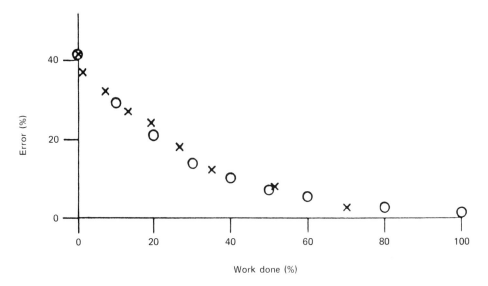

Fig. 5.5 – Reduction in error in forecast cost as work proceeds (error expressed as percentage of final cost): O, negative exponential reduction in error; x, actual reduction in error.

5.6 STEPS IN PROJECT EVALUATION

As we have seen in section 5.4, the first step in project management must be project generation (or concept formulation, in military terminology). In the military context, the suggested projects will be discussed among the likely user, the various defence committees, the research and development establishments and industry and as a result of this discussion the concept will be translated to a formal statement of operational need, called a **staff target**.

When the staff target has been defined, the Ministry of Defence will initiate one or more **feasibility studies**. The feasibility studies may be carried out at government research and development establishments or by private companies. Usually, contracts will be awarded for the work and often two or more firms will work competitively on the project.

The feasibility study is likely to be mostly a paper assessment of the project but modelling and experimental work may be a necessary part of the exercise. The output that is required from a feasibility study is as follows.

(1) Technical appraisals of alternative solutions to the problem posed by the staff target and an evaluation of the preferred solution.
(2) An outline of the performance characteristics required by the staff target and which will be necessary for project definition of the preferred solution.
(3) A statement of the areas of difficulty to be expected during the project and of the steps that will be ncessary to overcome them.

(4) Detailed plans for the phase of project definition which will follow the feasibility study and outline plans for the development and production phases which will follow project definition.
(5) Initial estimates of the likely time and cost of development, production and support.
(6) An assessment of any resources that will be required by the project.
(7) An assessment of the in-service life of the equipment and its potential for stretch.
(8) Any additional information necessary to formulate a **staff requirement**.
(9) Predictions of the foreign sales and the likelihood of foreign collaboration.
(10) The possibility of purchasing the equipment from overseas.

When the feasibility study has provided the above information, the decision will be taken by the Defence Staff to kill the project, to seek further information or to initiate the **project definition** phase. The decision to initiate project definition is made by issuing the staff requirement that derives from the information generated by the feasibility study.

The Ministry of Defence will probably award a contract to one or more companies for the project definition. The objectives which must be met by the project definition phase of the work will be as follows.

(1) A verficiation of the solution to the problem, proposed by the feasibility study. This verification will include the identification of high-risk areas and likely development problems.
(2) An analysis of the trade-offs between product performance, project times and costs.
(3) The finalized agreed performance characteristics of the equipment.
(4) Outline specifications covering engineering and performance specifications, trials and software.
(5) Firm plans for the full development programme, an outline plan for production and outline requirements for support when the equipment is in service.
(6) Realistic assessments of the cost and duration of the development programme and an estimate of the cost of the equipment in production, from stated assumptions.
(7) Proposals for the procurement strategy and contract action.

Project definition is normally carried out under the direction of a project manager.

If the project is complex, it may be necessary to conduct project definition in two stages: project definition 1 (PD1) and project definition 2 (PD2). PD1 will explore, particularly, the high-risk areas of the project and generate outline specifications and plans. PD2 will follow PD1 unless PD1 has indicated that further work is undesirable and the project should be killed.

Downey [6] recommended that the feasibility study should cost about $\frac{1}{2}\%$ of the expected cost of design and development and that PD1 should cost about 5% and PD2 about 10%. We thus have several stages of study and each stage costs more than the last. At the end of each stage we may decide either to kill the project or to continue. If we decide to continue, we commit ourselves only to the cost of the next phase. This procedure is shown as a decision tree in Fig. 5.6.

Large companies have problems that are similar to those of the Ministry of Defence and similar procedures may be used. Thus, deciding how much to spend studying a power

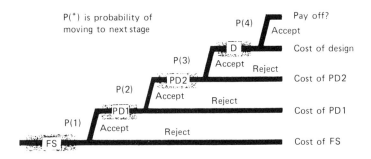

Defence projects

Downey 1968
Feasibility study (FS)
Project definition 1 (PD1)
Project definition 2 (PD2)
(for small projects PD2 is eliminated)
Design
Suggested that spend
before commitment is 5%
could be 20%

P(*) is probability of
moving to next stage

P(4)   Pay off?
Accept

D   Cost of design

P(3)
Accept   Reject   Cost of PD2

PD2
P(2)
Accept   Reject   Cost of PD1

PD1
P(1)
Accept   Reject   Cost of FS

FS

Costs probable rise exponentially

Fig. 5.6 — Stagewise project appraisal. $P(n)$ is the probability of moving to next stage; FS, feasibility study; PD1, project definition 1; PD2, project definition 2 (for small projects, this is eliminated). Downey [6] suggested that spending before commitment should be 5% but could be 20%.

station, a chemical works or a major production line, before committing the company to its full cost, requires much thought. Generally, then, civil companies will use stagewise decision processes before commitment to the whole of a new major project.

Smaller projects may be subjected to a modified version of stagewise decision making, especially when a company has many projects in hand at the same time. This modified procedure is the regular review of all the projects proposed or in hand. Typically, a committee, chaired by the technical director, will meet once a month to review every project, either proposed or in hand. Thus there will be no specific points in its life at which commitments are made to do more work; commitment may be deferred, more information may be requested, money will be made available for the next phase of work, or it may be withheld, but such decisions will be made at regular time intervals and not at pre-determined points in the life cycle of the project.

One of the problems of project appraisal is its cost. Generally, if a company is asked by the Ministry of Defence to make a feasibility study or a project definition, the work will be contracted for and paid for. At least, the work will be paid for if the negotiated price covers the cost. In such a case, of course, the taxpayer pays for the work to be done.

In the civil world, the work may be paid for by a customer who invites a supplier to tender for the provision of equipment but this is not often the case. Usually, the supplier is risking his own money in the effort required to make a good response to an invitation to tender or to evaluate a proposal from within the company. Suppose, for example, a company were to spend 15% of the estimated cost of a job in an effort to get the job; if only one tender in five were successful, an average £75 would be spend to get a job worth £100. If 5% of the estimated cost were spent getting the work, then £25 would be spent to get work worth £100.

5.7 PROJECT EVALUATION LOOKS FORWARD

It will have become clear that evaluation is not a simple process which tells us whether to accept or reject a suggested project. It is a process which provides the information without which the project could not be managed if it were accepted. It is almost incidental that the information required for project evaluation is largely that which is required for project management.

If we look at what is required of the feasibility study (p. 92) we see that it is engineering information, preliminary specifications, detailed time and cost plans for project definition, outline time and cost estimates of development and production, and assessments of necessary in-service support. The project definition phase must provide more engineering information, risk evaluation, more detailed specifications, plans for development, and outline plans for production and in-service support.

Project evaluation requires expensive work and yet it ends, rather than starts, with the detailed specification of what is to be done. The project engineer has engineering problems to solve, of course, but he must determine the following management problems.

(1) **Acceptance**. Equipment must be subjected to acceptance procedures to ensure that it meets the staff requirement (or the contractually agreed specification for a civil project). Sometimes equipment will progress through various stages of qualified acceptance before final acceptance is achieved. Acceptance criteria must have been set out in the technical specification in order to provide the basis for acceptance trials.

(2) **Post-design services**. The post-design process is necessary to control changes during and subsequent to production. These changes may arise as a result of user experience or manufacturing problems or to effect economies. The process will not involve major new design as this would create the need for a new project but it will include much cost reduction and product enhancement.

(3) **In-service support**. Equipment cannot enter service effectively unless in-service support has been planned and its cost budgeted. In-service support will involve the design of a system of operator traing and of the training of repair personnel, the design of operating and maintenance procedures, the manufacture of spares and the organization of a spares-provisioning programme.

(4) **Documentation**. Any intercourse between supplier and user will require documen-tation: documentation to describe acceptance, modification, quality management, defect reporting, and many other procedures.

(5) **Disposal or decommissioning**. In some cases, decommissioning can be expensive (what do we do with worn-out atomic power stations?) and project definition may

well involve consideration of the final disposal of the equipment or its manufacturing plant.

(6)   **The feedback of information.** Strictly, this should be considered as part of the problem of documentation design but the feedback of quality information, particularly, could require a management procedure of its own.

Project generation and evaluation require an organization and management structure of their own although these may be integrated with project management. Project management is not possible without the information obtained during evaluation but, because project evaluation can be costly (see p. 93) and may be closely allied to marketing, there is sometimes a danger of its being too far divorced from later management of the project.

SUMMARY OF CHAPTER 5

(1)   There are many reasons for generating a project. These range from the need to offer a major new system to the customer to the need for constant small changes to a product, to reduce its cost or to enhance its value.

(2)   Most large projects cost more than was predicted and, early in their lives, generate less income than was predicted. It nearly always becomes necessary to devise small projects that will bring the parent project back to its predicted earning capacity.

(3)   The learning (or experience) curve suggests that constant vigilance is required to generate small projects of cost reduction or product enhancement.

(4)   Major projects cannot be specified before work starts on them. In the early stages of the work, the specification of the project is subject to development just as is the product itself.

(5)   The cash flows that a project will generate cannot be predicted with acceptable accuracy before much work has been done.

(6)   The work needed to define a product and to predict the cash flows that it generates implies that knowledge of the project improves with time. Major discussions (e.g. whether to continue with a project or not) can therefore be made with increasing expenditure but decreasing risk. Military procurement uses stagewise decision making—concept formulation, feasibility study, project definition (1), project definition (2) and complete design. Companies in the civil field should also use stagewise decision making.

(7)   Some (scoring) methods of evaluating projects are available although there is no evidence that these methods are anything but heuristic. Again, while such methods may predict the value of a project they will not provide milestones against which the project may be managed.

REFERENCES

[1]   K. Hartley (1978) Cost escalation in UK aerospace projects. *Research and Development Management,* **8.**

[2]   T.P. Wright (1936) Factors affecting the cost of airplanes. *Journal of Aeronautical Sciences,* February.

[3]   P. Jefferson (1979) Private communication after unpublished paper. *Symp. organized by the Manchester branch of the Royal Aeronautical Society.*

[4] A. Hart (1965) A chart for evaluating product research and development projects. *Operations Research,* **13**, 550–569.

[5] J.R. Pope (1972) Evaluation of development—technical and managerial. *Proc. British Association Conf., Leicester.*

[6] W.G. Downey (chairman) (1969) *Development cost estimating*, Report of Steering Group for the Ministry of Aviation. HMSO, London.

[7] P. Pugh (1986) *The cost of sea power.* Conway, London.

6

Types of contract

6.1 PROJECT CONTRACTS

The relationship between the purchaser (customer) and the contractor is a reconciliation of two very different motivations. The customer requires a satisfactory project on time and as economically as possible: the contractor is striving in the long term, for increased profits. The project manager must therefore appreciate the legal basis of contracts in general as well as the particular conditions attached to those which are his special concern.

Throughout the life of the contract his interest is focused on three aspects: scope, time and price.

Today with projects being contemplated which are both novel and on a grand scale it is more than ever necessary to be absolutely clear about the performance requirements, the delivery programme and costs. These are becoming increasingly the subject of trade-off agreements designed to give the customer satisfaction, and the supplier some semblance of freedom, within a publicly accountable budget.

6.1.1 Contract writing

Every project engineer appreciates that an accurate specification is essential to enable the purchaser and supplier to work satisfactorily together but actual contract documents are often too inexact. The tortuous and ponderous language of legal documents can repel all but the most steadfast readers. Nevertheless, contracts are vital documents and their drafting assumes corresponding importance.

A contract has been defined as a promise which the law will enforce. It is also a means of communication between customer and contractor. The elements of a contract are an intention to create a legal relationship, the competence of the parties to enter into it, a lawful subject matter, a proper consideration in return for performance, and a genuine consent of the parties to do specific things.

It is essential for a project manager to understand the full context of the contract and the principles upon which it is based. Thus he may well wish to ask such preliminary questions as the following.

— When is a contract made?
— At what stage of our negotiations does an obligation of any kind come into being?
— Is it obligatory to use a particular form of contract, or is one entitled to use variants?
— Are there any terms that the law requires to be included in a contract?

If one is dealing with a foreign customer, it will be necessary to ask which system of law is applicable to the contract, bearing in mind that there are a number of critical issues, as well as a host of minor issues, on which the English law of contract differs from other systems.

6.1.2 The standard forms
Some branches of the Law of Contract have been codified by Act of Parliament; examples are the Sale of Goods Act (1893) or the Consumer Credit Act (1974). These Acts impose standard terms and formalities, some of which can be varied, and others of which cannot.

Engineering contracts are *not* subject to any such codes—the standard forms are norms derived from experience over years of negotiations. They save time and expense, but parties are free to vary them at will or abandon them altogether. In general, they strike a fair balance of interests between the parties, but they are not exactly similar to each other and some forms are fairer to one of the parties than others. Standard form contracts account for more than 99% of all contracts now made.

Some purchasers—public authorities, foreign governments and major industries— prefer to contract on their own terms, and contractors should always note the respects in which these differ from the standard form.

Some well-known standard forms are as follows.

(a) Model form A, general condition of home contracts for mechanical or electrical engineering works. Recommended by the Institution of Mechanical Engineers, the Institution of Electrical Engineers and the Association of Consulting Engineers.

(b) Standard forms of tender, contract and general conditions of contract for structural engineering works. Issued by the Institution of Structural Engineers.

(c) General conditions of contract, forms of tender, agreement or bond, for use in connection with works of civil engineering construction, approved and recommended by the Institution of Civil Engineers, the Association of Consulting Engineers and the Federation of Civil Engineering Contractors.

Project managers should also make themselves aware of the model form of new 'General Conditions of Contract MF/1' for home and overseas contracts 1988 for which a good practical guide for users now exists. For projects overseas they should also be acquainted with the Condition of Contract International Federation Internationale des Ingenieurs-Conseils. For building projects they must also know about different types of Joint Contracts Tribunal Standard Form of Contract.

Contracts come into being when a *firm* offer made by one party is accepted *unconditionally* by the other party.

Putting out to tender is not an offer, but an example of a prospective employer inviting offers. There is no obligation to accept any of the tenders.

A tender on the other hand is an offer, provided that it contains sufficient detail to make it certain on what terms the offer is made.

Acceptance is unconditional and creates a binding obligation. A party must accept exactly what is offered and cannot accept and impose modifications at the same time. Any attempt to do so would mean that a contract would not be created. The modified acceptance would, however, constitute a 'counter-offer' which the original tenderer could then accept in turn, if willing.

At the onset the project manager will check the following points.

-   Has a contract been made?
-   If so, when, and what are the terms?
-   What provisions have been made for dealing with contingencies?
-   What provisions does the contract make for handling grievances?
-   To what extent can one party limit liability?
-   How are third parties affected by the contract?

The project manager is primarily concerned with the scope of contracts in terms of money and time and any special conditions and warranty.

6.2 SCOPE

The first essential in drawing up a contract is to determine the extent of the work to be done and the requirements. From consideration of these the user's representative has to decide what form of contract will give his employer the cheapest job in the required time at the lowest price, which must be stated as definitely as possible.

If a contract is so complex that both parties must have an army of experts to interpret its terms, it is likely to contain so many conflicting objectives as to be unworkable. However, not all contracts can have definite terms. The risks attached to the contract are inversely related to certainty. In increasing order of technical certainty we can list research, feasibility studies, development, design and production.

Where the facts supporting the contract are clear, a contract for a specific lump sum will almost certainly be the best but, if certain of the important items covered by the contract are subject to considerable doubt, such items should be covered by a separate schedule and the price based on some agreed measurable variable.

The completion date of a contract must be clearly stated in the documents and will have an important influence on price, since it may necessitate overtime, premium rates, additional plant, etc. Completion on time is not something which just occurs, it has to be planned and worked for; the contract should provide an incentive to the contractor and and effective remedy to the employer for late completion.

'Completion' itself needs clear definition. It could be the date of

(a)   goods shipped (or ready for shipping),
(b)   delivery of goods to the purchaser's stores,

(c)   physical completion of construction on site or
(d)   plant and equipment commissioned and proved.

The type of contract depends upon the job, its completion date and the risks incurred. At one end of the spectrum there is the research and development contract where the uncertainty is high, leading to a lack of appropriate criteria for pricing. Until fairly recently, the traditional pricing basis for government research contracts was actual costs necessarily incurred, plus an agreed percentage profit.

At the other end of the spectrum, for instance, with a production contract, agreement is generally reached on a fixed price. Where production is continued over a period of time, actual cost can again be used as a basis. The learning curve may be built into the contract to reduce the price year by year.

Both the above policies have come in for persistent public and private criticism. The 'cost-plus' method encourages waste and rewards good and bad work alike. The 'agreed-price' formula for production work has been shown on occasions to lead to excessive profits. Great efforts have been made by the Government to introduce the incentive type of contract, with appropriate risks being shared by both parties. In such cases, indeed in all types of contract, the contract writer has to show clearly how such defined risks are to be allocated and identified.

6.2.1 Papers included in the contract documents
The contract documents usually comprise the following.

(a)   The invitation and advertisements to tender.
(b)   The conditions of tender.
(c)   The general conditions of contract.
(d)   The special condition of contract.
(e)   The specification.
(f)   The plans, drawings and other pictorial representations.
(g)   The schedule of rates.
(h)   The formal tender.
(i)   The correspondence which might take place in the final negotiation stages for the contract, or which accompany the tender.
(j)   The formal acceptance of tender.
(k)   A form of bond.
(l)   A contract agreement.

With a few exceptions, these items are indispensable and should never be separated from one another. After acceptance of a tender, the complete set of documents must be assembled and in Government work it is normal practice to seal them under a formal contract agreement. In industry a letter of acceptance is often considered sufficient. Before this happens, an overall critical review of all the assembled documents should be made to ensure consistency.

6.2.2 Quality of writing
The engineer who is responsible for preparing the contract specifications must bear in mind that they will be used by contractors in preparing their tenders. The fewer

ambiguities there are, the more competitive and closely priced the tenders will be. Tendering times are almost always short and only where the specifications are complete, explicit and logical will the contractor's staff be able to manage their work of tendering quickly and correctly. The customer obviously benefits from competent tendering.

If, on the contrary, the supplier has to spend money in clarifying the situation, the extra cost will eventually appear in the tender price, and so will any unresolved uncertainty.

6.2.3 Wording

The first requirement, as in all writing, is of clarity of intention in the mind of the writer. He should use clear concise grammatical English without colloquialisms. He should be consistent; too often, different words are used for the same item in the same documents, causing confusion. An example of this are words such as 'formation level', 'grade' and subgrade', which are commonly used in earthwork contracts.

Not all similar terms are synonymous; always distinguish between 'standard' and conventional' and between 'outcome' and 'consequence', for subtle differences in meaning can make great differences in price or performance.

Avoid circumlocutions such as 'in the case of', 'from the point of view', 'in regard to', 'with reference to', 'in this respect' and 'due to the fact that'. All such phrases can be used on occasions, but they result from, and lead to, sloppy thinking.

In general, verbs and nouns make for a clear style. Adjectives tend to clutter clauses and slow down the reading rate and adjectival nouns are ambiguous.

6.2.4 Drawings

The contract drawings, together with the written specification, should give a complete definition of the work to be done and of the quality of workmanship required.

Usually, the first graphic documents to be prepared are the design drawings. These must be complete, clear and logical, without undue cramping of details. Sheets should be numbered in a logical sequence and indexed. Wherever possible, scales should be identical for similar items.

It is very desirable that 'trades' should be separated, e.g. structural steel should be on a separate sheet from reinforced concrete work. The aim should be a graphic representation that builds up a story of what is required.

For civil projects, sheet 1 should show the locality, with access points to site clearly marked. This is followed by the site plan and general arrangement drawings.

In mechanical drawings, third-angle projection should be used, as this aids comprehension. Where necessary, perspective sketches should be introduced to clarify understanding.

Contracts are sometimes 'let' on incomplete drawings, and details prepared as the contract proceeds. This may save time by an early start, but very great care has to be exercised to get an accurate bill of quantities with unit prices specified.

6.2.5 Bill of quantities

The contract schedule, or bill of quantities, or material parts lists will be prepared from the plans or drawings. They are often the basis of contract payments and must, therefore, state the cost of each item.

Each item must also be defined simply and clearly, but care must be taken to allow for differences in quality of the same item, for instance, between soft and hard rock, which involve different costs in their removal.

Units of measurement must be explicitly stated, if possible, in terms of an accepted standard. If there is any departure from general practice, attention should be drawn to it.

Finally, care should be taken in each contract to provide for changing conditions which are beyond the control of the contracting parties. One typical example is value-added tax. The Institution of Civil Engineers, the Institution of Mechanical Engineers and the Institution of Electrical Engineers have now added Clause 71 to their general conditions of contract, to allow adjustment to the contract price to cover this tax.

6.3 TYPES OF CONTRACT

As previously mentioned in project work, the type of contract will vary according to the order of certainty. Generally speaking increasing order of technical certainty will carry such names as research, feasibility study, project definition (PD1 and PD2), full project development, and production. Financial uncertainty from the point of view of the contractor moves in the reverse order.

Engineering contracts can be separated into two main types: the fixed-price contract and the cost-reimbursement contract (which can include incentives). The form of a contract does not in every instance need to follow exactly these established types, although if any 'half-way' arrangement were proposed it would have to be very carefully thought out. Whichever type of contract is used, the intentions behind the contract should be clear and should remain clear and unvaried throughout the documents. This may appear so obvious as not to need saying, but mistakes have been made, with consequent serious financial liability falling on the purchaser.

There is only one type of contract which is purely a fixed price contract, and that is the one in which the contract is let for a fixed sum. It is commonly called a 'lump-sum' contract. There are, however, two other types of contract which are sometimes spoken of as fixed-price contracts because the price is based on a bill or schedule which is priced at the time of tendering. These two types of contract are the bill-of-quantities contract and the schedule rate contract. In such contracts the items of work are to be done for a fixed price or a fixed-unit price, but the overall sum to be paid is the aggregate payment for all the items as finally measured.

Included under the general broad heading of cost-reimbursement contracts are those contracts where the contractor is paid the actual cost of the works, plus a percentage of cost or a fee. There are certain variations of these contracts; for instance, a fee may be fixed, or it may fluctuate according to the closeness with which the contractor approaches a target cost for the works.

6.3.1 Fixed-price or lump-sum contracts
There can be no doubt that, where the circumstances permit, this is the most satisfactory type of contract for the employer, and also for the contractor (provided that the content of the works to which the lump sum relates is clearly set out), for the amount of payment is clear and specific. In such contracts a unit-price schedule is commonly called for, it being clearly indicated that this schedule is purely for the purpose of facilitating the

pricing of variations, whether these be additions or deductions; it is not intended for remeasurement.

Essentially, the condition which limits the application of a lump-sum contract to a particular work is the degree to which the work is clear and defined or, in other words, the extent of the risk to be taken by the contractor. If the plans and specifications have not reached a stage when they are quite clear and specific, then probably the employer is paying too high a price for risk. He would be better advised to use one of the other types of contract, where payments are made either on remeasurement of a bill of quantities or, perhaps, on a schedule of rates.

Any lump-sum contract which is let without the works being described clearly and specifically can be a most unsatisfactory contract and can cause much dispute. If the contract involves a risk (say, in respect of the type of country to be met) as civil engineering contracts often do, then the extent of that risk to the contractor may be reduced by paying him for that particular part of the work on a fixed schedule of rates.

In effect, this means that the schedule is warranted by the employer in respect of some features, e.g. such quantities as are specifically included within a limited field may be warranted as being in accord with the drawings. In the event that they prove not to be in such accord, payment for the difference would be made in line with the rates of the schedule. If this provision is made, it may reduce cost to the employer, but it must be very clearly set out.

Alternatively, the contractor may be required to assume the risk in his lump-sum price. If this risk is very considerable, then his lump-sum price will be high, and it may in the end be better business for the employer to assume that part of the risk in a priced item. This is a subject for nice judgement.

Quite large contracts for the supply of machinery or plant will commonly be on the basis of a fixed lump sum. Large civil engineering and building works, however, usually include construction variables which make it difficult to let the work as a straight fixed sum. This should nevertheless be the aim, even though one or more sections may be made subject to remeasurement on fixed rates.

6.3.2 Bill-of-quantities contracts

Contracts which include within the contract documents a bill of quantities are in very common use in civil engineering and building works. A detailed bill of quantities is prepared under itemized headings which will cover the complete work. The tenderer prices these items, and the contractor is paid at his tender rates for the actual quantities of work completed under each item. A typical bill is shown in Fig. 6.1.

Provided that everything goes well, this is a good type of contract. Indeed it is probably one of the most straightforward to administer, even when difficulties arise. Disputes arise in all types of contract when meanings are not clear, and the basis of contract therefore confused. When resolving such matters, the engineer must be judicial in his treatment.

It is essential in a bill-of-quantities contract to state that the items include the whole of the works; otherwise the position might arise later that the contractor will demand payment for work for which there is not a specific item. The danger of this could be reduced by the competence of the architect or engineer drafting the bill, and by the inclusion of a requirement that the contractor must include in the bill any further items of work which he believes to have been omitted. In general, if a bill is drafted with care,

			£	p
(a)	150 mm × 32 mm sawn softwood batten placed in lintel prior to fixing as ground for curtain rail	631 m		
(b)	225 mm × 32 mm ditto	53 m		
(c)	10 mm expanded polystyrene in vertical strip 210 mm wide placed behind dry lining, including polythene vapour barrier on the inside face of the polystyrene	634 m		
(d)	30 mm × 5 mm mild steel strap, 450 mm girth, twice bent, one end drilled and screwed to softwood and other end turned into joint in blockwork (WC24)	86Nr		
(e)	Ditto 1500 mm girth, ditto once bent, drilled and screwed to top of floor joinsts (WC24)	89Nr		
(f)	Galvanized mild steel anchor plate comprising 100 mm × 75 mm × 6 mm thick box section 225 mm long, twice drilled and bolted to concrete foundation (measured elsewhere) with and including two ragbolts 9 mm in diameter, 125 mm long, with nut and washer, including mortices in concrete and grouting in (WC24)	54Nr		

Joinery

			£	p
(g)	Include here or in the rates for the following.			
	Holes for pipes, bars, trunking and ducting and the like and all notchings (WC19)	Item		
	Treated wrought softwood unless otherwise described (WC19)			
(h)	175 mm × 50 mm plate	75 m		
(i)	100 mm × 75 mm ditto	100 m		
(j)	100 mm × 75 mm vertical post in support to porch roof screwed to anchor plate (measured elsewhere)	124 m		

To collection   £

Fig. 6.1 − A typical bill of quantities.

It is possible, and reasonable, to relate items of work within one or other of its items.

If the quantities vary substantially from the original bill (so that the price of the contract as envisaged by the parties at the time of letting it is substantially changed), then provision may be necessary, either for variation in the contract rates or for some other allowances in the contractor's payment. This is in fact one of the most fruitful sources of argument in a bill of quantities contract.

Architects and engineers must adopt a strictly impartial attitude and act with complete fairness in judging claims of this kind.

If an important item in the works is enlarged or decreased substantially, the contractor may have to rearrange his whole organization. To give an example, suppose that the bill of quantities is based on 1 000 piles of, say 20 ft in length, and in practice it turns out that some of these piles have to be 60–80 ft in length. It is evident that the contractor may have to obtain plant of a different type from that on which he based his price. To pay on a straight unit price, as given under the bill of quantities, may then be quite unfair. Likewise, if the quantity of piles is cut down so that perhaps there are 200 or 300 instead of 1000 or if the length is cut down from say 30 ft to 10 ft, then the payment of a unit price may again be unfair, and the engineer should give careful consideration to any claim that the contractor may make.

This applies to the more exceptional case. The engineer should, however, bear in mind that experienced contractors may be expected to foresee that variations will occur in underground work and may reasonably be expected to provide for these within the range of fair and normal expectations.

Perhaps one can illustrate the point by saying that a contractor's plant and organization should be sufficiently elastic to permit variations of quantities above and below those given in the bill—up to, say, 20%. Beyond such limits, some special consideration of plant, organization and establishment may well be fair and equitable.

6.3.3 Schedule-rate contracts
The term 'schedule-rate contract' is often used indiscriminately with a bill-of -quantities contract. A schedule-rate contract is the type of contract which is used widely for repetitive work, such as cartage, earth-moving contracts, kerbing and channelling, centre-line marking, drain laying and maintenance work. Quantities may be given only approximately—sometimes not at all. The contractor is usually asked to quote a price for establishment on and removal off the site, and this charge may recur. His rates should be fixed for a given time period.

6.3.4 Cost-reimbursement contract
As indicated earlier, where the time fixed for the completion of a project has not allowed for preparation of adequately detailed plans, specifications and a bill of quantities, it may be necessary to consider a cost-reimbursement contract. Such a contract may also be necessary at times when costs of materials and labour conditions are not stable, such as during a war or in the years immediately following.

In such contracts the contractor is paid the actual cost of the work, plus a fee. This fee may be a fixed sum, a percentage of the costs, or a fluctuating fee.

It will be evident that, unless the arrangements for assessing the costs of the works are clearly defined, much difficulty and dispute may arise; likewise, unless the arrangements for payment of the fee are carefully drafted, so that there is considerable incentive for the contractor to work economically, it may be difficult to obtain good value for money.

Therefore, the conditions surrounding any given case should always be thoroughly investigated to confirm that it is not possible to arrange some form of fixed-price contract; then careful thought should be given to including as much incentive for economy as possible. Such provisions should be built into the arrangements for the payment of the fee.

When tenders for such contracts are considered, more weight than usual should be given to the confirmed experience of the contractor; the adequacy of his resources, the availability of his plant, equipment and key personnel, and his reputation generally on contracts.

It should furthermore be remembered that contracts of this type involve the employer in very considerable expense in checking the contractor's methods and costs and auditing his records and accounts, because these are the basis of payment. It is important that the basis of charging be agreed before the contract is made, and it is wise to have this set out in the tender documents.

Cost-plus-percentage contracts
When the contractor is paid the cost of the works plus a percentage of this cost, there is little incentive for him to economize, either in time or in money. This type of contract should be avoided if possible. Where it is felt necessary to embark on such a contract, it is particularly important to ensure that the basis of charging be agreed in detail before the contract is made and be set out in the tender document.

Cost-plus-fixed-fee contracts
When the contractor receives a lump-sum fee for executing the work, it should be noted that this fee is not affected by the actual cost. If the quantities prove to be greater than estimated at the time of fee fixing, there may be a dispute and it is as well to include some provision to cover this situation. It is true that the contractor has some incentive, indeed an important incentive, to complete the works in good time, even when the fee is fixed. If he does so, his supervision and overhead costs are reduced to a minimum. Nevertheless, there is no complete safeguard against his adopting uneconomic or costly methods to complete the job in the shortest time, and therefore the employer is vulnerable.

It follows from the above that the fee for this contract arrangement should always be inclusive of the administrative and overhead costs of the contractor. He should not be permitted to make a separate charge for such services; otherwise even the incentive for completing to time will be lost.

Cost-plus-fluctuating-fee contracts or target-type contracts
Contracts of this type are designed to include incentives towards both economy on the works and early completion. The type of contract which has been developed to include these desirable features is the target-estimate contract. In such contracts, estimated cost and completion time are used as a basis for consideration at the time of tendering. The contractor's fee is increased as the cost is reduced below his estimate and, likewise, with any savings in time. On the contrary, the fee is reduced, according to some stated fomula, as the cost increases and as the time extends.

In devising this formula, great care must be taken to strike an intelligent balance, so that the contractor can aim to adjust his operations in order to produce optimum conditions—the maximum profit for himself and the cheapest work for the employer, consistent with completion on time.

It is worth reiterating, however, that the employer will be put to considerable expense in checking the contractor's costs against measured quantities and in satisfying himself as to the reasonableness and propriety of the costs put forward. If quantities vary, the contractor will seek an increased fee but, should quantities prove to be below those on which an estimate was originally based, he will probably resist strongly any suggestion that his fee be reduced for a reduced quantum of work. See Fig. 6.2 for a typical target-type contract.

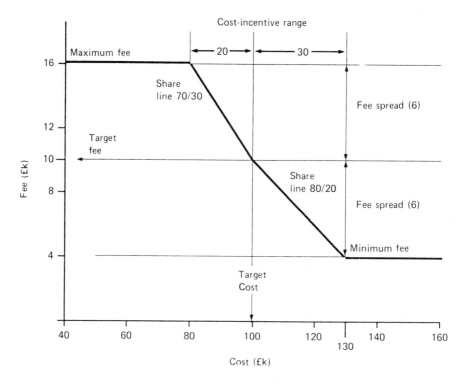

Fig. 6.2 – Target-type contract. If the final cost is £80k instead of £100k, the contractor gets £6k added to his target fee (the total saving is £20k; the customer gains £14k; the contractor gains £6k, i.e. gains are in the proportion 70/30). If the final cost is £130k instead of £100k the contractor has £6k deducted from his target fee and the customer pays £24k more than the target cost (i.e. losses are in the proportion 80/20).

A contract of this type calls for good and careful drafting of all the documents. In particular, there should be strict limitation of the grounds for variation of fee. Genuinely additional work (such as an extra building or an extra generator) would justify it, but mere expansion of the quantities in a particular item might not. It should be borne in mind that, after all, the contractor has been freed of virtually all risk.

Therefore between the extremes of a fixed-price contract (illustrated in Fig. 6.3) and a cost-plus contract (illustrated in Fig. 6.4) it is particularly important that the purchaser

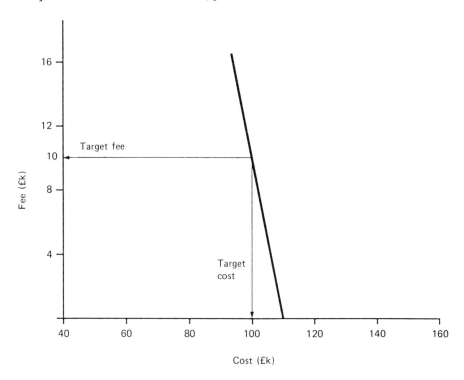

Fig. 6 3 – The fixed-price contract. If the contract is let for £110k and the target cost of £100k is met, the contractors fee is £10k. If the cost is £110k, the contractor gets no fee but, if the cost is £90k, the contractor's fee is £20k. Whatever the cost the customer neither gains nor loses and the gains are in the ratio 0/100.

of large sophisticated projects should employ an appropriate method of making it worth-while for the contractor to meet or exceed his requirements. For in essence a contract is much more than a piece of paper. It is a device which should harness and control the profit motive to achieve the results required by the customer in terms of price, delivery, quality and reliability.

There are really three main objectives which incentive contracts aim to achieve.

(a)   To keep costs as low as possible.
(b)   To achieve or better technical performance requirements.
(c)   To meet or improve delivery dates.

Hence it is possible to talk about cost incentives, performance incentives and delivery incentives. Of these, cost is the most frequently used. This is mainly because it is easy to devise but also because performance and delivery incentives are valueless under normal peacetime competitive conditions in the absence of a cost incentive.

Obviously there are grave dangers to agreeing fixed prices on unreliable cost estimates and the main alternative to this method in the past has been the cost plus contract. Here contractors are reimbursed for their costs with a percentage profit. The consequence of this is that there is no risk or loss for the contractor. It should therefore only be used where high risk is concerned as with an advanced development contract, but this type of

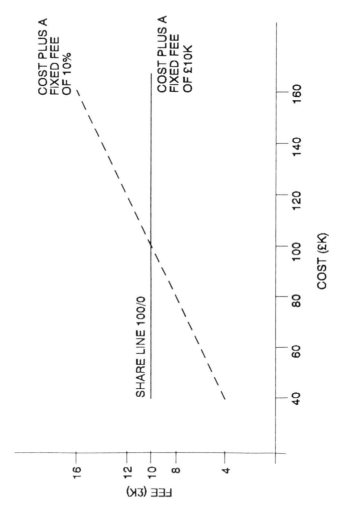

Fig. 6.4 — The cost-plus contract.

contract tends to reward good and bad performance alike. In fact, really bad performance is rewarded better.

If there is complete confidence in the cost estimates a fixed-price contract is an obvious solution. but with many projects there can be little assurance about the accuracy of cost estimates to make them suitable for fixed prices. Yet, on the contrary, the uncertainties are not always so great as to justify the use of the cost-plus type of contract, bearing in mind its disadvantages.

Hence it is necessary to devise some pricing mechanism between the two extremes which would limit the risks for both the contractor and the purchaser and yet at the same time provide adequate inducement to keep contract costs down.

A way of providing this is by having a target-cost type of contract which gives the necessary flexibility so that varying degrees of confidence in cost estimates may be accommodated.

The basic ingredients of a cost-incentive contract are threefold.

(a)   A target cost.
(b)   A target fee.
(c)   A share formula.

The target cost should be the best estimate determined mutually by the customer and the contractor of what the costs will be when the work is done.

The target fee will be the amount of profit payable if the costs come out at the target costs.

The share formula will determine how the excess cost (overexpenditure) or savings in cost (underexpenditure) in relation to the target cost will be shared between the customer and contractor.

The method of operation is then as follows. If the actual costs exceed the target cost, the contractor will be paid his costs, plus target fee *less a proportion of overrun* in accordance with the share formula. If, on the contrary, the actual costs are less than the target, the contractor will receive his costs, plus the target fee *plus a proportion of the underrun on spend.*

Typical cases of incentive contracts are as follows.

(a)   **Unlimited sharing** (Fig. 6.5). Here the target cost is £100k, the target fee £10k and the cost-sharing formula is 80/20.

If the actual cost equals the target costs, then the contractor gets his fee of £10k. If, however, the target cost exceeds actual cost, the contractor gets 20% of the savings (i.e. if the cost is £60k the contractor's fee is increased by £8k).

(b)   **Limiting the sharing** (Fig. 6.6). Obviously, if target costs are set too high and the contractor achieves much lower costs, considerably larger profit could be made and so some form of cut-off must be provided to limit the share arrangements.

At the overrun end the limitations take the form of either a maximum price or a minimum fee. A maximum price is normally appropriate when the confidence in the target-ccst estimate is fairly high. When there is a high degree of uncertainty in the cost estimate, it may be considered that the risks are such that the sharing arrangement on the overrun should be limited by a minimum fee. On the underrun

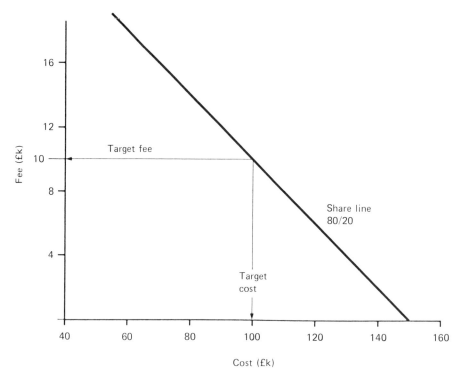

Fig. 6.5 – Unlimited sharing.

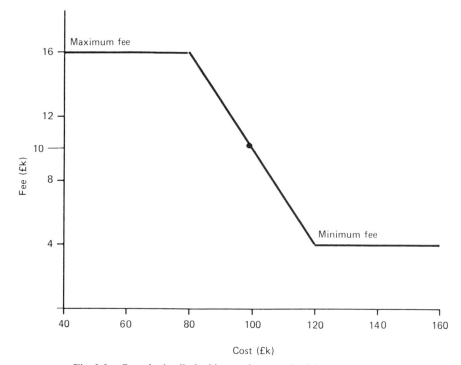

Fig. 6.6 – Cost sharing limited by maximum and minimum fees.

side of the target cost, the limitation on the sharing arrangement takes the form of a maximum fee.

(c)   **Fixed price** (Fig. 6.3). The cost–fee graph is of a fixed-price contract where the fixed price is £110k. Since it is a fixed price, the customer has no share in the savings (or it may be said to be a 0/100 sharing formula).

       If the final cost is £100k, then the contractor's profit is £10k. If, however, the final cost is £120k, the contractor's loss is £10k.

(d)   **Cost plus fixed fee** (Fig. 6.4). Here the fee is constant regardless of actual costs and it will be seen therefore that the contractor is guaranteed reimbursement of all legitimate costs plus a fixed fee so that the sharing formula may be said to be 100/0. Alternatively a fixed fee of 10% of cost may be used.

(e)   **Target-cost contract without a maximum price** (Fig. 6.6). Here the sharing arrangement is limited by minimum and maximum fees. A target cost is negotiated which should be the best mutually determined estimate of what the cost will be when the work is completed. Also a target fee is agreed to give a reasonable return for the work done and capital employed. In this case a target cost of £100k is set with a target fee of £10k. Limits of confidence in the target cost are then assessed to determine the lowest cost at which the work might be accomplished and the minimum reasonable estimate of cost. This assessment sets the range of possible deviations from the target cost over which the cost incentive provision must be effective. In this case the deviation is set at 20% of the target cost, i.e. the lowest estimated cost is £80k and the highest is £120k. Also the maximum fee is fixed at £16k and the minimum fee is set at £4k.

       Hence the fee spread is £12k and the cost-incentive range is £40k, so that the share line is 12/40 or 0.3 (or 70/30 if we apportion the savings between the customer and the contractor). In certain cases it may be desirable to have a varying share line as shown in Fig. 6.2.

(f)   **Target-cost contract with a maximum price** (Fig. 6.7). Here the maximum price represents the limit of the customer's obligation to pay the contractor for the work under contract. In this case the maximum price is £115k and above this cost, the share line becomes 0/100.

(g)   **Multiple-incentive contracts** (Fig. 6.8). Here incentives may be applied to each area of the contractor's effort, namely cost, performance and delivery. Where such incentives are applied to two or more areas of contractor's work, there will be an interplay between the differing incentives which determine the total profit.

       Here a contractor seeks to climb the so-called 'hill of happiness' by trade-offs between the three dimensions of achievement. The results are unlikely to please everyone but it does mean that negotiations take place within the set budget.

6.3.5 Design and build contracts

There should, perhaps, be some reference to 'design-and-build contracts'. Such contracts are used in some of the most important industrial applications and are usually based upon a service specification. The normal practice of a large oil company wishing to construct an oil refinery, for instance, is not to draw up its own documents nor to engage consultants for the purpose, but to approach firms who are experienced in designing and building refineries. The oil company compiles a detailed service specification of the work which the refinery will be called upon to do, and then they make their careful choice

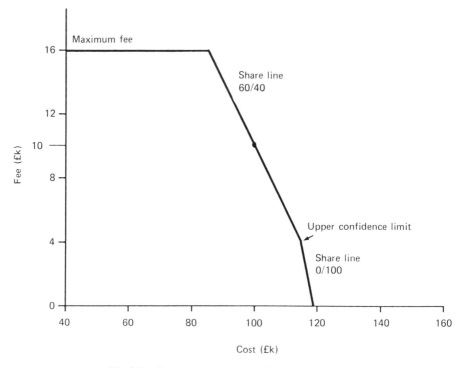

Fig. 6.7 – Target-cost contract with a maximum price.

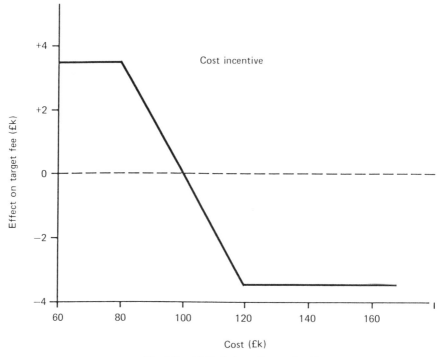

Fig. 6.8 – Multiple-incentive contracts.

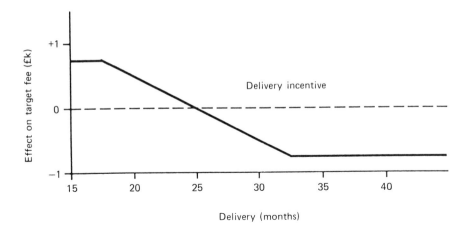

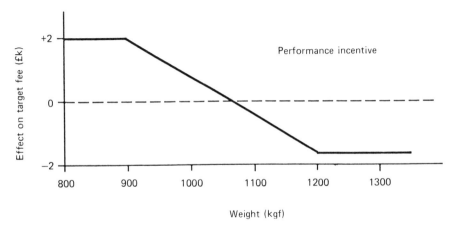

Fig. 6.8 – Multiple-incentive contracts.

from a restricted field. Having, after preliminary negotiations, chosen a contractor from this field, their expert engineers can keep in close touch with him throughout the design-and-build contract. Such contracts as these, when applied to special cases, have been found to be the best solution but, for the construction of the great majority of works, it is greatly preferable for the employer to engage competent professional advice to design his works, and to call for tenders from contractors (either on an open market or in a selected and restricted field) for the construction of these works.

A 'design-and-build' or 'turnkey' contract will be a satisfactory contract while things go well but, when they do not go well, difficulties may show up. The employer will then find that the engineer is the servant of the contractor, while he (the employer) is left without professional advice. Should he then engage such advice, his consultant will be without that detailed and continuous knowledge which can be so important at such times. This may lead to bad relations between the engineer and contractor, which will aggravate the difficulty of the situation.

6.4 TERMS AND CONDITIONS

Whatever type of contract is used in executing a project it is essential that the project manager is fully aware of the terms and conditions imposed in the contract. All contracts, including contracts of service, contain two types of term: those which are 'express' and those 'implied'. The term banning alternative or additional employment is 'express' whereas a term preventing an employee from competing with his company or firm is invariably 'implied'. Clearly it is not possible within the compass of this book to discuss all contract conditions but some of the main points are mentioned below.

6.4.1 Variations and omissions to contract

If a purchaser is likely to require variations after the contract has been let, then it is important that the contractor recognizes a satisfactory negotiating procedure for establishing variations in price. Not all variations lead to a change in price; some may require a redefinition of responsibilities and for such cases a variation procedure should be drawn up.

It is vital to appreciate that a variation instruction is only binding on a supplier when

(a)   it is in writing and signed by the engineer or his representative,
(b)   it is not so fundamental as effectually to alter the scope of the contract and
(c)   generally it must not be of such a value that, when added to variations already sanctioned, the sum is less than 15% of the contract price.

Should the supplier require additional time to execute the contract as a result of the variation, he must notify the engineer.

6.4.2 Escalation of costs

Once the costs of the proposed work have been estimated, the supplier must consider the effects of the duration of the work on the escalation of those costs. In a fixed-price contract then the responsibility rests with the supplier to estimate the escalation which might be expected to occur in the life of the contract and to introduce a contingency to cover such rises.

On long-running contracts, however, it is now accepted practice to include some form of contract price adjustment. The formula for calculating cost escalations may be simple such as that given by The British Electrical and Allied Manufacturers Association (BEAMA) or rather laborious such as the National Economic Development Office. Fundamentally all formulae for determining fluctuations are similar, differing only in the degree of detail and the reference index to be applied.

Basically each formula assumes that the increase in reimbursable cost area or expenditure is approximately equal to the product of the cost area times the change in reference index.

It is difficult to test any particular method except on a historical basis. The indices of material and labour costs are published by a variety of bodies, i.e. the Baxter indices by the Property Services Agency, part of the Department of the Environment, and apply to all civil engineering contracts which incorporate price fluctuation clauses.

The BEAMA formula is based on statistics from a broad range of BEAMA member companies on the incidence of labour employment, material employment and material expenditure during the contract and the proportion of 'inadmissible' overheads and profit. Indices of material and labour costs produced by the trade and industry are used to measure the percentage change between cost basis date (i.e. tender date) and a date determined as a specific proportion of the contract period.

For different types of engineering plant, other formulae have been evolved based on similar principles but with appropriate indices and reference data.

6.4.3 Penalties

Often, especially in continental contracts, penalty payments play an integral part in the contract which must be recognized by the supplier in budgeting. Penalties may occur owing to failure to meet the set programme or failure to meet the performance requirements.

If there is a breach of contract, there are various remedies available such as liquidated damages for delay.

While damages are the normal remedy awarded by the court for breach of contract, there are three other main remedies.

(a)   Specific performance.
(b)   An injunction.
(c)   *Quantum meruit.*

Both (a) and (b) are equitable remedies which may be awarded at the direction of the court to any person who has suffered a legal injury where damages would not be an adequate remedy. Specific performance is an order requiring a person to carry out a contractual obligation.

An injunction is an order of the court restraining the doing, continuance or repetition of a wrongful act. It may be obtained to enforce a negative contractual obligation where an order for a specific performance would not be available—thus if a designer agreed to work for a certain employer and then in breach of his contract agreed to work for a competitor. In such a case, although the employer would not have been able to obtain an order for specific performance of the original contract for personal services, he would be successful in an application to the court for an injunction.

Lastly '*quantum meruit*' is a claim for the value of work done under a contract. It rests not on the original contract but on an implied promise through acceptance by the other party of the benefit of the work done. If therefore a contract is suddenly cancelled, the contractor may apply *quantum meruit*.

6.4.4 Liquidated damages

The main feature of liquidated damages for delay is that they are a pre-estimate of the losses which, at the time of entering into a contract, it is estimated the purchaser would be likely to suffer were completion to be delayed, and which would arise directly out of such a delay.

The amount of such loss and therefore of the damages may and very often does bear no relationship at all to the value of the contract.

It is commercial practice for such damages to be expressed as a percentage of the contract price.

The reason for liquidated damages is not to provide the employer with an effective remedy but to protect the contractor by limiting his liability.

Hence the liquidated-damages clause, often, wrongly called a penalty clause can serve a number of useful purposes. The clause saves expense in litigation over the consequences of a breach and provides financial certainty for the contractor who then knows the limitations on his possible liability for delay.

6.4.5 Terms of payment

Again here it is essential that a supplier should establish the incidence of expenditure by his enterprise and compare this with the terms of payment offered by the purchaser. The cash flow generated by a project has been covered in Chapter 4 but it is vital that the buyer pays the contractor in a timely way and payments should reflect the rate of expenditure on the project.

A careful study has to be made by all suppliers to ensure that at various stages of the project there is not an undercovering of costs. If this proves to be the case, different terms of payment with the purchaser must be established or some external financing source such as the banks must be used.

Any supplier must understand any effects of retentions on his financing considerations. Final release of retentions may not be under the control of the supplier and great care is therefore necessary.

Progress payments

Most conditions of contract provide for payments on account. For civil engineering contracts these take the form of interim certificates covering estimated contract value to date of work on site and materials and plant delivered to site. For heavy capital plant equipment there are generally regular progress payments. In plant contracts the supplier may well include in progress payments items which have not been delivered to site maybe because the purchaser has prevented him doing so. There is therefore provision for such items and progress payments are generally made on account of manufactured work executed at the supplier's factory. In such cases 'vesting' clauses are extended to cover plant in suppliers factories and are earmarked as the purchaser's property before a progress certificate is issued.

Certificates of payment

For a supplier to obtain payment from a purchaser for any plant equipment there is a distinct procedure which must be adhered to as follows.

(1)   The supplier applies to the engineer for the appropriate certificate: **progress, interim, taking over, final.**

(2)   The engineer will issue the appropriate certificate to the contractors within 28 days.

(3)   The supplier presents the certificate to the purchaser.

(4)   The purchaser pays the supplier within *14 days* on a progress or interim certificate or otherwise within 1 month.

When the contract so provides, progress payments are made on account of plant manufactured and work executed prior to the commencement of deliveries to site; normally three payments are made when the value reaches 25%, 50% and 75% of the contract price and are limited to 90% of these values. Once deliveries to site commence, interim payments are made of 90% of the certified value of the work executed on site and plant delivered to site.

The final 10% (retention money) is released in two parts, first as 5% against the presentation of the taking-over certificate and second as 5% against the presentation of the final certificate.

SUMMARY OF CHAPTER 6

(1) A contract is a legally binding definition of what the project manager is committed to supply to the client.

(2) A contract must be accurate and unambiguous. Standard forms of contract, recommended by the major engineering institutions, help the project manager and his client to ensure that the contract is of an acceptable precision.

(3) Contracts may be 'costs plus', i.e. they require that the contractor makes a profit that is either a fixed sum or a fixed percentage of the cost of the work (whatever it costs). At the other extreme, contracts may be 'fixed price' so that the contractor will profit only if he is able to meet the client's requirements within the agreed price.

(4) While 'cost-plus' contracts provide no incentive to the project manager to limit cost overrun, they may be necessary where risks are greater than the contractor can be expected to accept.

(5) Between the 'cost-plus' and the 'fixed-price' contracts there are forms of contract which share the risk and profit (or loss) between the contractor and the client—if the project is completed for less than the original target cost, the gain will be shared and, if there are cost overruns, the reduction in profit (or the loss) will be shared. Such contracts preserve some incentive to work within budget while reducing the contractors' risk.

(6) It is essential for the project manager to understand the terms of payment and penalties that may be imposed during the execution of a contract.

7

Proposal preparation

7.1 PROPOSAL PREPARATION

A good proposal is vital to winning a contract or convincing top management of the need for a particular project. For large projects it is desirable for a project manager to help, or at least be party to, the proposal compilation. He will then be in a position to bring valuable experience from past-project execution to the proposal effort and will become aware of the 'whys and wherefores' of a particular proposal.

A proposal may be to sell to higher management a feasibility study, to change some production feature of a mass-produced product or to tender to some customer for a large portion of work.

From all these points of view a proposal may be looked upon as the means whereby a company, team of engineers or an individual sells ideas to a customer. The customer may be someone with the firm or outside. In either case the quality of any proposal establishes the group's or individual's reputation with the customer concerned.

Good proposals cost money to produce and must be designed to yield the results required, but poor proposals can also cost money and yield no return. Management at all levels must appreciate the importance of proposals and seek constantly to improve their quality. One international customer has reported that about 70% of the proposals which they receive are inadequate in one form or another, 20% are barely adequate and only 10% can be considered satisfactory. Considering the investment in money and time involved in proposal preparation and the importance of proposals to engineers and, in particular, contractors, it is surprising that nearly three out of four proposals seem to have little chance of succeeding from the start of the budgeted effort.

7.2 THE NEED AND FUNCTION OF A PROPOSAL

It is the function of a proposal to sell to the client, the managerial and technical ability of the company to execute the work required at a reasonable cost. It is not just the technical aspects of the proposal which count. The proposal must be a document which will convince the customer that the proposed solution to the problems presented is the best available, and that the company has an adequate organization and adequate personnel, managerial skills and facilities to complete the proposed programme on time and within the tendered price.

7.2.1 Spectrum of proposals

In certain instances, the technical proposal presented by a company may represent a substantial breakthrough in the state of the art and be clearly ahead of its rivals and in this case the technical section of the proposal is the deciding factor. However, in many cases it is not possible to give a clear-cut solution to a particular problem but rather to suggest the technical approach which the company would employ. Here the contractor is really selling the technical competence of its people, the skill of its management, and its overall general ability to develop an acceptable solution. The calibre of the personnel involved, both technical and managerial, is likely to be a more decisive factor than the technical proposals presented. Next there will be proposals where the weighting of the technical and managerial aspects are comparable. Finally, at the other extreme, there will be standard technical solutions to meet the customer requirements, and here management planning and control and estimating expertise will be most important. The complete spectrum of types of proposals might be represented as indicated in Fig. 7.1.

In compiling any of the above types of proposal, the combined parts of the proposal must show that the company has an understanding of the customer's problem and that the proposed design solution is not overdesigned or overpriced. It must convey the impression that the company has a real interest in the customer's problem and outstanding technical ability in the specific problem areas involved. It should stress economy consistent with the difficulties involved and should show that the company has adequate facilities for research, development, design, test and production. Emphasis here will depend upon the type of proposal. The managerial aspects must stress the ability to manage a realistic programme based on a logical plan together with the physical and human resources that would be deployed on the work. Finally all parts of the proposal must harmonize to make a complete whole which is easy to follow.

7.2.2 What constitutes a proposal

A proposal is an offer to supply a product or to perform a service, or a combination of both in response to an inquiry. Proposals may be very brief or they may require several volumes of many pages and diagrams. Consequently the costs of producing proposals vary by hundreds of pounds. It is also likely that a number of subcontractor's proposals will need to be prepared, considered and finally incorporated within the main proposal.

7.2.3 The tendering procedure

A tender is an invitation to trade. Before tenders are called, there should be a genuine intention to proceed with the work required by the ultimate issuing of a contract. A tender is therefore a proposal which constitutes a formal offer so that a contractor may be chosen and a contract placed.

The purchaser initiates a demand for a certain procurement to which contractors respond with their proposals and the best proposal is awarded a contract. Tenders are multipurpose documents which aim at describing and defining the plant, equipment,

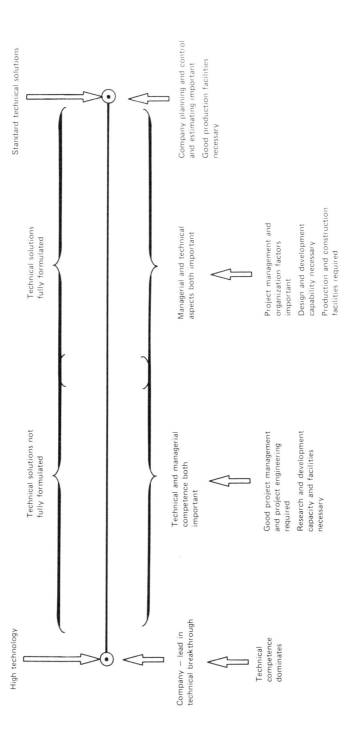

Fig. 7.1 – The spectrum of types of proposals.

service, etc., offered to customers. They go beyond mere description to the true aim which is to sell the company and its products, projects or services in the face of competition.

A further important purpose of the tender documents is contained in the paradox of contracting that the customer never buys the product or service that is offered in the proposal. In other words the tender is only a basis for subsequent negotiatons.

There are two distinct procedures used: the first is formally to advertise the requirement and to request bids from contractors; the second is to negotiate from the start.

A tender is therefore a most important piece of advertising for any contractor and the submission must

(a)   be attractive and well presented and
(b)   minimize risks and ensure a reasonable profit.

The purchaser will issue some inquiry documents, or letters of request and these may vary from a simple letter asking for quotations to be submitted to very large documents with specific tender forms which have to be completed. Before starting on a tender the contractor must ask himself certain basic questions about the enquiry, such as the following.

—   For what is he to be responsible—has the work been clearly defined?
—   To whom is he to be responsible—customer or main contractor?
—   What are the general and special conditions of the contract?
—   When is the work to be completed—are there any penalties for delays?
—   What are the terms of payment proposed?
—   Are there any nominated subcontractors?
—   How long is there for preparing the tender?
—   etc.

The production of a tender commits company resources and therefore has to be carefully considered. The decision making process is a two-stage affair: firstly a decision has to be taken as to whether the company wishes to take on the work (the bid or no-bid decision) and, if so, then a decision must be taken to commit resources to plan the proposal realization.

Consideration will need to be given to a number of factors at both stages of the decision process, as follows.

—   The price obtainable within reasonable certainty.
—   The credit required and on what items (credit insurance).
—   The possibility of presenting an appropriate technical solution likely to win the contract within the time scale allowed.
—   The hazards and risks involved.
—   The time available for producing the tender.
—   The nature of the competition.
—   Present company loading and financial position.
—   etc.

7.2.4 The benefits of good tendering

Any tender becomes an effort to sell against competition. For capital goods projects the cost of this effort can be considerable but there are benefits to be achieved. Continued tendering helps to maintain a design team and keep them abreast of current technical developments and in good morale, even though some of the tenders may be unsuccessful. Also, if the potential customer carries out a thoughtful analysis of an abortive tender there is the possibility of learning where one's weaknesses lie (technical, organizational, managerial, etc.).

However, the balance sheet is not nearly so favourable with foreign tenders where the analysis of rejected bids is far less helpful. A good example of the state of affairs can be gleaned from the atomic energy field where quite often a government will announce ambitious plans for power station construction and hastily call for tenders, without first securing the necessary financial backing. In the early days of atomic power these inquiries were of a general nature and could be answered by a brief descriptive tender, but over the years the various governments have recruited staffs of experts and the inquiries have tended to multiply, causing increased complexity. Only the need for commercial security has kept tenders within reasonable limits.

There is always the danger that a foreign power company or government, on receipt of a large number of detailed tenders will feel confident enough to build a station on its own. A delicate compromise between revealing secret technical facts and the need to sell the station has to be reached, but the balance can be upset by the customer's post-tender enquiries which the hopeful bidders dare not leave unanswered. Thus, any government can get an excellent education for its atomic energy authority by the simple expedient of calling for tenders and asking enough questions. In the meantime the bidder bears the cost of tender preparation and may reveal commercial information for which he has had to pay a considerable sum in royalties, etc.

The export market for reactors is changing and the number of bidders may increase. Under these conditions a company possessing or having built a reactor to an offered design enjoys an overwhelming advantage. Such a company offering a 'turnkey' contract may need to reveal very little important information and may point to a prototype as proof of design viability instead of answering detailed questions. It may be recalled that in the early days General Electric won the Italian SENN Station with a single—although thick—volume of tender documents backed by its own reactor performance. At that time some UK bidders for enriched reactors were submitting up to ten volumes of tender documents. Such efforts in those days cost over £100k each and with 30 or so bidders the money involved in producing tenders could have built (although not fuelled) several prototype reactors.

7.2.5 Categories of proposals

Proposals may be categorized by the type of effort deployed in their achievement. These will include feasibility studies, research and development, design and production. Broadly there will be four categories.

(1)   Research proposals to advance the state of the art. These may or may not have a project in view.
(2)   Development proposals for the design and development of specific hardware for specified requirements.

(3)   Production proposals for specific equipment which is already produced (i.e. the design is already frozen).
(4)   Study proposals involving desk research and some laboratory investigations.

There may also be supplementary proposals to put forward suggestions for support services to aid design, development and production.

7.3 ORGANIZATION FOR PROPOSAL PREPARATION

Since a company's future business and welfare depends upon successful proposals it is surprising how few really set out to organize their preparation efforts.

The failure to organize for proposal activity results from the attitude that many engineering orientated management have, that the only important element of a proposal is the technical part. This concept has never been true and is becoming less true with each passing year. In today's competitive market, customers and clients are having little, if any, trouble finding a number of technically qualified firms to compete for their business. On the assumption that a number of firms have submitted good technical proposals, the basis of selection is often on the peripheral technical areas such as configuration management, technical data, reliability, quality assurance, etc., and, most important of all, in the management ability, demonstrated in the proposal, to co-ordinate the many functions necessary for successful performance.

It is the correlation of the different skill efforts within the bidding organization that is the real success element. No longer is it sufficient to have an *ad hoc* system of proposal preparation because of its lack of efficiency and high cost. Too often many companies assign proposal preparation to a project engineer who understands only the technical aspect of the proposal. This is a poor management approach. Generally a project engineer who is well qualified to exercise control of the technical proposal is probably neither interested nor qualified to handle the multitude of other factors that any customer considers in his evaluation of proposals.

Management, and all levels of the company, must recognize that the content, composition and style of proposals may be the deciding factor influencing the future economic welfare and long-term survival of everyone connected with the enterprise.

7.3.1 The proposal organization
Where a firm is of sufficient size and the number of proposals justifies it, a proposal manager should be appointed with a permanent group of proposal co-ordinators. For the optimum organization of effort there will need to be a combination of non-recurring and recurring skill talents. If a small firm needs to prepare proposals sporadically, then it will be best to appoint a senior project manager to co-ordinate and correlate the effort. In either case the following functions have to be undertaken.

—   The group must be the focal point for all proposals, requests for quotations, etc.
—   They must establish the mechanics and procedures for the preparation of proposals and presentation materials.
—   They should establish a house style with appropriate format, reproduction and binding quality based on the type and value of the project.

- They can be responsible for writing small proposals, with appropriate input from other company skill areas, but for large proposals they must act in the staff role, co-ordinating and harmonizing the efforts of others.
- They must set up review procedures and evaluation methods for all proposals prior to submission to a customer.
- They must establish a method of coding information on all proposals so that it is available for future reference on proposal work.
- A detailed index of each proposal must be prepared by the group in advance of work being undertaken. This must list, in logical sequence, each section, subsection and subsubsection, drawings, graphs, schematics, pictograms, etc. It is essential to have a consistent system of paragraph numbering to permit advanced cross-referencing.
- Finally, the proposal group must co-operate with the marketing department in setting up and maintaining a detailed critique file based on customer briefing. This must be assiduously kept for both successful and abortive proposals.

The routing of a proposal manuscript may be depicted as a flow diagram as in Fig. 7.2. It should be noted that the heart of this work effort is the co-ordinator.

7.3.2 Organization of a proposal department
As previously stated, if the load warrants a proposal group on a permanent basis, then it should contain the following.

- A proposal manager to direct the work—depending on the size of effort required, there may need to be more than one proposal manager. The proposal manager could be a project manager whose work load is currently light.
- Technical writers who must be able to present technical information simply, concisely, accurately and rapidly. They may be specialized, e.g. control system writers, structural and civil engineering writers, etc.
- Technical illustrators to handle all drawings, illustrations, schematics and exploded views required in the proposals, which may be presented in writing or orally. These personnel may be located in the engineering department concerned and assigned to engineers in the respective skill areas. They must be capable of producing pertinent, clear and uncluttered diagrams quickly.
- Reproduction typists assigned as necessary who can use work processors to produce standard formats, margins, headings, spacings, paragraph indentations, etc.

7.4 THE RESPONSIBILITY FOR WRITING PROPOSALS

As Fig. 7.2 indicates, the proposal department has the onerous job of pulling together all the efforts from different skill areas and harmonizing them to make a smooth flowing proposal. The role of the department therefore is one of co-ordination and on no account must they be allowed to be a scapegoat on whose shoulders the skills areas place the entire responsibility for the proposal effort.

As in project management the proposal manager must secure input from the various 'in-house' and 'out-house' groups and there are two possible methods of approach.

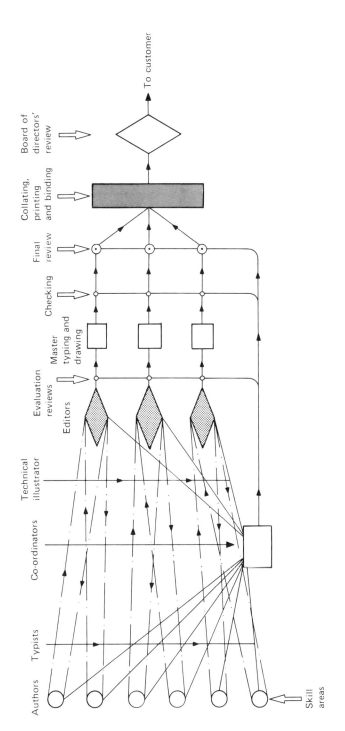

Fig. 7.2 – Flow chart of proposal preparation.

(1)   The proposal writers are responsible for securing information from the technical
       personnel and writing the various parts of the proposal.
(2)   The proposal organization plans and co-ordinates the proposal effort but ensures
       that the technical personnel concerned write the specialized portions for the
       proposal.

Method (1) suffers from not making the proposal effort a joint affair and method (2)
may lead to an unharmonized proposal which requires considerable polishing before final
production. On the whole, for large proposals, method (2) is to be preferred.

7.4.1 Responsibility of proposal team members
In reality, three distinct types of team member are required for the proposal department.

(1)   **Technical proposal members.** Here a temporary engineering group should be
       brought together consisting of the required engineers, systems analysts,
       mathematicians, specialist technologists such as metallurgists, chemists, etc., where
       required. They will be directed by a technical manager who, with them, will draw
       up the technical programme test-and-delivery schedule, the make-or-buy suggestions
       and the assessment of direct costs. Included within this group there may need to be
       personnel well versed in proposal work from other engineering support areas such
       as reliability, quality assurance, etc.
          Such temporary groups will need to be changed to meet the requirements of
       differing proposals.
(2)   **Cost proposal members.** Here the estimating and cost experts must review the
       technical programme produced and provide the cost format so that cost
       information can be developed and presented. This must conform to the client's
       or customer's request for a proposal. The elements of cost must tie in with the
       work statement and the firm's accounting structure. Any incentive or other cost
       indexes must also be clearly stated and fixed by this group.
(3)   **Management proposal members.** The management proposal must outline clearly
       the type and style of management that will be given to the technical programme.
       Information on past efforts may need to be quoted together with the relevant
       curriculum vitae of key management personnel, especially those concerned with
       project work. Special information on various support programmes such as value
       analysis, value engineering, safety analysis and security etc. may also be necessary.
       The team member of the proposal group must select wisely and write clearly about
       the organization, planning and control function to be used.

7.4.2 Responsibility of the proposal manager
The proposal manager has the overall responsbility for producing the best tender bid
within the required time. He must therefore be able to plan and organize effort over a
large number of individuals within the company. He must be able not only to manage his
team members but also effectively to lead and organize the working of the contributors
from the various skill areas.
    Often considerable resistance can be felt in these skill areas as proposal work
constitutes an additional effort which is superimposed on their normal day to day work
load. Hence the proposal manager must be able to exercise tact and diplomacy as well as

assertive drive and enthusiasm. Such drive must be constantly maintained in the face of a succession of lost proposal bids. He must always keep before him the need to devise and design new procedures and methods of producing timely proposals and above all to sell his company's capabilities. The overall compelling factor of his output must be that his company should be chosen for a particular assignment.

The proposal manager must also ensure that his group becomes the control point for initiating and terminating all proposal work and for this purpose he will need to establish a **request-for-proposal log** along the lines of Fig. 7.3. A further set of forms is then required to retrieve information from the various areas of the company. This necessitates a preliminary breakdown of the proposal content and will depend upon the nature of the work to be undertaken, the type of business, degree of complexity of proposal activity, etc. A typical example of such a form is indicated in Fig. 7.4.

The proposal manager must also be responsible for calling all the necessary reviews prior to final submission to the board of directors. In large companies a formal proposal review board would normally be constituted; for smaller concerns an informal group will be called together as required and should contain someone not concerned with all the proposal activity.

The broad responsibilities of such a board would normally be as follows.

- To review proposal preparation procedures.
- To review bid or no-bid decisions.
- To examine the experience and capabilities of technical, managerial and cost proposal personnel assigned to individual proposals.
- To overview the proposal outlines (Fig. 7.4).
- To monitor proposal activity to ensure that proper support is given to proposal activity in the various skill areas.
- To ensure that all proposals are reviewed by the board prior to submission to the customer.

The process outlined in Fig. 7.2 will demand several types of meeting in addition to the reviews previously mentioned and some of these are set out in Fig. 7.5.

7.5 PROPOSAL PREPARATION

Requests for proposals may come from a variety of sources—marketing channels, past customers, contract administration, production management, engineering, etc. Once the request has been received, it is vitally important that the mechanics of proposal preparation are set down and understood. Internal procedures will vary from firm to firm but should basically provide for the following.

- A quick preliminary analysis of the request for a proposal by the representatives of technical, manufacturing, construction, finance and other relevant departments to determine whether a proposal should be offered and to assess the extent of the effort that must be made to win the contract.
- The development of the initial proposal plan and outline; this will be a joint effort of the proposal manager and the technical and cost managers.

REQUEST-FOR-PROPOSAL LOG

Customer	Category of work	Date received	Proposal no.	Proposal manager	Due date	Date sent	Comments
ABC Co.	Feasibility study	June 1989	07214	Jennings	Jan 1992	15 Jan 1992	Prospect good
XYZ Partnership	Design	July 1989	07221	Elliott	May 1990		Doubtful, finance difficult
Former (Main contractors)	Design and development	July 1989	07223	Smith	–	–	–

Fig. 7.3 – Typical request-for-proposal log.

Proposal form A	Title	No.
Selection of work title		
Author	Date for completion	
Requirements		
Synopsis of idea:		
Main headings:		
Estimated length of text, diagrams required, etc.		

Fig. 7.4 – Typical form for preliminary breakdown of proposal content.

Meeting	To determine
(1) Review of request for proposal	Is it within the company's sphere of interest?
(2) Decision-making meeting: go or no go	Should it be taken on?
(3) Preliminary co-ordination meeting	Who and what will need to be contributed?
(4) Preliminary proposal review	Key points discussed
(5) Intermediate co-ordination meetings	Follow-up on who is doing what and by when
(6) Intermediate proposal reviews	Are all key points being covered?
(7) Final review and polishing	Does it all fit together?
(8) Final sign-off to customer	Proposal mail date

Fig. 7.5 — Types of meeting required for generating a proposal.

- The organization of a proposal team who should be briefed in the overall proposal plan.
- Fixing the format, style and quality level of the reproduction and binding of the proposal.
- Assessment of the following factors.

  - The performance risk. Where does the final (system not component) performance lie?
  - The value of partnership. Can a 'partner' spread the risk?
  - Whether the customer really wants what he is asking for. How can loss, costs or damage be contained if something goes wrong with the contract that has been won?
  - What capital expenditure will be necessary and whether there will be any residual value or re-use on other work.
  - What competition there is likely to be. How good is the competition? Do they have expertise that we do not?

At this stage, the company may decide not to bid for the work and go no further with a proposal.

A typical example of a network for this phase of the proposal work is shown in Fig. 7.6.

In making the key decision to bid or not to bid, the decision should be 'no' unless the company really needs the work, can withstand the risks involved and is willing to devote the necessary effort to generate a superior proposal. It is perhaps worth remembering that a well-written letter declining to make an offer is better than a weak proposal.

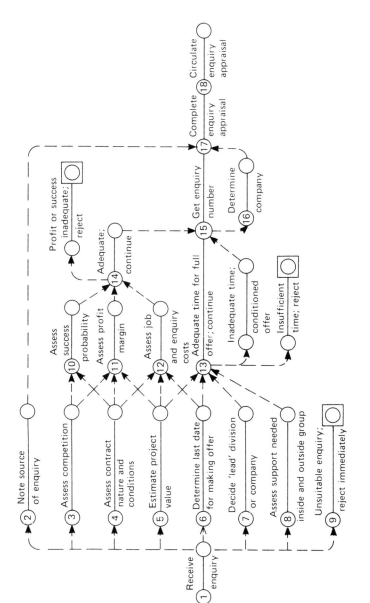

Fig. 7.6 – Phase 1 (the enquiry).

If it is considered worth while making a bid, then

— a list of all illustrations (drawings, schematics, graphs, etc.) should be compiled,
— a proposal time scale should be set down with appropriate milestones for reviews together with an estimated budget figure for proposals,
— check-lists for review meetings should be established and
— a properly constituted review board must be set up.

7.5.1 Phase 1: proposal preparation
After the request for proposal has been received, logged in and given a number, it must be immediately screened and a decision made as to whether to bid or not. Very careful proposal selection is desirable if money is not to be wasted.

The first examination must endeavour to assess the risks, e.g. as follows.

— Can we face estimating the risk?
— Is the project risk itself sensible? Does it fit our longer-term objectives?
— What about the payment risk? Can they pay? Will they pay? Will Export Credit Guarantees help?
— Finance. Shall we help him to pay? Again, will Export Credit Guarantees help?
— Contract. Which type should we use and why? Can we negotiate out liability or damages?

Proposals should only be generated where the company believes that it has a chance of obtaining a reward and where all elements of the company can wholeheartedly participate in the effort.

7.5.2 Phase 2: proposal preparation
On the assumption that the decision has been taken to go ahead, then the limited time available for the preparation of proposals makes it imperative that the proposal effort be planned in all aspects.

Initially the proposal manager must set the scene and outline the type of proposal required and stress the relative emphases to be placed on the various aspects of the work areas. The correct orientation of the proposal must be kept in mind; the viewpoint must always be that of the customer—what he needs and then why he needs us.

A typical example of a network for a large overseas project in this second phase is set out in Fig. 7.7. The detail of such a network will of course alter according to the nature of the business concerned. In the case cited, the enquiry was for a large civil, mechanical and electrical engineering complex in the Middle East.

The final form of the proposal must be determined; for small proposals, a single sheet may be sufficient and, for larger proposals, several volumes may be required. In the larger proposal of the type indicated in Fig. 7.7, it will be necessary to identify the required inputs from the various departments that will be concerned with the proposal development and an overall schedule must be evolved to budget both the time and the money available for the proposal preparation.

7.5.3 Phase 3: proposal preparation

The schedule should be flexible but it must include adequate time for the final overall polishing of the proposal. Too many firms spend so much time on the technical proposal that they leave too little or no time available for the preparation of the management and cost proposal and for the final editing and review of the proposal. This can lead to its being a collection of miscellaneous technical inputs, often lacking logical order and harmony, rather than a single coherent proposal. This is particularly important in overseas work where translation effort has to be included—an activity that is illustrated in phase 3 of the network in Fig. 7.8.

Any standard, mandatory or special aspects such as taxation problems, special restrictions in certain locations, security and patents must be carefully reviewed at this stage.

The principal activities of proposal preparation that must be scheduled are as follows.

(1)   Desk research work to gain the required background information.
(2)   The point at which the programme plan must be frozen.
(3)   The elapsed time allowance for adequately writing, editing and polishing the various inputs in order to present a coherent approach with respect to technical, managerial and cost factors.
(4)   The allowance of proper reviews to be co-ordinated.
(5)   Adequate time allowance for actual production, including any layout art work, printing, etc.

7.5.4 Format

Having fixed the timing of the proposal work the next step is to determine the actual format that the proposal should take so that appropriate binders, paper and captions can be prepared. The major cost of preparing any proposal will always be in the technical content and the cost of printing; paper, illustrations, binding, etc., will form a minor part of the proposal costs. It is the content and organization that are the most important and they must lead to a uniformly high-quality proposal regardless of costs. Since any proposal is the point of sale, it is manifestly false economy to cut costs on reproduction.

7.5.5 Development of the proposal plan

The technical team must review the request for proposal and identify key problem areas. They can then draw up their programme plan which must state clearly the objective to be achieved and a logical outline of the tasks to be performed. They should list the technical decisions required and assign responsibility for each task, estimate the manpower and facilities required, draw up a procurement plan and list any capital items likely to be required.

The cost team must draw up a cost estimate from the work statement and programme received from the technical team. Any cost plan must ensure that adequate control can be exercised if a contract is placed, and consideration needs to be given to the cost-reporting system required by the customer.

The proposal manager must review these development plans and ensure that all contractual terms and conditions are understood. He may well need to go back to the customer to obtain clarification of certain aspects of the proposed work or to seek additional information.

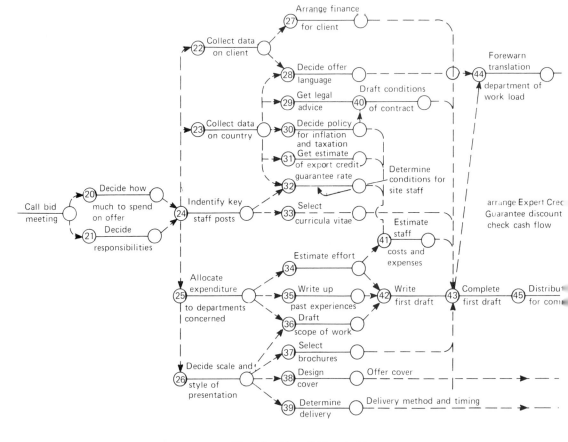

Fig. 7.7 – Phase 2 (first draft).

Consideration must also be given to the question of how the proposal or tender will eventually be sold to the customer. Will there need to be some political leverage, prior investigation of the site or any post-tender activity, etc.?

7.5.6 Proposal evaluation

Since the customer will inevitably carry out an evaluation of each contractor's proposal, it is wise for those offering bids to do an 'in-house' evaluation before submission. Experienced project managers can be of great value in conducting such evaluations, which may only amount to a simple rating system to enable comparisons to be made. The best method of achieving this is to assign a numerical weight to each area and criterion, which effectively reflects its proportional importance to the whole evaluation. The division of the points total between technical and business management aspects will depend upon the nature of the particular contract being considered. Of course, it is not possible to pre-determine exactly what the customer's evaluation factors will be and what weights he will assign to them but many of them may be general, and fairly shrewd guesses can be made as to the numerical rating assigned. A typical example of a rating scheme can be seen in Fig. 7.9.

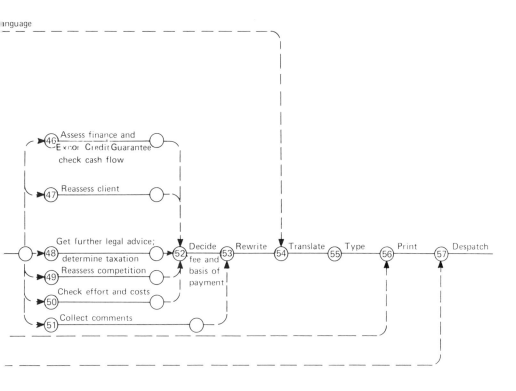

Fig. 7.8 – Phase 3 (completion).

SUMMARY OF CHAPTER 7

(1) Good proposals cost time, money and effort to produce.
(2) The function of a proposal is to sell, to the client, the managerial and technical abilities of the company to execute the required work at reasonable cost.
(3) The customer rarely buys the product offered in a successful tender. Generally, success in tendering is the basis for subsequent negotiation.
(4) A well-organized experienced multidisciplinary group is required to make good proposals.
(5) Making a proposal is, itself, a project and must be planned and managed like a project.

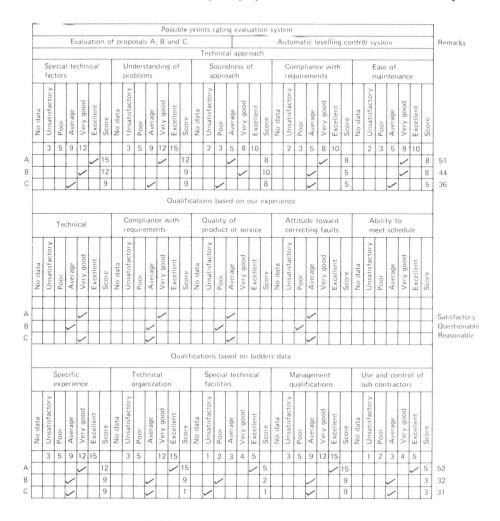

Fig. 7.9 – Typical example of a rating scheme.

REFERENCES

[1]   Marsh, P.D.V., (1987) *The Art of Tendering*, Gower Technical Press.
[2]   Horgan, M.O'c., (1989) *Competitive Tendering for Engineering Contracts*, E & F.N. Spon.

8

Negotiation

8.1 INTRODUCTION

The basic objective of nearly all negotiations is to reach an agreement which, for large project work, will enable a contract to be let.

A company, having prepared its bid in the form of a tender, has established a basis and background for negotiation to take place. The process can be depicted diagrammatically as shown in Fig. 8.1. If a project manager has been concerned with the proposal preparation, it may be desirable for him to take part in the negotiation phase. He does not necessarily lead the negotiating but can be a very useful member of the team. If the process is protracted, then a project manager, who will eventually take over the project once the contract is let, may be extremely important. The subtle points brought out as the negotiation proceeds may well be forgotten by those not responsible for the execution phase.

It is not intended here to give a comprehensive description of negotiating procedures but to emphasize one or two important aspects of negotiation which concern project management work. The successful planning, execution and conclusion of contract negotiations are vital to the ultimate achievement of effective project management.

8.2 THE BASIS OF NEGOTIATION

Negotiation may be defined as follows.

'The art of securing such an agreement as will enable the objective of the activity in question to be achieved on terms which, taking into account your enterprise's overall interests and looking both from the short- and long-term points of view, are the most favourable to your enterprise which reasonably can be obtained.'

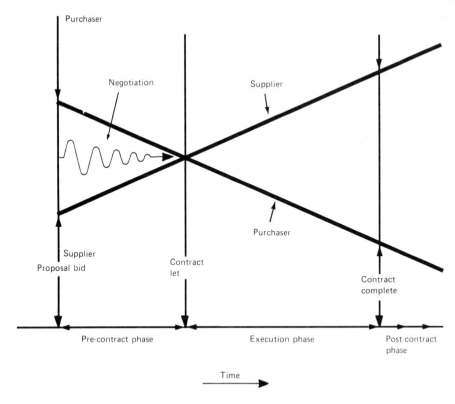

Fig. 8.1 — Process of negotiation. In the pre-contract phase the purchaser has the dominant
negotiating role but once the contract is let dominance passes gradually to the supplier.

From the above definition, it follows that, before any negotiation can proceed, the
negotiators must have defined or had defined for them the objective to be attained.
Whereas the definition of the objectives is not always as simple as one may think, it is
nevertheless surprising on occasions that senior management in some concerns are
prepared to enter into discussions or negotiations with no more conception of the desired
objectives than that they require to reach agreement on the basis for a contract.

Whereas the signature of a contract is no doubt a laudable objective, it is essential that
the individuals concerned have a greater degree of appreciation of what (for want of a
better phrase) may be termed the subobjectives—the fundamental points and possibly
inherent problems which may be faced in the negotiation. An agreed common line of
thinking and approach are essential on these fundamental points so that in fact these
individuals cease to be individuals as such but rather members of a *team*. We shall revert
briefly to this question of the team a little later.

It must be recognized that negotiation is not an end in itself but simply a means to an
end.

8.3 SHORT- AND LONG-TERM INTEREST

There is no point in negotiation which achieves a short-term advantage if in the long term
the outcome is likely to prove disadvantageous. Equally it may be necessary to insist on

the recognition of some point which, although of little significance, establishes a useful precedent for the future.

It is usually possible for a buyer, if he knows that a supplier is anxious for a particular order, to negotiate down from the price originally quoted or to impose conditions which he had not specified when inviting tenders, provided, of course, that his demands are not too onerous. The first time that he does it with a particular supplier he may actually achieve a genuine reduction or a better bargain, at least to start with, although by the time that the contract is over he may regret his actions. However, if he tries again with the same supplier or with another who has been put wise to his tricks, he will find that £2 have been added so that £1 can be given away.

8.4 REASONABLE TERMS

It must always be remembered that a bargain involves at least two parties, and each party has legitimate interests. Naturally, if you are the buyer, you want to purchase at the lowest price consistent with the quality, service, delivery, etc., that you expect. Equally, if you are the supplier, you want to make as much profit out of the transaction as you reasonably can but, if you are too greedy, you may lose it all or provoke the buyer into seeking competition where previously he was prepared to buy only from you.

Nobody can ever really give anything 'for free' in commerce. It is an illusion which dies very hard that there is any such thing as, for example, 'free' service or that defects are remedied 'free'. They are not; somewhere in the overheads there is an item to cover this. Service, research and development, design, financing the contract, and the taking of risks all have got to be paid for sooner or later. If they are not allowed as elements in the contract price, then either they cannot continue to be provided or the supplier must go out of business.

Being reasonable, however, is not just a question of trying to be fair to the other party; it is also being fair to yourself. It is not just ethics; it is also good business. You may have got him 'over the barrel' today but there is no telling how long it will be before he has you similarly placed. So a little commercial goodwill earned today may go a long way tomorrow.

8.5 PREPARATION FOR THE NEGOTIATION

Time spent in preparation is the most valuable time of all. It is fatal to enter into negotiation with a team that is not fully prepared to answer any questions that may arise. This means that the questions must have been predicted, the problems studied and the answers thought out before the negotiations.

The first essential step is to set down, in writing, the following.

(1)   Terms about which you consider there will be no disagreement.
(2)   Terms about which you consider there may be disagreement and divide these into three categories.

   (a)   Those which, if pressed hard enough, you will be willing to concede.

(b) Those which you would only concede if the other party made a major concession on another point.

(c) Those which under no circumstances you could accept.

In order to carry out this exercise, you will of course have had to decide on *all* the terms which are to be included within the scope of the negotiation and, if it is an actual contract which is being negotiated, the terms of the contract itself. Not all the terms have of course the same importance to both parties. Not unnaturally the importance of any particular terms will vary with the nature of the contract. For instance, on a contract to be performed in England, the **arbitration clause** is one about which there will be little dispute. You would not worry over which professional institute was to appoint the arbitrator in the event of the parties reaching disagreement but, on a contract to be performed in an undeveloped country abroad, this clause may be absolutely vital.

The more that you can get to know about the contract, the better—its background, its importance to both parties, its subject matter and its difficulties in execution. Time is the limiting factor. It is unlikely in practice that one can ever give the time to any particular deal which it demands and one may have to be fairly ruthless in deciding on priorities.

8.6 THE OBJECTIVE

Stress was laid earlier on the definition of the objective. This is an essential part of the preparations for the negotiation. Are you prepared to reach deadlock if you cannot get the other party to accept your essential terms? Alternatively is it important to reach agreement today even if it means sacrificing principles to do so? Is the other party's participation in the venture essential or only desirable? Have you any alternative sources to which you can go? This may apply to buyer and seller alike. You may be negotiatipg with a monopoly supplier, or you as the supplier may have been let down by other customers and be desperate to find work for your shops.

One of the worst circumstances to be in is to find, in the middle of a negotiation, that you just do not know the answer to the sort of question posed above. It may be that you yourself cannot give the answer; you may have to obtain it from your board or one of your directors, but to find this out in the middle of the meeting is disastrous and unpardonable when, with a little thought beforehand, it could have been avoided. You may of course decide deliberately to play 'hard to get' and be prepared to face deadlock, reserving the decision to another meeting.

8.7 BOTH SIDES OF THE ARGUMENT

Success in negotiations often depends on your ability to argue the opposing case as well as you can argue your own. A very valuable pre-negotiation exercise is either to act the part of 'devil's advocate' yourself or to get a colleague to do so. It is no use spending time talking about what a splendid case you have; it is the opposing case you should be worrying about and, in doing this, you must assume that the other party is at least as clever and well informed as you are.

Try to put yourself in the other party's position and see the situation through his eyes. Think of what his reaction is going to be to your arguments; then think of the counter. It is rather like playing a game of chess.

Finally, if you find yourself against the wall—his rifle trained on you—make sure you bleed when he fires. If you are prepared to give way in isolation on a significant point, it is always good to let him know he has scored a bullseye. A point of concession duly registered may, psychologically at least, represent a trading point for the future.

8.8 AVAILABILITY OF FACTS

Nothing is more annoying or disastrous than to have to stop in the middle of the presentation of an argument because you do not have some particular fact to hand, or to have to start rummaging through massive files to find a particular letter. Equally nothing is more impressive or demoralizing to the opposition than the well-timed production of factual evidence which cannot be contradicted.

Therefore, when rehearsing your case and that of the opposition, make notes of any factual points which are likely to arise or any arguments based on documents, particularly those which have originated from the other party. Get these looked up, make sure they say what you think they say and have them readily available. You may bring a colleague to a major negotiation whose sole jobe is to be able to produce at a moment's notice the right piece of paper. If he is unlikely to have a copy of his files with him, then have an extra copy or copies prepared to hand to him. A little gamesmanship in this direction can go a long way towards winning the day.

Whilst things which are matters of opinion are always going to be argued about, things which are matters of fact are capable of being decided upon and cannot, in the ultimate, be contradicted.

So far as you can, therefore, when preparing the case try to turn everything into a matter of fact and get the facts available to you. If you think that the other party is going to make loose statements such as 'the weather during November and December was terrible, much worse than we could possibly have expected', then have the average rainfall figures for those months with you, going back over, say, 5 years.

8.9 ADVANCE NOTICE OF POINTS

It is often a matter of nice judgement to decide how far to give, to the other party, advance notice of what points you are going to raise. On the one hand, to be forewarned is to be forearmed; on the other hand you do not want to invite the comment 'I'm sorry I didn't know you were going to raise that issue today and I am afraid that the meeting will have to be postponed to enable me to consider the matter'. That just wastes everybody's time and achieves nothing.

On balance, therefore, it would seem preferable to give advance notice of any major points which you are going to raise, particularly where you think it probable that the other party's negotiators will either want to get instructions from their board or to bring someone to the meeting who would otherwise not have attended. It is also evidence that you are 'playing fair' and you may be able to make some capital out of that.

8.10 PERSONALITIES

Turning now to the question of personalities, wherever possible find out as much as you can about the reputation of the persons with whom you are dealing, their strong points and their weak ones. People often have pet tactics or foibles, such as a calculated loss of temper. One should be ready to deal with these.

If you have not previously dealt with the other parties to the negotiation, use the first fiew minutes of social chatter before the negotiations start to try to assess their characters. Remember also that they are probably trying to do the same thing.

If you do not know, find out at the start what authority they possess and who is the captain of their side and also whether there is any chance of dividing their team.

8.11 THE NEGOTIATING TEAM: ITS COMPOSITION AND NUMBERS

Whatever its composition your team must be a balanced one and have a status appropriate to that of the negotiation itself and the team with which it is likely to be faced. Factors affecting team composition and status are as follows.

(1) Do not 'send a boy to do a man's job'. If the negotiation is to be at director level, then have someone of equal status on your side, i.e. unless, as a matter of deliberate tactics, you do not want the negotiation to decide anything but merely to get the other side to reveal its hand.
(2) If technical questions are going to be raised, e.g. in engineering, finance or law, then make certain that you have an expert on your side; otherwise you will be at a disadvantage.
(3) On the other hand, it may often pay not to have the experts in at the negotiation itself but to have obtained their advice beforehand. This applies more particularly to lawyers and acccuntants. Engineers and commercial people are often far happier negotiating without their legal and financial advisers present. The decision on this must depend on the nature of the negotiation, and the knowledge you possess of the other party's character.
(4) The characters who would form the team must be compatible and prepared to work together. It is fatal to have as the 'strong man' of the team someone who should merely be there as an adviser.
(5) The team must not be too large. Three is probably the maximum number who can act effectively. If there are any more than three, then unless they are very strong willed and prepared to be silent for most of the time it is almost certain that they will start an argument amongst themselves which can immediately be worked on by the other side.

8.12 THE TEAM CAPTAIN

Someone must be selected to act as 'team captain', and there can only be one captain. Sometimes the captain will select himself but it is not essential that he should be the most senior person present from the company. It depends on the nature of the negotiations. If for instance it is the terms and conditions of contract that are being negotiated, then it must be the senior commercial executive, even if the team contains a technical executive whose personal status in the organization is higher. For that part of the negotiation his role is that of an adviser.

On occasions, as where the agenda contains a wide range of subjects, the captain may, for certain items, hand over his authority to lead to another member of the team but the summing up at the end of that item should be made by the captain, and it is he who should then take the discussion forward to the next item. Where this is to happen, it should, ideally, be worked out between the team members in advance.

8.13 WORKING TOGETHER

There is a definite art in working together and for that reason a company which is continually involved in a certain type of negotiation would be well advised to develop certain working partnerships between its executives. Once two people (and two make an ideal team) have carried through a series of negotiations together, each will have learnt how the other thinks and what his reactions are likely to be, when to let the other hold the floor and when to come in himself.

One of the most effective techniques which the two can develop is that of the 'unreasonable chap' and the 'reasonable chap'. In seeing what is the best bargain that you can achieve, you may start with proposals which represent the most favourable bargain you think it is possible but unlikely that you will obtain. Having presented arguments to justify those terms, it is often difficult for you personally to withdraw too far, without giving the inference that you are a person who is prepared to withdraw any proposals you may make. That is the point at which your colleague comes in with 'Well, I think we could stretch a point here although it is of course departing from our normal policy, as my colleague has explained.'

The game can of course be played the other way round. The 'reasonable chap' makes the running so far and then his colleague comes in and says 'I am afraid having regard to my colleague's generosity on the points we have discussed so far, this is something to which our company could never agree.'

Sometimes it may be necessary to use the 'bogey' of the board, or a 'Mr. X' who is not attending the meeting, in order to back up the stand that one has taken on a particular point. This can be effective but it does carry the danger that, if used too often, it detracts from the personal authority of the negotiator himself and may lead the other side to withdraw from the negotiation or refuse to give their own final agreement.

8.14 RESERVATIONS, TIMING AND CALLING IT A DAY

There comes a time in the discussion of any point when either

(1)   you have reached agreement or
(2)   it is obvious that on the basis then being followed you are not going to reach agreement.

It is absolutely essential to recognize when this point has been reached. If you have got agreement, then note it down at once and pass on to the next point. Never go on explaining or introducing fresh ideas or thoughts or in any way prolonging the discussion on that point. If you do, then the other party may reopen the negotiation and you will find that you no longer have agreement on that issue. It is often easier to argue yourself out of agreement than into agreement.

It is, equally, no use going round and round a particular point, repeating arguments which have failed to impress. You have got either to start the discussion again on a completely fresh approach to the problem or to put that point aside for further discussions later on, perhaps when agreement has been reached on other issues. The old phrase 'it's no use flogging a dead horse' is particularly apt and recognition of this would reduce the time wasted in discussion tremendously.

A sense of timing is a most valuable attribute for a negotiator to possess. Particularly when the subject is money, there is usually a crisis point in the negotiations when it is possible for agreement to be reached, on the most favourable terms. If you snatch at it too soon, you will get agreement but not on the best terms. If you allow it to go past that point, then the other party's resistance will have stiffened again and you will find that either his terms have hardened or you may not be able to get agreement at all.

Very often most of the time is spent in discussion of one or two vital points and you are left at the end of the day with a number of minor items and not much time left. How you play this will depend largely on what has gone before. If you believe that you have scored a victory on the major points, particularly as this may be embarrassing to the other party's negotiators in their personal positions in their company, then to save their face and gain their personal goodwill you may concede the minor points quickly. It may also help to tip the balance on their ready acceptance of what has gone before to do this.

8.15 ECONOMICS AND EMOTION

Emotion, unless it is entirely artificial, is a bad companion at the negotiating table. It is only rarely that displays of temper or harshness can achieve worthwhile results. It is often wise, if one person who would normally be a member of the negotiating team has become emotionally involved in a dispute, to leave him out of the side.

It is sometimes necessary to pursue a point, not for its cash value but because a matter of principle is involved, but one must be very careful. Victories on points of principle can so easily become Pyrrhic ones. Before comitting yourself to a particular line because of a point of principle, make an honest and objective analysis of your own motives to determine exactly what is the principle involved, and a careful and objective assessment of the cash value of the point and the price that you are likely to have to pay for achieving it.

The value to you of any particular item in the negotiation, in terms of cash, should always be estimated, as should the value of any concession which the other side either offers you or requests you to make. You should not be afraid to work out sums in the middle of the negotiation before making a decision. Adjourn the meeting temporarily rather than give a snap answer, the cash value of which you are unable to estimate.

If you are satisfied that the economic effect of a particular concession is insignificant, then be prepared to give it, if it assists you to achieve your overall objective, even although this may be against legal or other advice which you have received. Advisers are bound always to be conservative and to cover themselves.

SUMMARY OF CHAPTER 8

(1)   Negotiation between the tendering company and the customer takes place before the contract is let.
(2)   Negotiation is required to obtain terms that are *reasonable* to *both* parties.
(3)   It is necessary to spend time preparing (or even rehearsing) for negotiation.

(4) Facts must be gathered, arranged and assessed before negotiation and must be available during negotiation.
(5) Negotiators must be of a status appropriate to the job. They must be capable of making the decisions required.
(6) A negotiating team will be made up of members from different disciplines.

REFERENCES

[1] Scott, W.F., (1983) *The Skills of Negotiating*, Gower Publishing Co.
[2] Kennedy, G., (1982) *Everything is Negotiable*, Arrow Books.
[3] Marsh, P.D.V. (1974) *Contract Negotiation Handbook*, Gower Press.

9

Organizing for project work

9.1 ORGANIZATION AND PROJECT MANAGEMENT

Organization has been defined as 'the arrangement of the people in a business so that they can act as one body'. Any organization exists so that people can work harmoniously together to obtain effective corporate results.

Reference has already been made to the fact that project work demands an outlook and behaviour that are different from the normal modes established by a conventional structure of a company. The situation is confused by the fact that the project manager is not always assigned complete responsibility for resources. Generally he has to share these with the rest of the organization.

The main characteristic of project organization is the exceptionally strong lateral working relationships demanded, necessitating close co-ordination between many individuals in differing functions. In achieving this a project manager will need to exercise sound common sense and tolerance if he is to succeed in the scramble for existing resources no matter what the organizational arrangements are. There will also be a vertical component to all project management work as additional expenditure will need to be approved by senior management who will also wish to know the current progress.

Certain organizational uncertainties are inevitable and many a project manager may find that his working relationships with functional department heads have not been clearly defined. Tricky questions can arise such as the urgency of design release, new project features or modifications after field testing, spare parts scheduling, etc. All these can be potential problem areas. At the same time a project manager may have to juggle with conflicting internal schedules laid down by departmental heads, to say nothing of customer changes and subcontractor variations.

Before describing some of the standard types of organization that have been tried by industry to meet the above difficulties, some general observations on organizations might prove beneficial.

9.2 CHARACTERISTICS OF ORGANIZATIONS

9.2.1 Bureaucracy

This type of organization has the typical structure of a pyramid with a heavy vertical chain of command. It was perfected during the industrial revolution, is based on the division of labour into specialisms and operates within a system of rules and procedures that can deal with any work situation. The great strength of bureaucracy lies in its capacity to deal with the routine and predictable. The threats to such a system of organization are many but perhaps the greatest is rapid and unexpected change, and it is this together with the additional complexity of modern technology, where integration across departmental boundaries with professionals of very diverse specialisms has to be co-ordinated, that has led to different types of organization. Organizational values are being changed to replace the purely mechanistic value system of bureaucracy. In short, today we are seeing the need to humanize the organization and to allow for personal growth so that self-realization can occur. An organic-adaptive structure is required where there is harmony between the individuals' needs for tasks which are meaningful, worth-while, creative and satisfying and a flexible organizational structure capable of dealing with a variety of new tasks.

9.2.2 Problems of present-day organizations

Anyone concerned with developing appropriate organizations to handle the above problems is faced with the key problem of how to structure human groupings in a rational way and at the same time to avoid any undesirable side effects and to give maximum satisfaction to all those so organized. Of course, as Drucker [1] has pointed out, 'good organization structure does not of itself produce good performance . . . but a poor organizational structure makes good performance impossible . . .'.

9.2.3 Integration

There is a problem of how to integrate individual needs with managerial goals. Such issues as incentives, rewards and personal motivation are relevant here. It seems likely that, as technology advances, society will require a more human approach and may well be willing to sacrifice some efficiency to obtain it.

9.2.4 Collaboration

Management has to understand and be able to resolve conflicts. As organizations grow, they become more complex and they fragment and divide into water-tight compartments. Interface conflicts quickly arise as tightly knit 'in-group' attitudes develop.

9.2.5 Adaptation

The rapid changes taking place in society create a turbulent environment which upsets the placid, stable and predictable environment of yesteryear. The old structures with power vested at the top and procedures laid down to cater with the routine can no longer adapt and they start to decay. The increasing interdependence between working groups calls for new forms of structure that have resilience and an ability to reshape quickly. In order to ensure survival, organizations must, however, do more than merely respond passively to changes. They may need to take the initiative and to try to shape the environment to meet their needs. This involves creating demands and needs where none existed before.

9.3 STRUCTURAL CONSIDERATIONS

In talking about organizational structures it must always be borne in mind that the appropriateness of an organizational structure must always be the extent to which it furthers the objectives of the firm, and not the degree to which it conforms to a prescribed pattern.

9.3.1 Line-and-staff approach

Depicting any organization relies on certain assumed conventions, e.g. that a vertical position on the chart indicates relative authority levels and horizontal lines depict collaborative linking. Staff are usually represented by horizontal lines off the main line functions as at A in Fig. 9.1. This line-and-staff principle emanates from military practice. The line officers are those who stand in the lines of combat but the staff provide the support activities. Actually the staff perform two distinct functions.

(a)   The general staff, which is analogous to the board of directors of an enterprise, formulate policy and make major decisions.
(b)   The staff that provide general support, e.g. Signal Corps, Supply Corps in the Army, or, as in Fig. 9.1 at 'A', represent management services of one sort or another.

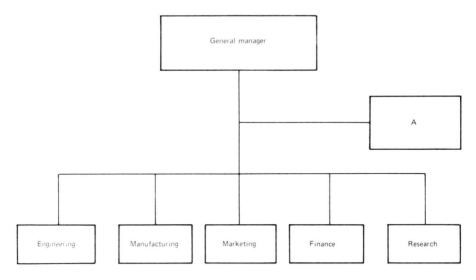

Fig. 9.1 — General management (functional) organization.

Today in many manufacturing companies the projects and products are created by what are often looked upon as being staff functions, e.g. research and development, engineering and finance, and this seems to be a wrong concept. Even the military have found the line-and-staff concept to fail under the accelerated communication systems available today. In short, improved communication has tended to polarize authority at the top while the power of decision making by subordinate line managers has been weakened, although they now have to co-ordinate and to get co-operation in response to issued orders from the top. The staff, on the contrary, can report directly to the chief executive or his delegates and have therefore had their influences extended.

Clearly the line-and-staff type of organization shown in Fig. 9.1, which might be called a general management functional organization is not really well suited to project management. The advantage that such an organization has is its ability to preserve and enhance its technical skills and expertise, and it is really well suited to mass production work of product items to a given standard specification. Where slow evolution produces small product changes and derivatives, it does allow all projects to benefit from advanced and new technologies. However, in order to get people working harmoniously together to achieve 'task' goals, as well as 'functional' goals, it is important to look to other forms of organization.

9.3.2 Systems approach
Any function-based structure of the type shown in Fig. 9.1 assumes that the required communication between personnel in different functions will develop but the very nature of this approach produces a degree of isolation between functions which then become incapable of handling the complexities of modern technology and market requirements.

A systems approach would take specialist groups and management services as a system requiring consideration as a whole, rather than looking at their individual roles. The interactions between the different parts of the system enable appropriate decisions to be taken and the best organizational structures will seek to promote links within the system. By taking individuals out of their functional roles and putting them together into project teams, communication can be improved and greater emphasis can be placed on the tasks that are to be done (and which do not usually fall within function boundaries). There are various arrangements for creating such teams, the most commonplace being as follows.

(1) **Line or aggregate project management** (Fig. 9.2). Here direct control over all project matters is under the authority of the project manager who has his own team of specialists. In effect, each manager responsible for a project is running his own business. While this method does provide strong control by a single project authority and has therefore a quick response time, it may fail to develop technical skills for perpetuation and there may well be a lack of interchange between project teams.

(2) **Staff project management** (Fig. 9.3). Although at first sight this might seem a hopeless type of organization, it can be successful at the small end of the project spectrum where there is a need for strong technical leadership as well as good management ability, but it is useless for larger projects and can prove frustrating and unrewarding to all but the highly technically competent.

(3) **Matrix project management** (Fig. 9.4). This seeks to combine some of the advantages of the aggregate organization with those of the functional or general management organization in Fig. 9.1. In this concept all the functions are in their normal positions beneath the general manager. Each functional group is headed by a departmental manager responsible for maintaining technical performance excellence within his function. To the left of the chart there is a project manager for each project currently being undertaken. Each manager here has programme responsibility within each functional area of the company. In effect the project manager directs an element of each functional department for matters concerning

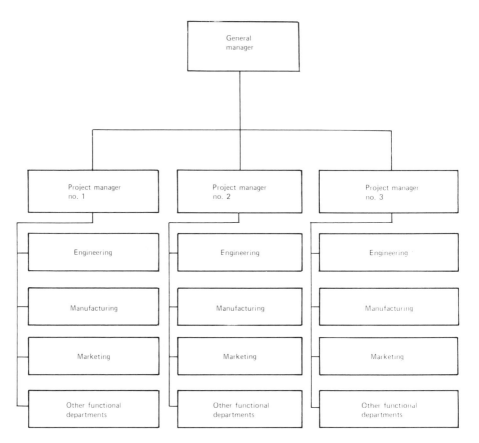

Fig. 9.2 – Line project management. Project managers have the authority, personnel and facilities to perform all functions (direct control).

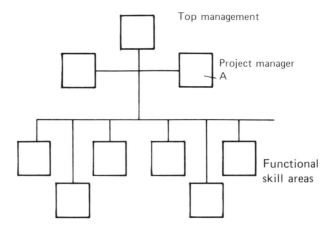

Fig. 9.3 – Staff project management (influence control).

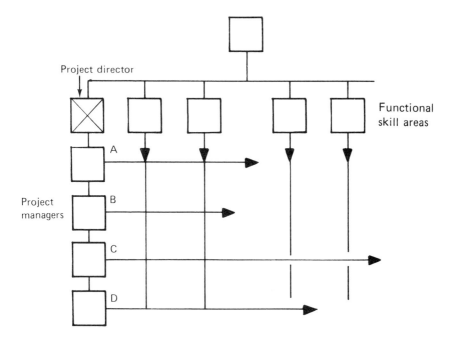

Fig. 9.4 – Matrix project management (dual control).

his particular project or projects. All personnel are permanently assigned to be functional area and are responsible to their departmental heads on technical matters—the *how*. At the same time they are completely responsible to the project manager for *what* they do and *when* they do it.

The penalty paid for such a system is in the degree of control and response time; however, it has the great advantage of building up the survival element of the enterprise and provides career continuity but can make it difficult for specialists to operate under a dual accountability system. Annual reviews and project priorities can also be constant sources of confrontations.

(4) **Hybrid project management** (Fig. 9.5). Again this structure seeks to comprise the best of the 'line' and 'matrix' type of organization. In this case, functional specialists are seconded to specific projects for the duration of the specialist work. On completing this, they return to the functional department. This produces better control reaction time but may lack flexibility to deal with sudden disturbances and fail to develop techniques.

9.4 THE MERITS AND DEMERITS OF PROJECT MANAGEMENT STRUCTURE

The four examples of the systems approach to organization design shown in Figs 9.2, 9.3, 9.4 and 9.5 can be reviewed from the point of view of advantages and disadvantages as shown in Fig. 9.6.

Burns and Stalker [2], in their classical study of traditional Scottish firms seeking to introduce electronic development work, concluded that an 'organic' type of organization

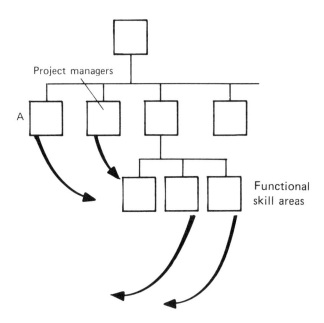

Fig. 9.5 – Hybrid project management (variable control).

was appropriate to unstable conditions in which new and unfamiliar problems frequently arise and where the work cannot be broken down and distributed among existing specialists.

A 'mechanistic' organization, on the contrary, is suitable where relatively stable conditions obtain and where the problems and tasks can be broken down into specialisms within which each individual carries out his assigned, precisely defined task. A summary of these main differences is given in Table 9.1.

Table 9.1 – Difference between mechanistic and organic organizations.

Mechanistic (inflexible)	Organic (adaptive)
Rigid structure (bureaucratic)	Flexible structure
Formalized control systems	Informal control
Prescribed roles (fit people to jobs) Defined contributions	Adaptive transient roles and groupings (build jobs around people's strengths)
High conformity	Entrepreneurial, innovative effort
Emphasis on vertical relationships	Emphasis on lateral relationships

9.4.1 The conventional mechanistic organization
Almost all organizations today are structured on a single line of command (vertical relationships).

	Line or aggregate project management	Staff project management
Advantages	(1) Strong control of a single authority (2) Rapid reaction time (3) Good for performance, cost delivery, trade-offs (4) Leadership easy, personnel loyalty high (5) Good customer contacts	(1) Very strong technical control (2) Moderate reaction time (3) Develops in-house technology, and know-how (4) Very good for developing project engineers
Disadvantages	(1) Fails to develop technology for survival (2) Opportunity for technical interchange between projects small (3) Inefficient use of manufacturing and construction facilities (4) Difficulty in balancing work loads as projects come and go (5) Lack of career continuity	(1) Poor schedule and cost performance due to multiproject situation (2) Often poor customer relations (3) Technical overload often reached (4) Excessive time consumed on persuasion (5) Little project-orientated planning
	Matrix project management	Hybrid project management
Advantages	(1) Helps to advance and keep new technology (project feedback) (2) Facilitates technical interchange (3) Good utilization of resources (4) Good external relations (5) Moderate reaction time	(1) Very good development of personnel on project (2) Better utilization of collective experience (3) Technical performance high (4) Career development good
Disadvantages	(1) Dual accountability (2) Conflict of interest between project and functional line (3) Profit and loss accountability more difficult	(1) Appraisal of individual's work more difficult (2) Problems of personnel returning to line work (3) Loyalties can conflict

Fig. 9.6 –Some of the advantages and disadantages of types of project management organizational structures.

This form of bureaucratic hierarchy works well in stable conditions and where the predominant tasks are sequential, routine and repetitive, e.g. manufacturing assembly lines, and invoice departments. Such mechanistic structures are often necessary to achieve co-ordination of effort.

To summarize, the realities of conventional bureaucratic organization are as follows.

(1)   Hierarchic structure of control, authority and communication, i.e. decisions are made at one level but implemented at others.

(2)   Specialization and differentiation of tasks, i.e. tasks are undertaken by different functions and become distinct and separate. Authority and accountability are prescribed and competence becomes specialized. Objectives tend to be set in isolation from those of other functions.

(3)   Emphasis of vertical interaction, i.e. paired relationships of superior and subordinate predominate. Problems are referred, or delegated upwards.

(4)   Expectations of loyalty, conformity and obedience, i.e. compliance, predictability and reliability are seen as being essential.

(5)   Structures change more slowly than function, i.e. individual roles and contributions often outgrow formalized back-up. The organization chart does not reflect the reality of the organization.

(6)   Emphasis on stability (tendency to rigidity), i.e. inadequate response to changing pressures and conditions, inability to adapt readily, and reinforcement of sanctified rituals and beliefs in time of crisis.

(7)   Availability of necessary talent, i.e. normal structures and hierarchies tend to impede the bringing together of the best brains and abilities to resolve major and complex problems.

9.4.2 Organic project organization

When change is accelerated, and more and more novel 'first-time' problems arise, traditional forms of organization prove inadequate and can no longer cope.

Highly creative departments (e.g. design engineering) require flexible adaptive arrangements of people and tasks and hence the critical need is to organize to get the job done and this usually means breaking hierarchical boundaries.

A growing response to the problems created by bureaucratic structures is that of 'project management' and the project organization.

People, instead of filling fixed slots in the functional organization, move back and forth. They often retain their functional 'home base' but are detached repeatedly to serve as temporary team members.

Basically, this amounts to what Toffler [3] describes as the creation of 'disposable' work teams, i.e. the organizational equivalent of paper clothing and throw-away tissues.

Some of the principal realities of project teams are as follows.

(1)   They are adaptive structures and organizations which are most effective for coping with

      — change,
      — innovation,
      — critical situations and
      — major one-off problems.

      Herein lies the main case for project management.

(2)   Almost expressly, they

      — deny the benefits of stable formal systems, designed to protect members (and clients) through published and consistently operated rules,

- rely heavily on the goodwill, motivation and commitment of the members,
- reward innovative rather than conformative behaviour and
- place higher value on initiative and commitment than on traditional 'loyalty'.

(3)   They may be seen by many members as

- unfair,
- threatening and insecure,
- changing for change's sake,
- meritocratic,
- insensitive to personal needs and wishes, and
- 'jobs for the boys'.

Some of the problems in operating project teams are the following.

(1)   People who are used to single line-of-command structures find it hard to serve more than one boss, especially co-equal bosses (e.g. as in Figs 9.4 and 9.5).
(2)   Members may give lip service to teamwork but do not always know how to develop and operate as an effective project team, i.e. they tend to go their own way and retreat into previous long-established patterns of working.
(3)   Project and functional managers (e.g. as in Fig. 9.4) may compete rather than co-operate. Where there are disparities in grade, formal status or political influence, one may dominate at the expense of the other.
(4)   Individuals must learn to act more as 'managers' than as specialists or administrators, i.e. they must develop a strong sense of personal accountability for results and therefore be largely self-starting and self-directing. This represents a major departure from traditional bureaucracy where there is a great deal of vertical dependence on superiors.

9.5 GROUP BEHAVIOUR AND MOTIVATION FACTORS

It becomes apparent that organization is almost as much a process as a structure. It is a process of delegation and communication, and a process of adaptation—people adapting to the organization and adapting the organization to their needs. It is a process through which power, authority and influence are exercised, accepted or rejected. Project managers often have to influence teams of people as well as individuals to further the performance of their projects. It is vitally important therefore that project managers understand something of the needs of individuals.

9.5.1 Human factors in organization
Many thinkers and managers overemphasize the rational approach to organization. It is assumed that, because the structure is rational, behaviour also will, at all times, be rational. There is a surprisingly widespread belief that man will permanently suppress his emotions for the good of the organization.

There is also the conviction that man, being rational, will welcome increasing doses of specialization, since he must clearly see the logic of doing the same thing all the time. He will also, in the interests of specialization, suppress the complex of talents and capabilities which are his.

It is not sufficient to provide a logical framework for man to work in. He must be allowed to develop in his job, in the emotional as well as in the intellectual sense. This requires of the manager an understanding, learned or intuitive, of those factors which condition emotional response as well as intellectual response. The manager must learn to tolerate, and indeed encourage, emotional conflict, without causing cataclysm.

A good deal of attention has been given to the needs of the individual as part of the organization, and research, at one stage, tended to concentrate on how best to satisfy these needs. One particular concept of human motivation which has proved particularly useful in understanding individual behaviour is Maslow's [4] hierarchy of needs. One is aware of the dangers of oversimplifying and also of the fact that there are some serious flaws in the hierarchical approach to explaining motivation, but the concept does deepen understanding of individual behaviour.

A manager can try to provide opportunities for need satisfaction and hence motivation through doing the job itself so that people will enjoy doing good work. In order to do this, a manager must have a general understanding of the basic types of human need.

(a) **Physiological needs**. People desire food, drink, absence of fatigue, etc. It would be important for the manager to take note of the general working conditions of his employees in order to satisfy these needs, e.g. lighting, temperature, ventilation, and design of equipment.
(b) **Safety needs**. People have needs for protection against danger and threats. When workers feel threatened, they have strong needs for security. In times of change, a manager must realize that these needs will be very strong in most workers. Total security may not be possible but reasonable security is desirable.
(c) **Love needs**. The love, affection and warmth of family and friends. The need to belong and the need both to give and to receive love.
(d) **Social needs**. Workers like to be thought well of by their fellow workers and they also have needs for a certain amount of social contacts during the day.
(e) **Status and self-esteem needs**. People desire to be thought well of by

  (a) colleagues and
  (b) managers.

  There are often conflicting needs. Self-esteem and self-confidence form part of these needs. Here the manager can give praise and recognition for work done well by his subordinates.

A manager will also have to use negative motivation in order to prevent some problems arising or to remedy some problem which has occurred. In order to be effective, any disciplinary measures which the manager uses must be accepted as fair and reasonable by his subordinates.

To motivate his working group, the manager must have an understanding of his people, including their needs and problems. The manager should then use whatever available incentives he has which will work best in a given situation. There are some incentives which are not in the power of the manager to provide, e.g. money, but good leadership and understanding of employees are in the compass of every manager (see Chapter 14).

9.5.2 Group behaviour

Man achieves through group action what he cannot achieve alone. He also achieves satisfaction from membership of groups. He belongs to groups which are external to the organization in which he works and he belongs to subgroups within the organization. The needs of the individual are qualified by the needs of the groups to which he belongs.

Groups differ in cohesiveness, i.e. the strength of the bond which binds the members of the group together. Some groups are loosely bound and can only exercise minimum influences on their members, other groups are highly cohesive groups and can put considerable pressure on their members.

The organization is an overall group and the way in which the organization works is modified by the behaviour of the subgroups within it. Conflicts of objectives arise between the organization as an overall group and the subgroups. Conflicts also arise between the subgroups themselves.

For an organization to work satisfactorily it is necessary to recognize the existence of these informal patterns within it and to use them to achieve objectives.

Project people are concerned with change, and project managers should understand how teams can be used to achieve a desired change.

The group as a medium of change

(1)   If the group is to be used effectively as a medium of change, those people who are to be changed and those who are to exert influence for change must have a strong sense of belonging to the same group.

(2)   The more attractive the group is to its members, the greater is the influence that the group can exert on its members.

(3)   In attempts to change attitudes, values or behaviour, the more relevant they are to the basis of attraction to the group, the greater will be the influence that the group can exert upon them.

(4)   The greater the prestige of a group member in the eyes of the other members, the greater the influence that he can exert.

(5)   Efforts to change individuals or subparts of a group which, if successful, would have the result of making them deviate from the norms of the group will encounter strong resistance.

The group as a target of change

(1)   Strong pressure for changes in the group can be established by creating a shared perception by members of the need for change, thus making the source of pressure for change lie within the group.

(2)   Information relating to the need for change, plans for change, and consequences of change must be shared by all relevant prople in the group.

(3)   Changes in one part of a group produce strain in other related parts which can be reduced only by eliminating the change or by bringing about readjustments in the related parts.

SUMMARY OF CHAPTER 9

(1)   Project management requires communication between groups of different disciplines within the company (largely horizontal lines of communication).

(2)   The traditional hierarchical (or pyramid) organization in a company has a strong vertical chain of command and is not, generally, suited to project management.

(3)   A simple extension of the hierarchical organization is to introduce project management as a staff function. This can work when projects are small, particularly if they are also very technical, but is not suitable for the management of large projects.

(4)   Line project management is an organizational structure in which every project is managed by a project manager who has his own team of specialists. While this ensures good project management, it does not make for the flexible use of special skills and it may not develop new technical skills.

(5)   Matrix and hybrid management structures are both compromises between the extremes of hierarchical structure and the dedicated project management structure of line project management.

(6)   Group behaviour, human factors and motivation must be considered in the design of organizational systems and in their management.

REFERENCES

[1]   Drucker, P.F., (1968) *The Age of Discontinuity*, Harper and Row, New York.
[2]   Burns, T. and Stalker, G.M. (2nd edn. 1966) *The Management of Innovation*, Tavistock, London.
[3]   Toffler, A. (1970) *Future Shock*, The Bodley Head, London.
[4]   Maslow, A.H. (1954) *Motivation and Personality*, Harper and Row, New York.

10

Planning and programming a project

10.1 THE PLAN

It has already been emphasized that project managers and engineers tend to be disturbers of standard organizations and practices and it is in the nature of their work that such changes must be not only created but also controlled.

The project manager must first establish the results that he wants to achieve in terms of key objectives. Any objective without a plan is a dream. A plan is the means by which it is proposed to convert a present position or situation to some future condition or situation which is the set objective, and it is a set of statements, prepared in advance of what has to be done. A programme is a set of schedules setting out a plan with its required timings.

If an objective can be achieved without a plan, then it was really not an objective but a predicted certainty. Managers are not employed to allow and follow predicted futures but to design alternative futures, to appraise them and to select the best one, which then becomes the objective. They must then work to achieve this objective by a plan, and any plan will require a series of activities that connect, in some logical way, the various major events.

This identifying objectives, generating and selecting plans, allocating resources to the achievement of the plan and then implementing the plan is shown diagrammatically in Fig. 10.1.

Above all the project plans there is, as we have seen, the corporate plan with its long- and short-range objectives for the company. In fact, it is the total of all the project plans which together form the company's corporate strategy. In establishing a project plan, its interaction with the other projects in the company must be considered—its competition for resources, its contribution to common objectives, the fact that other projects are not viable unless this one is successful, etc. However, generally, once a project plan is

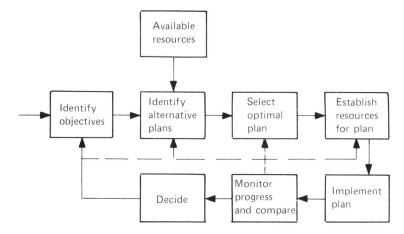

Fig. 10.1 – Planning a project.

developed within the company's corporate strategy, it should provide the framework within which almost all the management decisions needed to bring the project to a successful conclusion will be made. This does not mean that there will never be problems caused at the interface with another prcject; there will always be a danger that resources will be taken from one project to help another that is in a crisis or that changes to one project will force changes on another, but a well-designed plan will establish a procedure for change.

Essentially, the plan will break the project down into a number of activities, each of which may be programmed in its use of time and material resources. The logical sequences of these activities will thus create a series of milestones at which the use of time and resources may be monitored, and successfully reaching the final milestone will ensure that the project is completed on time and within budget.

10.2 THE PLAN AND THE PROJECT LIFE CYCLE

It is helpful, when discussing the planning and control of a project, to consider its life cycle. The life cycle has been discussed in Chapters 2 and 3 as a sequence of activities which generate cost and revenue and these activities will, as shown in Fig. 10.2, form manageable chunks of work which may be broken down into well-defined statements of work. Management is then concerned with planning the statements of work against the milestones that their defined use of time and material resources provide. Once the milestones have been set, the management of the project becomes the monitoring of achievement against those milestones and the application of controls to meet the milestone requirements when monitoring shows it to be necessary.

No project can succeed if there is an inadequate strategy for tackling the basic problems. A programme is a statement of intention setting out the milestones of achievement towards clearly defined objectives. It will be clear that any such statements of intent have a large element of uncertainty written into them, since what is to be tackled

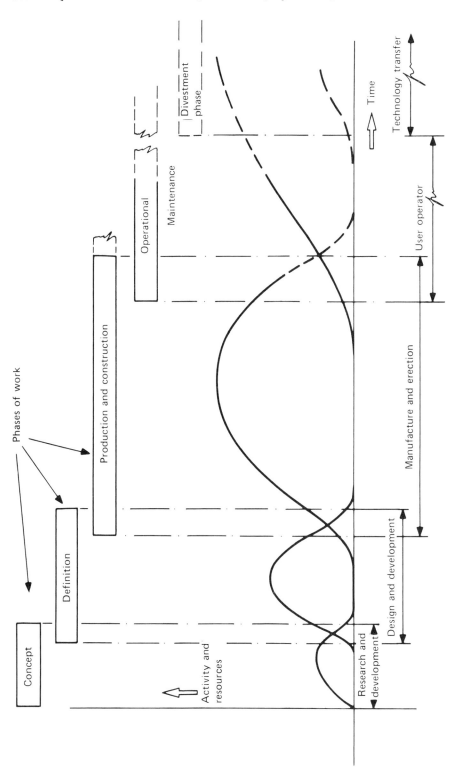

Fig. 10.2 — Project phases and activity report.

has probably never been attempted before, either on such a scale or in such a manner. Any project programme must therefore be flexible to take account of any changes which take place as progress proceeds through the various project stages.

10.2.1 The programme

The programme specifies what work has to be undertaken and, therefore, it defines the scope of the project and acts as a yardstick against which performance achievement can be monitored for control purposes. Because of uncertainty the initial programme for any project may well have to be altered as a project proceeds, but the criterion of a good programme lies in the ability that it allows for adaption to catastrophes as they occur. The dimensions of any programme will be in terms of resources required, and time and cost allocation. The project manager will be responsible for laying down the programme to be achieved, and for this purpose he will have to consult with the task performers in all phases of the contract. As a task setter he may often require specialist project engineers to make up part of his own team.

Programme objectives can be broken down into a series of tasks with definite achievement goals or milestones. These are generally called activities and events; activities represent time, and events represent finite achievements and, therefore, have no time duration. The development of project evaluation-and-review techniques (PERT)* and the critical path method (CPM)* did, in fact, originate out of large-scale complex technical projects, such as the Polaris missile, the Manhatten project, large chemical plant work and early aerospace and guided-missile work.

It is the essence of such techniques that the activities and events are fitted together to form a network which represents the complete logical structure of the project as a whole. Such an overall display then allows those responsible for the various activities to estimate durations and resources, be they material or human, that are needed. This information enables the project manager to predict completion dates of the project and/or parts of it and so to ascertain how interactions between his programme and other concurrent programmes will be managed. It is vitally important for a project manager to break down a project into activities that can be identified and tackled by individuals or particular departments or subcontractors. By this means he establishes a sound proper operational relationship with the specialist group skills. The worst mistake that can be made is to list an event as an activity (perhaps the word 'milestone' should be used instead of 'event' because we are less likely to think of a milestone as an activity). This sometimes happens when there are large technical areas of ignorance. The opposite may, however, occur when activities have zero duration (dummy activities). These dummy activities are merely devices for maintaining the integrity of the network and act rather like triggering linkages in mechanisms.

10.2.2 The work-package structure

The complementary roles of the project manager and the functional manager centre around the work to be accomplished—the work package. A work package is an integral subelement of the project, a subsystem, a subproduct, etc. Fig. 10.3 shows the confluence of the project and functional effort around a project work package.

---

* PERT and CPM are discussed quantitatively in Chapter 12.

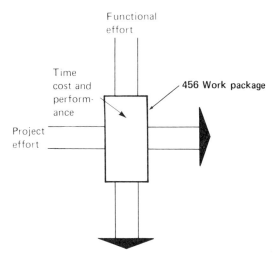

Fig. 10.3 — Confluence of the project and functional (skills area) effort for a particular work package.

The work package grows out of a work-breakdown analysis that is performed on the project. When the work-breakdown analysis is completed and the work packages are identified, a work-breakdown structure comes into existence. A work-breakdown structure can be represented by a pyramid similar to that used for describing the traditional organizational structure. Stated another way, the work-breakdown structure represents the breakdown of the work targets that must be achieved in order to meet the objective. Such a structure can be broken down by portions of hardware and then by functions associated with each aspect of the work. A typical work-breakdown structure for a missile is indicated in Fig. 10.4.

In the context of an engineering project, the work-breakdown analysis and the resulting work packages provide a model of the products (hardware, software, services and other outputs) that completely define the project. Such a model enables project engineers, project managers, functional managers and general managers to think of the totality of all projects and services comprised in the project. This model then can be used as the focus around which the project is managed, reporting the progress and status of engineering efforts, resource allocations, cost estimates, procurement actions, etc. More particularly, the development of a work-breakdown structure with accompanying work packages is necessary to accomplish the actions in the management of a project. The work breakdown analysis requires

(1)   summarizing all products and services comprised in the project, including support and other tasks,
(2)   displaying the interrelationships of the work packages to each other, to the total project and to other engineering activities in the organization,
(3)   establishing the authority—responsibility matrix organization,
(4)   estimating project cost,
(5)   performing risk analysis,
(6)   scheduling work packages,

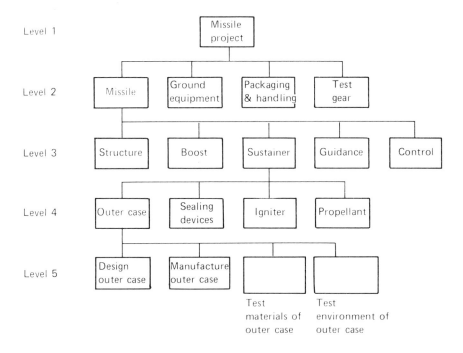

Fig. 10.4 – A typical work-breakdown structure.

(7)   developing information for managing the project,
(8)   providing a basis for controlling the application of resources to the project and
(9)   providing a reference point for getting people committed to support the project.

10.3 PLANNING THE PROJECT LIFE CYCLE

All projects need a plan, but planning without action is futile and action without planning is fatal. The plan clearly defines what is to be done, why and by whom, when and for how much. The plan outlines the strategy of how future events are to be undertaken. Essentially it is purposeful anticipation in action. Purpose is associated with a single organization or individual and suggests adaptability and a continuing initiative while anticipation suggests a modest word for forecasting. The project plan becomes the standard for the control system but, unlike physical standards, often changes in the light of performance. The project manager has constantly to adjust the plan to combat disturbances and regulate action.

Throughout the project's life cycle the plan becomes a key communication document for the co-ordination of the various work packages that have to be undertaken.

10.3.1 Essential elements of a project plan

No matter what size of project is being undertaken the essential elements of an engineering plan are as follows.

- A summary of the essentials of the project written in such a manner that anyone can get a grasp of the project. It states briefly what is to be done and how it is to be done, and it lists the end product or service.
- A work-breakdown structure that has enough detail to identify the relationships of work packages, work units and job numbers.
- A citation of tangible key milestones that can be counted, measured and evaluated in such a way that there can be no ambiguity as to whether or not a milestone has been achieved. There should be a correspondence of milestones to project budgets to facilitate adequate monitoring.
- An event logic network (an activity network) that shows the sequencing of the elements (work packages, work units and job numbers) of the project and how they are to be related—which can be done in parallel, series, etc. Such a network may have to be turned into bar charts where the plan and the schedule are in one and can be easily followed by those working with them.
- An organization interface plan that shows how the project relates with the rest of the world—customer, line-and-staff organizations, subcontractors, suppliers, and other clientele that have some role in the project.
- A plan for reviewing the project—who reviews the project, when and for what purpose.
- A list of key project personnel and their assignments in the project.

While the project plan need not be elaborate for a small project, there still has to be a plan which should be depicted in the simplest possible way. The danger with large projects is that the plan too often gets too large too soon, it then becomes too difficult to exercise control.

When the plan has been formulated, a programme of work can be produced as a set of time schedules so that the 'when' and the 'how much' of each work package can be determined. Separate budgets and schedules may be drawn up for every project element and given to the individuals who are to be held responsible for them.

10.4 PROGRAMMING AND MONITORING THE AGREED PLAN

Any project programme requires analysis, expresses policy and should lead to control. The programme must be depicted so that it strikes a balance between the necessity to include essential information and the requirements of simplicity. If the chart is too complicated, it loses its value because it cannot be readily understood; if it is not easy to read, regular monitoring for the duration of the project tends to lapse and the chart falls into disuse.

There are several forms of presentation which can be used.

10.4.1 Network analysis
Network analysis is a method of preparing programmes in such a way that they can be analysed to identify both the critical and the non-critical activities and their inter-relationships. A network diagram is a generic title for programmes produced by this method. Examples of such diagrams are as follows.

(1)   The **critical path diagram** (sometimes known as the **activity-on-the-arrow diagram**) (Fig. 10.5).
(2)   The **precedence diagram** (alternatively known as the **activity-on-the-node diagram**) (Fig. 10.6).
(3)   The **cascade diagram** (more often known as the **linked-bar chart**) (Fig. 10.7).

Such diagrams are prepared to determine the logical sequence, interrelationships and timing of the activities and the shortest time in which the programme can be completed. However, apart from a well-drawn linked-bar chart, such diagrams are usually large, complicated and obscure, to all but the drafter and other planning engineers. Inevitably they are poor media for communication to and interpretation by the people who are going to use them. In general, it is better to break the networks down to small 'fragnets' which are then depicted as bar charts.

Basically a network diagram is a programming tool. It only becomes a control tool if it is regularly monitored and updated (see Section 10.5). In the past, programmes in the form of critical path or precedence diagrams have fallen into disrepute, not necessarily because of any lack of accuracy in initial programming logic, but through management's failure regularly to update the programme to reflect actual progress.

The most effective method of monitoring such a network programme and measuring the effects of delay is to ensure that the programme is continuously updated after each progress review, preferably by computer: firstly with a time analysis[*] to assess current progress in relation to the completion date and secondly, where there is a projected overrun and it is not possible to extend the end date, a revised resource[*] analysis rescheduled with the additional resources and programmed to maintain the existing completion date.

Such monitoring is, however, relatively expensive, requires the continuous attention of a programmer, the commitment and full understanding of the programme team and, if possible, the availability of a computer to provide a programme update after each progress review. Furthermore, even on some of those projects where regular updating is carried out, neither the contractor's team nor the project design team have the resources to make full and effective use of the programme review data.

In practice either the updating is not carried out and the programme rapidly becomes out of date or the updating is carried out but the implications are not fully understood and the appropriate action is not taken as it should be. In either case the programme loses credibility as a control tool and is left on the wall to fade away in the course of time whilst the team get on with the job with the aid of 'meaningful' bar charts.

The main lessons that have been learnt for using networks are set down in Fig. 10.8.

A critical path or precedence diagram, despite its value as a programming tool to work out the duration and sequence of operation and the timing of a project, may need to be redrawn in bar chart form, preferably as a linked-bar chart, in such a way as to continue to show the interrelationship and timing of the activities and the critical path.

---

[*]   The mathematics of time analysis and resource analysis is described in Chapter 12, where both normal and computer-aided methods are given.

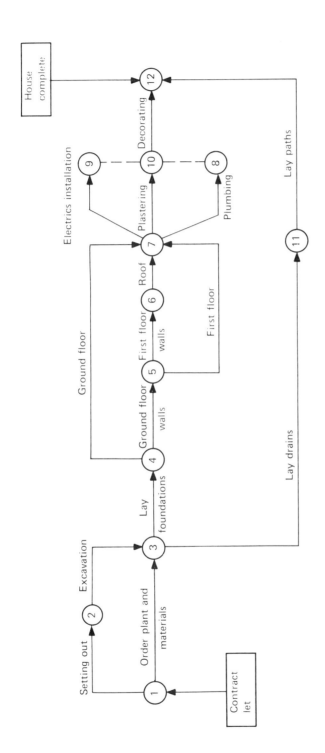

Fig. 10.5 – Arrow network for building a house.

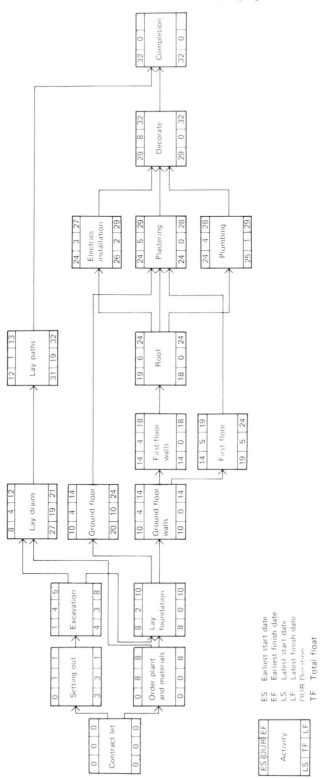

Fig. 10.6 – Precedence diagrams for building a house.

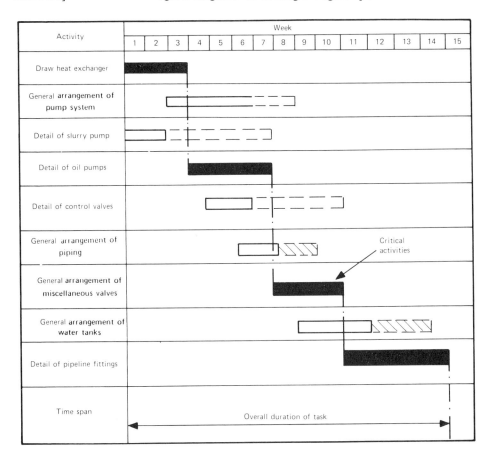

Fig. 10.7 – Bar chart for pumping station, showing critical activities.

(1)   Keep it simple – not too large too soon.

(2)   Use a hierarchy of networks if necessary.

(3)   Present in a way as near to a bar chart as possible.

(4)   Use standard networks where possible (ladders).

(5)   Keep old networks.

Fig. 10.8 – Lessons from the application of arrow networks.

10.4.2 Bar charts

Activities are set against a time scale as in Fig. 10.9. Here it is seen that the project consists of nine activities and each activity takes 4 weeks to complete. The first activity starts at the beginning of week 1 and is scheduled to be completed at the end of week 4, the second activity is scheduled to start at the end of week 1 and be completed at the end of week 5, etc. The scheduled date at which each activity will start is derived from the

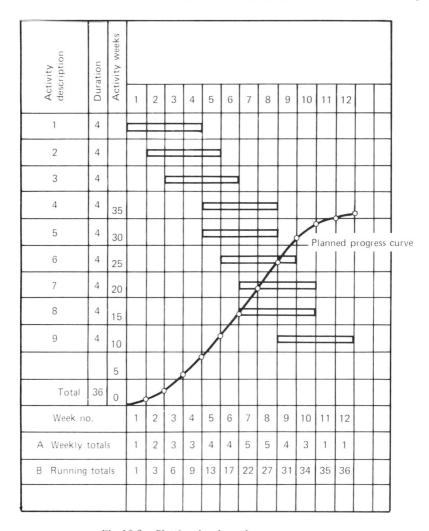

Fig. 10.9 — Plotting the planned progress curve.

logic of the plan; thus activity 4 is not scheduled to start before the beginning of week 5 because activity 1 must be completed first; etc. In order to set up a bar chart, therefore, we need to know the definition of each activity, the duration of each activity and the earliest date at which work on each activity can start.

Often the start date of an activity is well defined. For example, it is not possible to test a prototype until

(a)   the prototype has been made and
(b)   the test schedule has been written.

However, there will be occasions when the start of an activity is not absolutely defined by the completion of an earlier activity. For example, it would be simplistic to argue that a component cannot be made until the drawings have been produced and it is common practice to commence manufacture when *some* drawings have been issued because only by doing so can an acceptable completion date be achieved.

The construction of a bar chart is not, therefore, the application of simple logic to set the activities in their places. Engineering and managerial judgement are required to programme times that are both achievable and acceptable.

A curve representing the planned progress of completion of the 'activity weeks' throughout the programme can now be plotted on the programme. Fig. 10.9 shows the horizontal axis using the programme's time scale. The vertical axis is plotted upwards from the base-line to a convenient height using a scale of the total number of 'activity weeks'.

If a progress check is made at the end of week 4, it will be seen from Fig. 10.9 that for activity 1 the progress target is 100% (4 'activity weeks'), for activity 2 it is 75% (3 'activity weeks') and for activity 3 it is 50% (2 'activity weeks'), a total of 9 'activity weeks'.

A record of actual progress can also be plotted against the planned progress and this is illustrated in Fig. 10.10. Here it can be seen that for activity 1 the actual progress at the end of week 4 is 50%, for activity 2 it is 75% and for activity 3 it is 25% as shown blocked in on the bars.

The progress of each activity is readily seen but overall progress is not so apparent. However, by totalling the 'activity weeks' achieved, 6 'activity weeks' can be recorded at the appropriate position (at week 4) along line C and, by plotting this value on the graph, the overall position can also be identified.

Plotting this achieved value and reading off horizontally indicate that a target of 6 'activity weeks' should have been achieved a week previously, week 3; therefore an assumption can be made that overall progress is 1 week behind programme.

Fig. 10.11 shows the bar chart with a further assessment of progress made at the end of week 8, also arrowed. The target is 27 'activity weeks' (read from line B); the progress achieved is 15 'activity weeks' (read from line C). Plotting this value on the graph and reading off horizontally, it is seen that 15 'activity weeks' were planned to be completed approximately $2\frac{1}{2}$ weeks previously; therefore overall progress has now fallen approximately $2\frac{1}{2}$ weeks behind programme. The rate of overall progress in comparison with the rate of planned progress is now clearly evident from the graph.

Fig. 10.12 shows the addition of another vertical scale from 0 to 100 so that percentage completion can also be read off the graph. At week 4, target completion is 25%, as determined by the position of the planned progress curve relative to the percentage scale; actual completion is 17%, as determined by the corresponding position of the achieved progress curve. At week 8, target completion is 75% and actual completion 42%. The above explanation of Bar Charting has been set out in the **PSA** document Planned Progress Monitoring. See reference [1] and is reproduced here by kind permission.

10.5 PROJECT CONTROL

For any project the art of control by the project manager is to regulate the pace of working so that the desired client objective is achieved. In doing this the project manager may exercise his prerogative by suggesting trade-offs between time, cost and performance. Control is more of an art than a science and the following are some practical guidelines to aid project managers in this art.

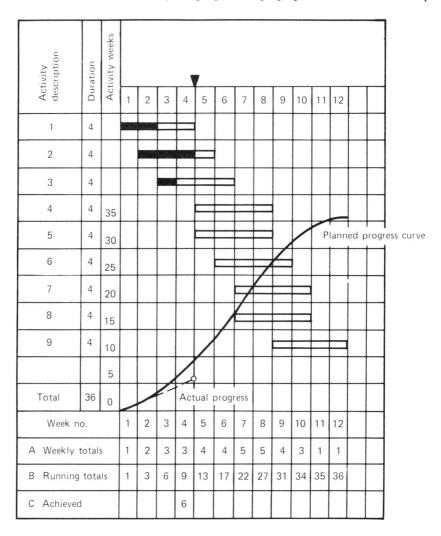

Fig. 10.10 – Monitoring progress at week 4.

10.5.1 Can a project be finished sooner?

To trim a project's schedule, find critical tasks that can be eliminated or done in parallel or finished in less time than they are scheduled for.

(1)   Eliminate a task. Make sure that every task is necessary for the project.
(2)   Replan dependent tasks to be done at the same time, i.e. in parallel.
(3)   Overlap sequential tasks, e.g. when producing a book, say that it takes 10 days to typeset some copy, and then 10 days to print it, adding up to a total of 20 days. By splitting the manuscript into two parts, some of the work can be done in parallel, saving 5 days.
(4)   Decrease the duration of critical tasks. Perhaps a task's duration can be decreased by applying more resources.

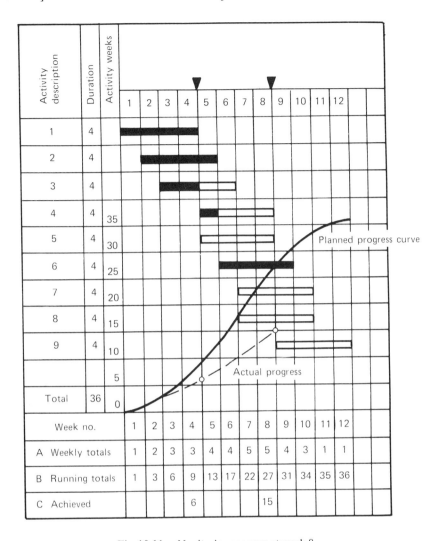

Fig. 10.11 – Monitoring progress at week 8.

10.5.2 Which tasks should be shortened?

The 'critical' tasks are the most important to shorten, since they affect the completion date of the entire project. Here are some suggestions to find tasks to shorten.

(1) Shorten the tasks that occur early in the project. This gives more flexibility later in the project, when it will probably be needed.

(2) Shorten the longest tasks. Often a certain percentage can be squeezed out of any task's duration. Therefore, the greater the duration a task has, the more time you can remove from it.

(3) Shorten the easiest tasks. Look for tasks that have been done successfully before. Find places where there are fewer unknowns or where one can be sure of the resources' capability or dependability.

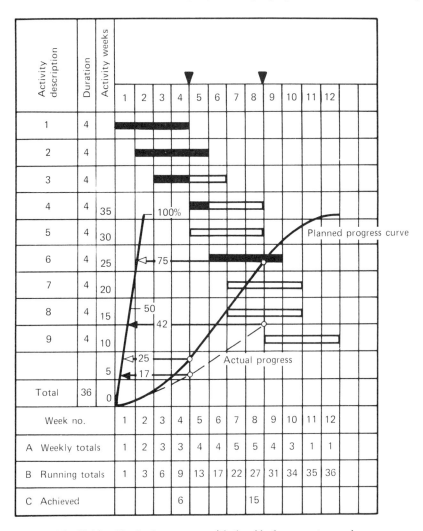

Fig. 10.12 – Monitoring progress with the aid of a percentage scale.

(4) Shorten the tasks for which there are more available resources. For example, you may know that you can easily use freelancers for proof reading and that task can therefore be shortened.

(5) Shorten the tasks that cost the least extra money to speed up (very important!).

(6) Shorten the tasks that can be directly controlled. It is usually easier to control work done within an organization than work contracted out. However, as with any good rule, there are exceptions. Sometimes a premium can be paid to get the work done faster by an outside contractor.

10.5.3 What can be done if people or other resources are lost or added?
If someone leaves, the project can be juggled to spread the work out among other resources. If resources are added to the project, existing resources may be overloaded, and then it is necessary to reassign tasks to the new resource.

(1)   See how tasks are divided between resources and consider reallocation. See who has free time and who is overloaded and consider who can be redeployed.
(2)   Add or remove a resource from a task and consider the effect on the project.
(3)   Remove a resource from the entire project (to affect costs but what will be the effect on the end date?).

10.5.4 What happens if a task finishes late

If a task finishes late because it took longer than expected, increase the task's duration. Note that this increases the time that each resource spends on the task; so it may increase the resource costs for the task.

   If the task finishes late because it started late, what time can be made up to preserve the completion date?

10.5.5 Keep the cash flow positive

The project must be driven to give a positive cash flow wherever possible (Fig. 10.13).

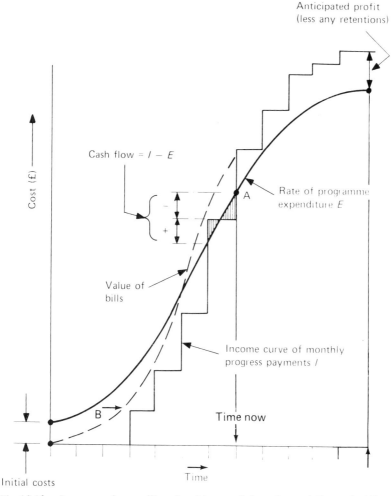

Fig. 10.13 – Programmed expenditure E and income I planned completion against time.

Care should have been taken at the negotiation stage to ensure that adequate progress payments are assued so as to achieve a positive cash flow as soon as possible. In Fig. 10.13 this occurs at point A. However the value of the work done, indicated by the chain line B, shows that at, time now, the actual expenditure exceeds the planned programme expenditure and that a positive cash flow will only be achieved with the next progress payment.

It is also necessary to check expenditure against milestones of completion to ensure that proper progress is being made.

SUMMARY OF CHAPTER 10

(1) The objectives of a project cannot be achieved without a plan. The plan requires the identification of objectives and the allocation of resources.

(2) The project plan is a part of the corporate plan.

(3) To be effective as a management tool, the plan must be broken down into a sequence of activities. Each activity will have a well-defined statement of work so that there will be no doubts about when an activity has been completed (and whether it is late) and what resources it has used (and whether it has overspent).

(4) The logical sequence of activities forms a network which shows the dependence of each activity on the others.

(5) The network of a project is usually too large for easy use and must be broken down into a number of smaller 'fragnets' for the operator.

(6) Smaller networks and 'fragnets' are more simply depicted as bar charts. These are easier to use than networks and contain more immediately available information.

(7) Management of the project involves monitoring achievement against the network, measuring the effects of delay and then bringing the project back onto its originally determined programme.

REFERENCES

[1] Lott, B.D. (1979) *Planned Progress Monitoring*, PSA Department of the Environment.

[2] Wearne, S.H. (2nd edn.) (1989) *Control of Engineering Projects*, Thomas Telford Ltd.

[3]   McKenzie, G. (1967) The Time and Resource Aspects of Project Management, *The Chemical Engineer* No. 209.

11

Cost prediction and establishing milestones

11.1 BUDGETS AND COST PREDICTION

The association between the cost of an activity and the time at which that cost occurs has been referred to in terms of the time value of money in Chapter 4. There is also a need to associate costs and revenues with the times at which they occur in the production of a master budget by the organization promoting the project and its contractors. A master budget takes an overall view of the income and expenditure of an organization and is formed by the aggregation of individual budgets, e.g. the sales budget, administrative budget, the research and development budget and project budgets. An essential part of the master budget is the cash budget. This is a statement of expenditures and incomes and includes information on when those incomes and expenditures will occur. It can be as detailed as identifying the daily cash flows or may be on a weekly, monthly or yearly basis but, as we have seen in Chapter 2, the company's master plan is a basket of projects and the production of the master budget relies on estimating, as accurately as possible, the costs and durations of individual activities in projects. The budgets provide some of the information required for project control and, on a corporate level, for the organization's management of its funds.

There are a number of methods for estimating the costs and durations of projects and the primary difference between these is between top-down estimating and bottom-up estimating. There are other methods but these are considered to be less legitimate than the two main approaches. These other methods include 'price-to-win' estimating and Parkinsonian estimation [1].

The price to win is the tendering price for a contract based on estimates of how much a customer is prepared to pay for the work required, or on how much the competing tenders are likely to be. Parkinsonian estimation is based on the hypothesis that 'work expands to fill the time available' [2] or, for software projects, Utz' 'law', which says that 'any given program will expand to fill all the available memory' [3]. The estimates are then based on the resources available rather than the resources which may actually be required. These methods of estimating do not attempt to make a realistic forecast of the true effort or cost required by a project.

In top-down estimating the overall cost for the project is derived from its global properties. A total cost for the whole project is estimated first and then this may be broken down into the various components of the project. One advantage of a top-down estimating system is that it can be applied at an early stage of project definition, when the lower-level functions of a project have yet to be defined. Even at later stages of project definition, when there is more detailed information available, top-down estimates have the advantage that the costs of smaller functions or parts, and of integrating these, will not be overlooked.

The disadvantages of this method are that it does not identify low-level technical problems that are likely to escalate costs, that it provides little detailed basis for justifying the estimate and that it may be more prone to error than bottom-up estimating where estimating errors for the component parts have an opportunity to cancel each other out.

In bottom-up estimates a project is broken down into component parts. The cost of each component is estimated and these are then summed to arrive at an estimated cost for the overall project.

The weaknesses of top-down estimates tend to be the strengths of bottom-up estimates and vice versa. Bottom-up estimating tends to cover only the costs for component parts of a project and may overlook such costs as those of project management and of integrating the individual parts. Individual component parts may also be overlooked. There may be a tendency for bottom-up estimates to be underestimates as a result. A bottom-up estimate can only be undertaken when a project is sufficiently well defined to have identified its components in some detail. Bottom-up estimates also require more effort than top-down estimates but, as each job can be costed by the person responsible for it, the estimate may be based on a more detailed understanding of the work to be done. The estimate may, however, be subject to some 'adjustment' as it passes up the organizational structure to the manager with overall responsibility for the project. Estimation errors in bottom-up estimating have an opportunity to balance out.

A further distinction is between subjective and objective methods. Objective methods can be divided again into parametric, comparative and synthetic methods and the choice of which particular method to use depends to a great extent on the quantity, quality and type of information available [4]. As a result, different methods are appropriate at different stages of a project.

The estimating process may incorporate more than one of these methods so that the 'final' estimate at any time may be formed by the aggregation of individual estimates arrived at by different methods.

Knowledge of the equipment or product that is being estimated will improve as the project develops. However, there is a need to define what exactly is being estimated at an early stage of the project, even if certain assumptions may have to be made about the project. The assumptions made at each stage should be recorded so that they can be amended as the project progresses and the estimates refined. These assumptions concern, for example, the volume and rate of production, design specifications, the type and quantity of special tooling, prototype design features, the costs of materials and parts, and allowances for testing.

11.2 SUBJECTIVE ESTIMATES

Subjective estimating can be used when there is little or no information on previous similar projects or some of the activities within a project. It is a characteristic of estimating for capital expenditure or for research and design expenditure that the programmes are carried out only once and in a changing technical and business environment, and so data on previous similar projects may be scarce. The subjective method of estimation attempts to overcome this problem and in application can vary in sophistication depending on the ability of recall and judgement that an estimator has of previous experience. At its simplest level an estimator can provide a single point estimate of the cost and duration of the scheme being considered. On a higher level of application an estimator can provide single point estimates of the costs and durations of each of the activities which constitute a project and these can be combined in an appropriate way to produce estimates of the total cost and duration. Inaccuracies arise in such estimates not only because of the assumption that the single point estimate is correct and immutable but also because of biases in estimating. However, psychologists, decision analysts and management scientists have attempted to improve the quality of subjective estimates by developing methods which take some account of uncertainty and aim to identify and reduce bias.

11.2.1 Uncertainty in subjective estimates

Uncertainty arises when there is some doubt about the duration or cost of an activity. This may be because of doubt over a factor which will influence cost or duration. The weather is such a factor which will certainly affect a construction project but other sources of risk are technical complexity, technical novelty, the success of trials, changes in specification and resource availability. There are a number of approaches to finding the subjective probabilities of a particular outcome.

(1)   One way in which uncertainty can be incorporated into estimates is to use the idea of the '**expected value**' of the uncertain quantity [5]. This method requires a number of estimates of the uncertain value and the probability that each of those estimated values will occur. These estimates are combined to form the 'expected value', which is then treated as a single point estimate, known with certainty. The following example illustrates the method for calculating the expected value.

Table 11.1 shows probability assessments for the cost of an activity in a scheme. The first step is to check that the sum of the probabilities associated with costs is one. Next, the pairs of probabilities and costs are multiplied together, and finally the sum of these products is found. This is the expected value of the uncertain quantity, in this case £379 000.

Another way in which uncertainty can be incorporated into estimates is by making three estimates for each unknown quantity which are then combined to produce a single expected value. The three estimates required are the most likely, the pessimistic and the optimistic estimates. The **project evaluation-and-review technique** (PERT) approach (see Chapter 12) to combining these three estimates assumes that they are from a β distribution which has a standard deviation of one sixth of the difference between the optimistic and the pessimistic values. The pessimistic and optimistic values correspond to the bounds of the β distribution

Table 11.1 – Calculation of the expected value of the cost of an
activity of a project.

Factor	Cost (£)	Probability	Probability × cost (£)
Activity cost	250 000	0.1	25 000
	350 000	0.2	70 000
	400 000	0.6	240 000
	440 000	0.1	44 000
		Expected value	£379 000

and the most likely value corresponds to the mode of the distribution. Based on
this assumption, an approximate value of the mean can be calculated which is given
by

$$\text{expected value} = \frac{p + 4m + o}{6}$$

with the assumed standard deviation of

$$\left| \frac{p - o}{6} \right|$$

where p is the pessimistic estimate, m is the most likely estimate and o is the
optimistic estimate. The expected values are then combined in the same manner as
if they were point estimates. An idea of the standard deviation of the final estimate
can be achieved by adding the variances of the individual cost estimates in the
budget and by adding the variances of the durations on the critical path of a project
activity network, where the variance is the square of the standard deviation.

In PERT this means that we determine the expected duration of each activity;
these are then used as point estimates to determine the finishing date of the project
but the derived standard deviation of each of the activity times enables us to
determine the variance of the completion date.

The following is an example of the application of the PERT procedure. The
pessimistic, optimistic and most likely estimates of the duration of an activity are
shown in Table 11.2 and are as follows.

$$\text{expected duration} = \frac{50 + (4 \times 36) + 10}{6}$$

$$= 34$$

$$\text{standard deviation} = \frac{50 - 10}{6}$$

$$= 6.67$$

$$\text{variance} = (\text{standard deviation})^2 = 44.44.$$

Table 11.2 – Estimates of the optimistic, pessimistic and most likely durations of an activity.

Likelihood	Duration (days)
Optimistic	10
Most likely	36
Pessimistic	50

By assuming that the duration of the activity is normally distributed, with a mean of 34 days and a standard deviation of 6.67 days, we may use the probability paper of Fig. 11.1 to calculate the probability of meeting any given due dates.

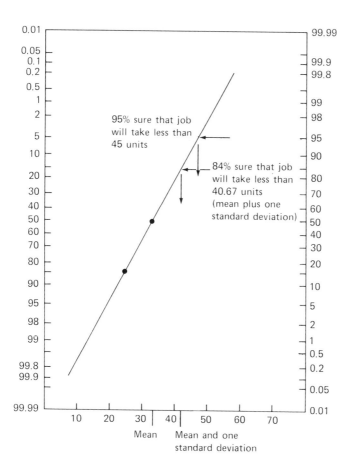

Fig. 11.1 – Cumulative normal distribution.

(2)   A subjective estimate and the probability associated with it can be represented
       graphically in two ways; by a probability distribution curve and by a cumulative
       distribution curve. Figs 11.2, 11.3, 11.4 and 11.5 show two curves for each of four
       different distributions and give an indication of the range of shapes possible. The
       normal distribution is symmetrical about its mean and mode (which is the highest
       point on the curve) which occur at the same value, one of the two normal
       distributions shown in Fig. 11.2 has a mean at 0 and the other at a value of 3 of the
       uncertain variable. The distribution which has the sharper peak has a smaller
       variance than the flatter distribution which indicates that there is less uncertainty
       associated with it. A characteristic of the normal distribution is that it is not
       bounded at either its upper or its lower ends, which means that there is a possi-
       bility, however small, that an extremely high or extremely low value of the
       uncertain variable occurs.
           Fig. 11.3 shows two log-normal distributions. Unlike the normal distribution,
       the **log-normal distribution** is asymmetrical. It is bounded at the lower end, which
       in the case of the two distributions shown occurs at 0, so that a value of the
       uncertain variable of less than 0 is not possible. The distribution is unbounded at
       the upper end so that there is a very small probability that a very large value of the
       uncertain variable occurs.
           Fig. 11.4 shows two examples of the Weibull distribution, which has been used
       for representing probabilities associated with the economic life of capital equip-
       ment. This distribution is also bounded at the lower end but not at the top end.
       The **exponential distributions** (Fig. 11.5) are bounded at the lower end but not at
       the upper end and the probability that an uncertain variable occurs decreases as the
       uncertain variable increases.
           Fig. 11.6 shows a distribution which is bounded at both the upper end and the
       lower end, at values of 10 and 50 of the uncertain variable. The maximum
       frequency occurs at a value of the uncertain variable of 36 which is the mode of the
       distribution. The relative frequency of other values of the uncertain variable can be
       read so that, for example, a value of the uncertain variable of 25 occurs 0.4 times as
       frequently as the value of mode.
           Fig. 11.7 shows a cumulative distribution curve which is a graph of the
       cumulative frequency of the uncertain variable. The graph represents the same
       information as in Fig. 11.6 but presented in a different way. Fig. 11.7 shows the
       proportion of occurrences which are equal to or less than the value in question of
       the uncertain variable. For example, Fig. 11.7 indicates that, when the uncertain
       variable is 30, the cumulative frequency is 25%. This means that 25% of
       occurrences of the uncertain variable will have a value of 30 or less. From the graph
       we see that about 50% of the occurences of the uncertain variable will have a value
       of 34.5 or less. This value of 34.5 corresponding to 50% on the vertical axis is the
       median of the uncertain variable. Of the two types of curve, it is the frequency
       distribution curve which is most commonly used to assess subjective probabilities,
       as it is more easily interpreted visually than the cumulative probability curve.

(3)   Estimators are not usually able to draw the entire curve of the probability
       distribution or of the cumulative distribution but it is more often possible to
       estimate the location of several points on the curve and, by drawing a smooth line
       between these points, to obtain the remaining values. There are a number of

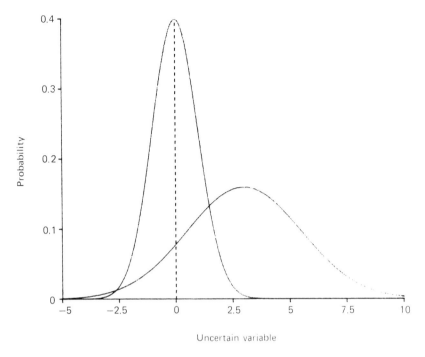

Fig. 11.2 – Two typical normal distributions.

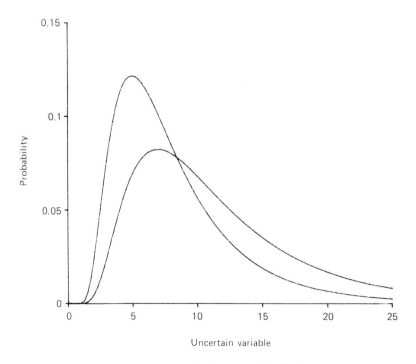

Fig. 11.3 – Two typical log-normal distributions.

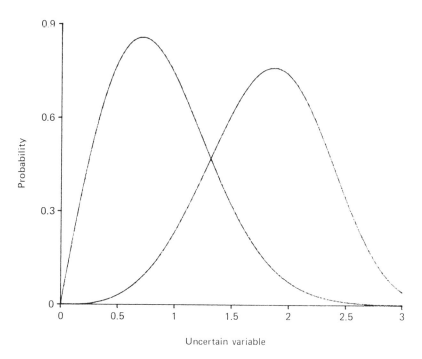

Fig. 11.4 – Two typical Weibull distributions.

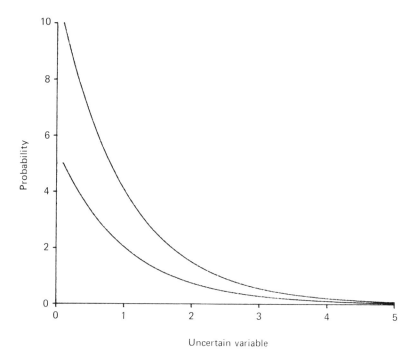

Fig. 11.5 – Two typical exponential distributions.

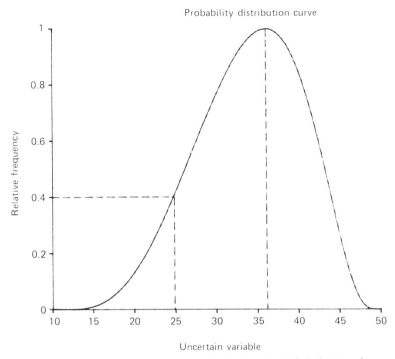

Fig. 11.6 – Distribution bounded at both the upper and the lower end.

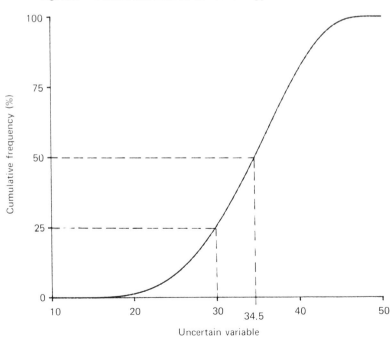

Fig.11.7 – Cumulative distribution curve which is a graph of the cumulative frequency of
the uncertain variable.

different methods for locating points on a probability distribution curve. One, the **method of relative heights**, is also known as the **histogram method** [5]. In this approach the most likely value of the uncertain quantity being estimated, e.g. duration or cost, is specified and then the likelihood of other values of that quantity is assessed in relation to this value. Thus the estimator is required to associate probabilities with particular values of the uncertain quantity. By drawing a histogram of the relative frequencies of the values of the uncertain variable, such as in Fig. 11.8, the estimator can see how the different estimates for each value of the uncertain variable relate to each other. These relative heights may be used to find the expected value or may be combined in a more sophisticated way if the project demands it. A smooth line drawn between the points defined by the histogram in Fig. 11.8 will approximate to the probability distribution curve shown in Fig. 11.6.

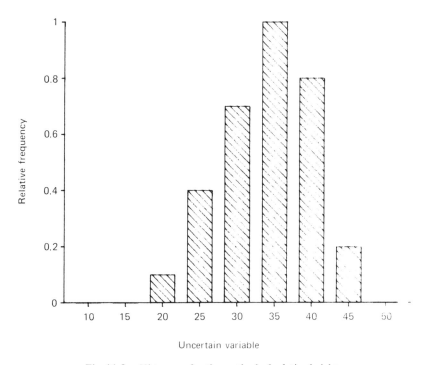

Fig. 11.8 – Histogram for the method of relative heights.

Another method is known as the **percentile method** [5]. Variations on this method are the fractile and tertile methods which differ from the percentile method in detail only. In the percentile method the estimator assesses values of the uncertain quantity associated with a number pre-determined percentiles of the distribution. For example, the estimator can be required to state a value such that the uncertain variable is as likely to be above as below the stated value; this is the fiftieth-percentile point or median. Alternatively, he may state a value such that there is a one-in-ten chance that the uncertain variable is less than the stated value; this is the tenth percentile point. In the fractile method the same approach is used except that the percentiles are replaced by fractiles, so that the percentiles referred to in the example become the half and tenth fractiles respectively. Fractiles in common use are the quartile (or twenty-fifth percentile) and the tertile. Tertiles divide the range into three equally probable intervals, so that, for example, the third and two-thirds fractiles would be assessed, followed by the one ninth, two-ninths, four-ninths and five-ninths fractiles, and so on. In these methods the estimator is required to provide values of the uncertain quantity for particular probabilities. These definitions are illustrated on Fig. 11.9.

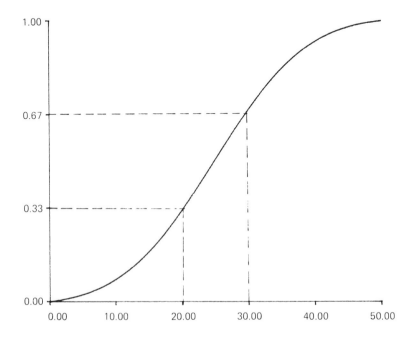

Fig. 11.9 – Tertile method for estimating a probability distribution. 1. The estimator believes that on one-third of the occasions a job will take less than 20 hours. 2. He also believes that on one-third of the occasions (two-thirds of the occasions) the job will take more than (less than) 30 hours. 3. The estimator may continue to argue that on those occasions when the job takes less than 20 hours, on one-third of those occasions the job takes less than 10, and 4. also on two-thirds of the occasions when the job takes less than 20 hours it takes less than 14 hours. 5. Continuing this process an assessor will define the estimates to a cumulative distribution shown by the continuous curve.

(4)   A third approach which is difficult to apply even by those estimators acquainted with statistical distribution theory is to estimate the parameters which affect the shape of the probability distribution of the uncertain quantity. This method requires the estimator to make certain assumptions about the general shape of the distribution, e.g. that it is a normal distribution or that it is a β distribution, and then to estimate the parameters, or the moments, which define its shape, such as the mean and the standard deviation for a normal distribution. Computer programs exist which allow an estimator to see the shape defined by this method and allow the parameters to be altered until the desired shape is arrived at. A major dis-

advantage of this method is the difficulty of estimating the parameters of complicated functions, even by estimators who have a good statistical background.

(5)   The **Delphi technique** is another method of arriving at an acceptable value for an uncertain quantity [6]. In this procedure a group of people produce estimates independently of each other. These estimates can then be combined and some information, e.g. the mean and the interquartile range, fed back to the estimators, who can then reconsider and alter their original estimates if they wish. The process is repeated until the range of estimates becomes acceptably close. Either the mean of this range of final estimates can be accepted or the estimators can meet to agree on a final estimate. Disagreements between individuals or the domination of a group by an individual or by a small group are avoided by the Delphi process. It has been applied to problems concerning business and social policy, technological forecasting and feasibility studies.

11.2.2 Sources of error in subjective estimating

Two main sources are responsible for errors in subjective estimating. They are bias and overconfidence.

Bias in making subjective estimates

Three sources of bias are the most common in estimating uncertain quantities, namely availability, adjustment and representativeness [7].

(1)   **Availability**. In some circumstances, people's estimates of uncertain quantities are affected by the ease with which examples can be brought to mind. For instance, an estimate of a cost may be influenced by an estimator's ability to recall excessive costs more easily than moderate or low costs, hence biasing the estimate produced towards higher costs. The availability of examples of circumstances can be influenced by the frequency of an occurrence as, the more often it occurs, the more easily it can be brought to mind, with the result that less frequent occurrences are overlooked. Ease of imagination can also influence the perception of probability of an occurrence; the more easily it can be imagined, the more likely it is thought to occur. The effect of witnessing a car accident, for example, will increase a person's subjective probability of the frequency of traffic accidents.

  Another example of the type of error caused by ease of imaginability is that many people think that more committees of two members can be made up from a group of ten people than can committees of eight. In fact, 45 committees can be formed of either eight or two members. This error arises because it is easier to imagine more combinations of two than it is to imagine combinations of eight.

(2)   **Adjustment**. In some situations, people formulate their estimates by starting from an initial estimate and then adjusting this value to arrive at a final estimate. In general, estimators tend to underadjust their estimates. Subjects who were asked to estimate the value of $8 \times 7 \times 6 \times 5 \times 4 \times 3 \times 2 \times 1$ within a time limit of 5 s gave a much higher answer than those asked to estimate the value of $1 \times 2 \times 3 \times 4 \times 5 \times 6 \times 7 \times 8$ [7]. The median estimate for the descending sequence was 2 250 and for the ascending sequence 512. The correct answer is 40 320 (the respondents were obviously not bellringers all of whom know that 40 320 is the number of changes that can be rung on a peal of eight bells).

(3) **Representativeness.** This type of error arises because people have a tendency to make incorrect associations between apparently similar occurrences. This effect is also sometimes known as the 'halo' effect; an idea can be perceived to be good or bad simply by its association with an individual or another project which has been seen as either a success or a failure. An example of an error due to representativeness is a belief in the 'law of averages'. Suppose that the mean cost of producing an article is £100. In a study of the production cost of 50 of these articles chosen at random, the first item is found to have cost £150 to make. What do you expect the average cost of the sample to be? The correct answer is £101, but a surprising number of people believe that the expected average cost of the sample will be £100.

As an exercise, estimate the populations of the following countries.

(a) Iran.
(b) Indonesia.
(c) Burkina Faso.
(d) Libya.

It is quite likely that your estimates will have been influenced by the quantity and type of other knowledge you have of each country. In fact the population of Burkina Faso is 8 million but, as you may not have heard of that country, you probably assume that its population is much less than that of Libya (3.5 million) which you will have heard of. Indonesia has a population of 157.5 million and Iran 48 million.

(4) **Overconfidence and underconfidence.** A further source of error in subjective estimates is that of overconfidence or underconfidence [7]. The confidence of a person's estimates can be measured by comparing a known probability distribution with that estimated by the assessor. Two measures of comparison are usually applied: the interquartile index or the surprise index. The **interquartile index** is the percentage of items for which the true value falls within the quartile range of the subjective estimates. The quartile range of a distribution is the range of the uncertain quantity which lie between the twenty-fifth- and seventy-fifth-percentile points. Estimators are asked to provide subjective probability distributions for quantities for which the true value is known. A person who is perfectly calibrated will have an interquartile index of 100%. The **surprise index** is the percentage of true values which fall outside the extreme values of the assessed subjective estimates. Again in this measure of estimating ability estimators are asked to provide subjective distributions for a quantity for which the true values are known and the proportion of estimates whose true value lies outside this range is expressed as a percentage of the total number of estimates made. In this method of measurement, a perfectly calibrated person has a surprise index of 0. Estimators in general tend to be overconfident, although training can reduce overconfidence and bias and improve the quality of subjective estimates.

11.2.3 Analysis of subjective estimates
The analysis and combination of estimates of costs and durations are straightforward when they are point estimates. In that case they are combined in the conventional manner to produce a budget and timetable for the project.

When the costs and durations generated incorporate some information on uncertainty in the form of a probability of their occurrence, the analysis is more difficult. One method which has already been described is the PERT method. Another is to calculate the mean of each distribution and treat this 'expected value' as a deterministic estimate and continue with the construction of the budget and timetable as if these costs and times were known with certainty. Yet another approach is to combine the probability distributions mathematically, although this can become a long and difficult process especially when there are many activities and the probability distributions are not of the better-known standard forms. The computational problems can be overcome by combining the estimates by simulation which requires that a random sample of each of the distributions is taken and combined as for point estimates and the result recorded. The process is repeated a large number of times (e.g. 10 000) and the results can be tabulated in the form of a probability distribution. Simulation requires access to computing facilities and software. A random number was generated from each of the three activity cost distributions in Figs 11.10(a), 11.10(b), and 11.10(c). The three activity costs that were generated were added to give a possible total cost of the project. Fig. 11.10(d) shows the cumulative distribution that was derived from 100 such simulations, arranged in ascending numerical order.

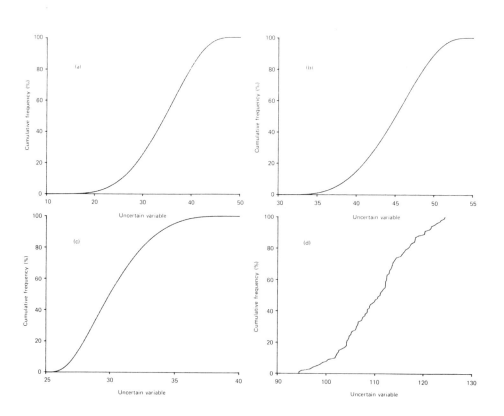

Fig. 11.10 – Combining probabilities by simulation.

11.2.4 Practical application of subjective assessment methods

In practice a number of steps can be taken to reduce the errors of estimating subjectively.

(1) Estimators should not arrive at estimates on their own. A disinterested analyst should conduct the process with the estimator or estimators individually, possibly using some kind of procedure such as the Delphi technique.

(2) Estimators should be aware of exactly what they are estimating and of the terms used so that no ambiguity arises.

(3) Estimators should have a knowledge of the concepts of probability.

(4) Estimators should not be concerned about inconsistencies in their estimates as the analyst should construct the enquiry to identify and clear up any discrepancies.

(5) Estimators should be trained in the methods of subjective estimating so that the effects of bias and overconfidence are minimized.

11.3 OBJECTIVE ESTIMATING

Objective methods of estimating can be applied when there is an adequate amount of information available on the costs and durations of previous similar projects undertaken [4]. The estimating procedure depends to a great extent on the volume and type of information available about previous, current and future projects. As a project runs its course, the quality and type of information change so that the most appropriate method of estimating may also change. The three main objective methods are the **comparative, synthetic** and **parametric** methods.

11.3.1 Comparative estimates

This method involves comparing the project with those undertaken previously and adjusting the costs and durations of the previous project or projects to account for differences between them. The method uses a process of extrapolation from data on previous projects to produce estimates for the project in question and relies on the existence of detailed records from previous projects. The method may be used to estimate the costs and durations of a project as a whole or to build up a total estimate from estimates of its constituent parts.

The first problem in applying this method is to decide which previous projects, or part projects, can be considered sufficiently similar to the current project. Even in projects which involve new technology, many activities will have been carried out previously. Initially the selection process should not be too specific. It is better to find that a number of previous projects match the present project loosely than to find that none matches it exactly and to narrow down the selection criteria if a number of similar projects are found. It is important to keep records of previous project and activity costs so that they can be referred to in the future and methods for doing so are covered in sections 11.5 and 11.6 of this chapter.

Differences in the projects can be allowed for by multiplying comparable activities by a factor which can take into account such differences as technical complexity, relative size, cost inflation and other price adjustments. A comparison of technical complexity, for example, is a subjective factor, but factors for cost changes can be calculated from published cost indices.

11.3.2 Cost indices

An index is a statistical measure designed to show changes in a variable, or a group of related variables. It shows the relative change rather than the absolute magnitude of change. Many indices available are produced by government departments, e.g. the index of retail prices, price adjustment formulae for construction building contracts, aerospace and electronics cost indices. The private sector also produces indices, e.g. *Financial Times* indices, *Economist* indices and Barbour indices.

Possibly the most widely quoted is the **Retail Price Index**, which attempts to measure the change in the price of goods and services and is often used as a basis for wage negotiations. Some savings certificates and pensions are index linked.

Index numbers are important statistical tools but should be used with care.

The Retail Price Index is not suitable for calculating changes in costs for all industries, and special indices are produced for the needs of particular sectors of industry, e.g. the Baxter Index for Civil Engineering price adjustment, printed monthly in the *New Civil Engineer* [8] and the aerospace and electronics cost indices [9]. This type of information is available directly from the Central Statistical Office but is also available from journals such as *Business Briefing* [10] which now publishes some of the cost indices formerly published by *British Business*, the last edition of which was published in September 1989.

An example of the use of cost indices

An airframe manufacturer has been asked to produce an airframe which was last made in April 1983, and for which only general cost information is available. It is now April 1986.

The index number (base 1975) for combined costs of the aerospace industry airframe sector in April 1986 is 322.4. The corresponding index number in April 1983 was 265.6.

The relative price increase is given by

$$\text{relative price index} \ = \ \frac{\text{index number in April 1986}}{\text{index number in April 1983}}$$

$$= \frac{322.4}{265.6}$$

$$= 1.214.$$

The cost in April 1983 should be multiplied by 1.214 to find the cost in April 1986.

11.3.3 Synthetic estimates

Generally, synthetic methods, whether applied in work measurement or in estimating, break a complete process or project into its most elemental parts, for which the costs and durations are estimated. It is likely that many of the work elements will have been carried out on many previous occasions and that cost and time data will be available for them. Any estimate which is built up from the elements of a whole project can be called synthetic, but a distinction is drawn by the number and detail of the divisions that a project is divided into and by the degree of accuracy with which the quantity estimated is known.

Synthetic estimating requires that the main project is divided up into many small parts, and it is easy to overlook some potentially important elements of work in the process. Problems also arise because the elements are looked at in isolation; costs in terms of money or time may be incurred by the interaction of two or more component elements and by the process of combining the elements to form a whole.

Synthetic methods are better known for their application to work measurement and method study. In certain circumstances it is also possible to apply these techniques to estimating the costs of a new project. Human movements can be broken down into fundamental elements, such as reaching, grasping and placing, which are used repeatedly, and a standard time for a task can then be built up using a pre-determined time for these motions. Various systems have been devised to calculate these times, such as the pre-determined motion–time system and the data are available from a number of specialist consultancy firms if this type of information is not available from within a company. The methods have been developed so that they can be applied not only to manual tasks but also to clerical and creative work. One main disadvantage in using such data to build up time and cost estimates is that the minute detail of the work to be carried out needs to be known before the technique can be applied. Clearly the details of, for example, production cannot be known before a detailed design has been completed. However, estimates can be made for the shorter-term future when these details are known, and also for activities which have been carried out previously.

11.3.4 Parametric estimates

Parametric methods for estimating cost and duration rely on the relationship between the physical and technical characteristics of a project and the cost and duration of part of or all the project [4]. The mathematical relationships are derived by estimating dependencies based on historical data from projects carried out previously. Typical examples of parametric costs are as follows.

(1)   Estimating the cost and duration of a building from its floor area. The cost may be assumed to be for example £200 per square metre for a particular type of industrial building (although no two buildings will be precisely the same cost per square metre).

(2)   Estimating the cost of motoring in terms of pence per mile (although no two motorists will run their cars in the same way).

(3)   Estimating the cost of designing and developing a gear box in terms of its estimated weight.

Each of these three examples only has one variable which affects the total cost, but more complicated relationships can be found for complex projects. For example, the cost of a building is related not only to its floor area but also to the amount of land that it occupies, its construction method and the materials from which it is built, and extra parameters such as these may be included in a parametric cost-estimating model for buildings.

Principles of parametric estimating methods

The first objective of the parametric method is to derive a cost-estimating relationship (CER), which relates the relevant characteristics of a scheme with its cost. The most common forms of CER are linear, logarithmic and exponential relationships. Other possibilities also exist, such as a mix of these equations e.g. logarithmic linear.

For linear relationships,

$$Y = a + bx_1 + cx_2 + \ldots .$$ (11.1)

For logarithmic relationships

$$\log Y = a + b \log x_1 + c \log x_2 + \ldots .$$ (11.2)

For exponential relationships,

$$Y = a + bx_1^c + dx_2^e + \ldots .$$ (11.3)

Y is the quantity being estimated and $a, b, c, d, e, \ldots$ are constants and $x_1, x_2, \ldots$ are physical, technical or performance characteristics.

A good intuitive understanding of how costs vary with the parameters is helpful when choosing the form of the estimating relationship. A 'short list' of estimating relationships can then be compared by statistical methods, e.g. the correlation coefficient, the standard error of the estimate, the t test, the F test and the most efficient one chosen [11].

The **correlation coefficient** is sometimes used as a measure of how much linear relationship there is between one variable and another. Its value always lies between -1 and $+1$. A value of -1 indicates a perfect linear relationship with the value of one variable increasing as the other decreases. A value of $+1$ indicates a perfect linear relationship with an increase in one variable corresponding to an increase in the other. A value of 0 indicates that there is no linear relationship between the two variables. Care must be taken with correlation coefficients as a high value does not *necessarily* mean a good correlation or a low value that there is no correlation.

Computer programs exist for fitting curves to data, and these routines can be applied to empirical parametric data.

Data must be defined consistently before they can be used in a parametric model. This is particularly important with respect to costs as inflation has meant that even identical articles manufactured at different times have different costs. A base year should be chosen for the model and all costs adjusted to that year. This can be achieved by the use of cost indices as described in section 11.3.2.

An example in the construction of a parametric model
The data shown in Table 11.3 are taken from an article on a steam jet ejector [12]. The data show cost, capacity, suction pressure and steam consumption.

A logarithmic CER in the form

$$\log C = a + b \log Q + d \log P + e \log S$$

where C is the cost, Q is the ejector capacity, P is the suction pressure and S is the steam consumption was applied to the data in Table 11.3 and the values of a, b, d and e found by solving the four simultaneous equations obtained by substituting the data into the CER, giving

$$\log C = 3.844\,346 + 0.460\,846 \log Q - 0.495\,935 \log P + 0.1336\,116 \log S.$$

Additional data for steam jet ejectors are shown in Table 11.4 together with the costs estimated using the CER derived, and the error in estimating the cost.

Table 11.3 – Cost and technical characteristics of steam jet ejectors.

Ejector number	Cost (£)	Capacity ((kg dry air) h^{-1})	Suction pressure (Pa)	Steam consumption kg (kg air)$^{-1}$
1	300	32	20 000	3.4
2	700	109	13 332	6.2
3	410	181	40 000	1.2
4	600	227	26 664	2.1

Table 11.4 – Actual costs, estimated costs, technical characteristics and the percentage error of the calculated costs for steam jet ejectors.

Ejector number	Capacity ((kg dry air) h^{-1})	Suction pressure (Pa)	Steam consumption (kg (kg air)$^{-1}$)	Actual cost (£)	Calculated cost (£)	Error (%)
5	109	13 332	6.2	700	699	0.08
6	181	20 000	3.4	670	666	0.64
7	73	33 300	1.6	300	307	2.38

The example demonstrates the main principles of parametric estimating although it does not display some of the difficulties encountered by more complex problems. The unknown constants in the example (i.e. a, b, d and e) can be derived accurately from the four sets of data; there are four unknowns and four simultaneous equations can be solved to find their values. In many cases the amount of data available exceeds the minimum amount required to derive values for the constants in the estimating relationship, and then the curve represented by the estimating relationship is fitted by using statistical methods.

Fig. 11.11 shows data points, and the line of best fit to these points, for the costs associated with 20 similar products of different weights. The line of best fit for these points is

cost = 2549.75 + 58.19 × weight.

The correlation coefficient of this line of best fit to the data is 0.9845 and its standard error is 1246.2568. This line of best fit to the data can then be used as the CER. For example, if the weight of the equipment to be estimated is 400 units of weight, then the CER estimates its cost to be £25 825.08.

It should be noted that the data in Fig. 11.11 lies in the range from about 100 to 600 units of weight, and it is within this range that the CER is most accurate; outside this range its estimates become more less reliable.

An estimating relationship may prove to be unsatisfactory for a number of reasons. One possible reason is that the data used to generate the relationship are inadequate or inaccurate. Another possible reason is that not all the 'cost drivers' have been identified,

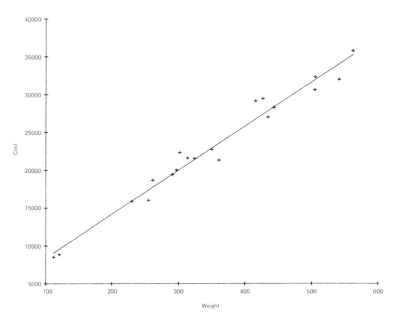

Fig. 11.11 – Graph of cost against weight.

or that spurious variables have been included. The approach then is to review the cost drivers to see whether any have been overlooked or included when they should not be.

Another possible error in parametric estimating is caused by using the estimating relationship to predict the unknown quantity beyond the range over which the relationship is valid. Extrapolation should be done with care and bearing in mind the limits of the estimating relationship. Interpolation within the range of the existing data will provide more robust estimates.

Generally, the more 'cost drivers' that we use, the more likely we are to be able to fit a curve to our data but the more dangerous it will be to extrapolate from the curve. It is desirable to have a large number of data points in order to determine a cost relationship in which we can have much confidence but this must not lead us to collect data points which are not related to one another. For example, if we were to use parametric costing to predict the design and development costs of a new aeroplane in 1990, could we use cost data obtained from aircraft built in the 1960s and 1970s?

Problems such as those mentioned can be time consuming and difficult to overcome. Computer software manufacturers have developed parametric cost-estimating packages, e.g. PRICE and FAST [13], to ease the workload of the analysis. These packages require as input a number of pre-determined parameters, e.g. total weight, operating environment, complexity and density. The cost drivers required vary from package to package and between the type and purpose of hardware being estimated, although some are common to all. Computerized parametric estimating models can also estimate the life cycle costs of hardware, estimate costs for producing and supporting computer software and handle timetables so that a budget can be produced for the scheme. These packages incorporate data derived from the experience of the software manufacturers and their manufacturers and their previous customers, to which estimating relationships have already been fitted. A user organization's particular characteristics can be incorporated by calibrating the model so that estimates produced by it are adjusted by a factor derived from knowledge of that organization's previous projects and their costs.

The parametric cost-estimating methods is effectively a mathematically formalized form of the comparative method and it has achieved varying degrees of success. It often does not give good absolute predictions of costs but may still be used for the ranking of two or more alternative solutions to the same project specification. It should also be borne in mind that the method is most useful compared with other methods when projects are at an early stage of definition.

11.4 SELECTION OF ESTIMATING TECHNIQUE

The main types of cost- and time-estimating methods described are not totally independent of one another; each one incorporates elements of the others. Parametrics may include a subjective estimate of complexity, skill or efficiency as a cost driver, for example. A synthetic estimate may be made up of cost or time elements derived by any of the other methods available. Each method has its own merits and the most appropriate method for one project may not be the most appropriate for another. A combination of methods may prove to be the most suitable in many cases, and the choice will depend on the detail to which a project has been defined, the type of project and its degree of novelty. Table 11.5 gives a guide to the methods which may be the most suitable at different stages of the project.

Table 11.5 – Suitable estimating methods at different stages of a project.

Stage	Subjective method	Comparative method	Synthetic method	Parametric method
Feasibility				
Full development and manufacture				

11.5 PROJECT BREAKDOWN

The degree to which a project should be broken down into its constituent parts which are to be shown as activities on planning networks or as individual entries in a budget can be difficult to decide upon. If the breakdown is not detailed enough, then efforts to predict and then to monitor the costs and durations will be frustrated by lack of detail. Important activities may be obscured and overspending of time and money may not be pinpointed easily. Conversely, if the breakdown is too detailed, estimating and then monitoring the costs and durations of many activities which are short and cost little is time consuming and expensive and often does not yield more management information that those with less detail. Programmes and budgets which are too detailed can be large and contain activities which cannot be distinguished sharply from others and this volume of detail may cloud the overall view of what is happening during the course of a project. The degree of breakdown varies from project to project depending, for example, on its size or complexity.

11.5.1 Work-breakdown structure

A project or work-breakdown structure provides a consistent method of dividing up a whole project into its parts. A scheme is divided into groups of related activities broken down into levels of increasing detail. Two main criteria for division are used: product orientated, and function or systems orientated. With product-orientated division the project is broken down into levels of hardware, e.g. main equipment, major assemblies, subassemblies, and major and minor components. With a systems-orientated or functional-orientated division the project is broken down into levels of organizational discipline, e.g. management, manufacture, design, mechanical design, electrical design, high voltage and low voltage.

A project is thus broken down into the appropriate detail by dividing it into its parts step by step, each step becoming more detailed than the previous one. Each level of detail is appropriate for a different purpose; the more general levels provide an overview for senior management to monitor and plan in the longer term, and the more detailed levels provide information on targets and goals and their achievement, in the shorter term, possibly even daily, to more junior personnel.

In many cases it is appropriate to use a combination of the two breakdown methods. The higher-level divisions of a project, i.e. the less detailed, tend to be made by differentiating products, and the lower-level divisions made by differentiating the types of work or function carried out. Somewhere between the highest and lowest levels of the work-breakdown structure a change will be made from product-orientated division to functional-orientated division. The level at which this change should occur will depend on the individual project and also on the structure of the organization; however, the change should occur at the same level in all branches of the work-breakdown tree.

Several factors will influence the number of levels of work breakdown for a project.

(1)   The stage to which the project has been defined. As a project becomes better defined, it will become possible to break it down into more detail and hence into more levels of the work-breakdown structure.

(2)   The size of a project; for a larger project, more levels will be required to reach the same degree of detail as for a smaller project.

(3)   The amount of uncertainty in an element of work is an influence. Although in general it is preferable to divide all parts of a project down to the same level of detail, it is sometimes desirable to divide elements for which there is more uncertainty into more detail than the others. For instance, in the case where an assembly has many components which have been produced in large quantities previously, and a few components which are new in design or manufacture, the work associated with the new components may be broken down into more detail than for the others.

If a system of cost control is to be used and actual costs and durations are to be compared with those estimated and planned for, then the elements at each level of the project breakdown provide a basis for constructing the activity network of the project. This topic is addressed in Chapter 12.

11.5.2 Milestones

The work-breakdown structure can be used to identify significant events for control and management of the project. These key events are known as milestones and they represent events which indicate the completion of a significant and clearly definable part of a project. Milestone events can be used as a way of monitoring progress and as events for which progress payments are made. It is very important that milestones are defined precisely so that there can be no doubt when they have been achieved. One way in which any ambiguity can be eliminated is to define all activities which must have been completed before a milestone can be reached.

Table 11.6 shows one way that a timetable for the achievement of milestones can be presented. The table lists the milestones in date order and shows the planned date and actual date of achievement of the milestones. There is also a provision for showing revised forecast dates for achieving milestones not yet reached. A disadvantage of this type of presentation is that slippage of the project, i.e. the amount of time each delayed milestone has been delayed, cannot be seen clearly. For this reason, bar charts are frequently used for planning and control. Bar charts are easy to draw and understand, although their simplicity does have some disadvantages. Fig. 11.12 shows a bar chart of a project which has as milestones the achievement of the design, manufacture and trials stages of the project.

Table 11.6 — Achievement of milestones.

Milestone no.	Milestone	Date planned	Date achieved	Revised date
1	Start design	1 September 1988	1 September 1988	–
2	Start construction of fuselage	1 June 1988	1 June 1988	–
3	Start construction of wings	2 August 1989	12 August 1989	–
4	Start construction of tail	20 August 1989	–	1 September 1989
5	Equip wings	30 September 1990	–	30 October 1990
6	Fit engines	1 April 1991	–	–
7	Roll out demonstrator	5 June 1991	–	–
8	First flight	30 June 1991	–	–

The bar chart can be kept up to date by hatching or colouring the bars in proportion to the amount of work completed or of the progress achieved. The difference between the time at the end of the coloured area and the 'Time now' indicates the deviation from

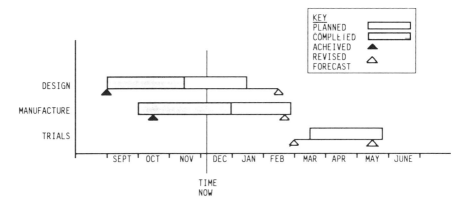

Fig. 11.12 – Bar chart showing planned, achieved and revised milestone dates.

the planned timetable. A drawback of this simplicity is lack of detail and this can result in misinterpretation of the progress as shown on the bar chart. For example, if the progress achieved is expressed as a percentage of the total work to be done and this is indicated on a bar chart by colouring in the same proportion of the bar, then this implies that there is a linear relationship between progress and time. This is not always the case; the first 10% of the work of an activity may take longer than a tenth of the work which comes towards the middle of the activity. A bar chart which is completed on the assumption that there is a linear relationship between the proportion of work completed and the proportion of the allowed time which has elapsed would then show incorrectly that the activity is behind schedule for its first part. More seriously, the mere logging of man hours used between milestones will not show whether the activity is meeting unexpected difficulties. Thus a job for which 100 man hours has been allowed and 90 spent may well have hit problems which will extend the time needed to 1000 man hours. More information is needed to show such problems than a record of man hours used so far.

In another sense, the bar chart is an oversimplification because, as we have seen, the predicted time or cost of an activity will be probabilistic. Built into any prediction of time (or cost) will be the assumption that there is a probability of the activity taking more or (rarely) less time than the bar chart shows. This can be dealt with to a limited extent by PERT, as will be shown in Chapter 12 but, broadly, it must be realized by project managers that times and costs cannot be predicted with precision and deterministic methods of project management (such as the use of bar charts) will provide a framework within which the manager will use his common sense, judgement and experience; they will not, of themselves, produce the right answers.

11.5.3 Coding
Once a project has been broken down into sufficient detail, each element can be allocated an unique work identification code.

Requirements of a work identification code
(1)   A work identification code must identify an element of work uniquely.
(2)   The association of a group of elements at one level of the work-breakdown structure with a common element at a higher level should be reflected in the code.

(3)   Similar work undertaken elsewhere in the same project or as part of another project should have a similar code number, but differing in some simple manner which indicates the main project and the higher-level elements of which the work forms part. This will ease the process of collecting data on similar activities in future, either for control or management purposes or for collecting data for estimating some future project.

(4)   The code should be in a form which can be entered into a computer database. Some databases have restrictions on character formats and these should be accounted for in the design of the code.

(5)   The code should be neither too short, so that the detail of output and its adaptability to differing projects is impaired, nor too long, so that it becomes difficult to use. Typically a code will consist of between nine and 15 characters in groups which represent different functions. There is merit in having some mnemonic quality in the code. This will reduce transcription errors and ease the recognition of work from its code and vice versa.

Structure of the code

Once the basic contents of the code, i.e. the work and cost elements, have been decided upon, then the structure of the code can be decided upon. The exact manner of numbering in a code will depend on how it is anticipated that the data represented in the code will be used in future. If it is intended to hold data on a computer database, then it is possible that certain constraints on the code's structure may be imposed by the nature of the database itself or by the way that the database will be interrogated; different interrogation packages may have different requirements.

Significance in a code means that the elements represented by the code can be identified from the parts of the code. The advantage of a code which has significance can be shown more easily by explaining the disadvantages of a code which lacks significance. A code which lacks significance would for example be a random number of the required number of digits. No information can be imputed from this code, it has no meaning in the context of the project. A code which does have significance does hold some information. For example, a code in the form AB–YZ can represent the start and end nodes of an activity in a critical path network.

Example of a work identification code

This section gives an example of a coding system for a project.

Table 11.7 shows the structure of a coding system where XX represents a two-digit number. The code consists of seven sets of two-digit numbers. Each pair of numbers has a different function in terms of representing parts of a project, and these are described in the following.

Table 11.7 – Sample coding system.

Project code	Breakdown level 1	Breakdown level 2	Operational department	Standard grouping	Subgroup	Detail
XX	XX	XX	XX	XX	XX	XX

(1) **Project**. The first two digits represent the main projects undertaken by an organization.

(2) **Divisions of the project**. In this example the first two levels of work breakdown are made by differentiating products, and these two levels are represented by two pairs of numbers.

(3) **Operational department**. This pair of numbers represents the department which will carry out the work.

(4) **Standard groupings**. These are types of expenditure which are common to all divisions of a project and reflect the elements of costs and incomes chargeable to each. Eight main types are the most common. These are as follows.

   (a) Employee expenses, i.e. direct labour costs, salaries, wages and other personnel costs, e.g. National Insurance contributions.
   (b) Expenses related to premises.
   (c) Expenses related to transport.
   (d) Supplies and services, i.e. direct material drawn from stores or bought in bulk.
   (e) Contracted services, i.e. hired plant and services.
   (f) Central, departmental and technical services, security, and financial services.
   (g) Capital financing costs.
   (h) Income.

(5) **Standard subgroupings and details**. These are divisions and subdivisions of the standard grouping.

   (a) **Employees**

Subgroup	Detail
Operational	Salaries and wages
Support	National Insurance
Premises related	Superannuation
Transport related	Advertising
Administrative and clerical	Training
Other	

   (b) **Expenses related to premises.**
   Repairs and maintenance.
   Energy costs: electricity, gas.
   Rents.
   Rates.
   Water services.
   Insurances.
   Cleaning.
   Fixtures and fittings.
   Apportionment of expenses of operational buildings.

   (c) **Expenses related to transport.**
   Direct transport costs: purchase, running costs, repair and maintenance.
   Hire.
   Insurances.

   (d) **Supplies and services.**
   Equipment, materials and furniture.

Clothing, uniforms and office expenses.
Computing.
Communications: postage, telephone.
Expenses.
(e) **Contracted services.**
Hired plant and services.
(f) **Central, departmental and technical services.**
Administrative buildings expenses.
Central support services.
(g) **Capital financing costs.**
Leasing charges: building, transport, plant and equipment.
Debt management expenses: interest.
Depreciation.
(h) **Income.**
Customers' and clients' receipts: fees, sales.
Interest.
Transfers from other items.

11.6 DATA COLLECTION

It is essential to collect accurate and up-to-date information on the costs and times of the activities in a project, not only to be able to monitor the progress and costs of current projects but also as a basis for making estimates in the future. Information is available from a number of sources: from records of payments, by word of mouth and from elsewhere. Information gleaned from different sources is prone to variations in accuracy and is sometimes open to different interpretations. Each method of collecting information has a different purpose and each has its advantages and disadvantages. Meetings are time consuming but often raise important points which may otherwise have been overlooked and which can then be cleared up in the presence of all the interested parties. The time taken up by meetings can be reduced by including in the agenda a progress report which has been circulated some time beforehand. The following list indicates the main content of a work progress report.

11.6.1 Specimen content of a project progress report
— Date.
— Report title and reference.
— Project title.
— Author.
— Distribution list.
— Summary. Project progress and expenditure compared with budget comprising of

(1)   the total to date and
(2)   in the period since the last report.

— Present status. More detailed information than the summary.
— Work completed since the last report. Achievements including milestones, a report on the problems encountered, e.g. staffing, productivity, problems with materials or drawings.

- General comments.
- Future work to be completed in the next period. Targets including milestones, anticipated problems of staffing and productivity.
- Intended and recommended actions.
- Appendix. Staffing levels; man hours (total to date, planned, overtime); detailed breakdown of percentage completions; receipts and issue of drawings; detailed changes of planned work; unplanned work; changes to future work.

Informal sources of information are less reliable and can contradict data from other sources. Such information should be verified to avoid embarrassing problems later.

Information required for monitoring the progress of a scheme falls into three categories: costs, time and resources.

(1) **Costs.** The costs collected should be as up to date as possible. Cost collection systems should be reviewed if there is a significant delay in obtaining cost figures; a commitment accounting system may need to be introduced if there is not already one in operation. Costs of completed work should be separated from costs of work in progress, and revised estimates of future work should be collected.

(2) **Time.** Activities which have been completed, with start and finish dates, and any past activities which were added to, or deleted from, the programme. Activities which have been started but not finished, with start and estimated finish dates. The estimated start date of activities yet to start. The dates on which milestones were achieved, and any revisions of the durations of future activities.

(3) **Resources.** Revision of future resource availabilities and requirements.

SUMMARY OF CHAPTER 11

Chapter 11 is concerned with cost and time estimating for projects. The problems of making such estimates are considered and methods of overcoming these, appropriate at the different stages of a project are studied. Sources of cost and time data are noted, and methods of dealing with the uncertainty and risk associated with making cost and time forecasts are dealt with.

An overview of methods of separating projects into parts for estimating budgetary and management control is conducted. Work-breakdown structures and the importance of milestones in project management is covered. Methods of arranging a work identification code and a sample coding system are included.

REFERENCES

[1] B.W. Boehm (1981) *Software engineering economics*. Prentice-Hall, Englewood Cliffs, New Jersey.
[2] G.N. Parkinson (1957) *Parkinson's law and other studies on administration*. Houghton–Mifflin, Boston, Massachusetts.
[3] (1986) *Economist Style Book*. Economist Publications, London.
[4] (1969) *Report of the Steering Group on Development Cost Estimating*. HMSO, London.

[5] P.G. Moore and H. Thomas (1976) *The anatomy of decisions*. Penguin, Harmondsworth, Middlesex.

[6] H.A. Linstone and M. Turoff (1975) *The Delphi method*. Addison-Wesley, London.

[7] A. Tversky and D Kahneman (1982) *Judgement under uncertainty: heuristics and biases*. Cambridge University Press, Cambridge.

[8] *New Civil Engineer*. Institution of Civil Engineers, London.

[9] Business Statistics Office, *Business monitor Monthly statistics MM19 aerospace and electronics cost indices*. Government Statistical Service, HMSO, London.

[10] *Business Briefing*. Association of Chambers of Commerce, Soverign House, 212a Shaftesbury Avenue, London WC2H 8EW.

[11] P. Kennedy (1985) *A guide to econometrics*. Basil Blackwell, Oxford.

[12] J.C. Tallman (1953) Ejectors show low cost first. *Chemical Engineering,* **60**, 176–179.

[13] F.R. Freiman (1983) FAST cost estimating models. *Transactions of the American Association of Cost Engineers*, G.5.1–G.5.13.

12

Network analysis

12.1 INTRODUCTION

The use of analytical techniques has become an essential part of modern-day project management. The development of sophisticated user-friendly software on micro-computers means that even small-scale operations have access to facilities previously only available on minicomputers or mainframe computers. Whether the project involves the planning and organization of the 1988 Winter Olympics, the design and operation of a major distribution system or the construction of a single building, the need for these analytical techniques to calculate project duration, manpower and material requirements and cash flows has become established. There is, of course, no longer any real need for manual analysis of projects; however, in order for the best use to be made of computerized[*] project management, an understanding of the analyses performed is required. This chapter introduces the reader to the analytical techniques known as time analysis.

12.2 CRITICAL PATH METHODS

A project consists of a series of distinct jobs or activities. Each activity will have a certain duration and resource requirement (of course the duration may be dependent on the resources allocated and this is discussed later). The activities which make up the project will also have a logical order in which they must be carried out. The diagrammatic representation of these activities is called a **network**. Even though the analysis of the project will be carried out by computer the manual construction of the network is an essential starting point.

The network consists of a series of nodes connected by lines which determine the logical ordering of the activities. There are two distinct network representations.

---

[*] Some commercially available programs are listed in the bibliography and Appendix 12A demonstrates the use of a program written by the authors.

(1) **Activity-on-arrow network**. In this representation each node represents the end of one activity and the beginning of the next. The connecting lines or arrows represent the activities.

(2) **Activity-on-node network**. In this representation each node represents an activity and the connecting lines define the logical order in which the activities take place.

Aruguments have raged over many years as to which representation is superior. Each method has its advantages and disadvantages but, as the network will almost certainly be analysed by computer, the required representation will usually be defined by the particular computer program being utilized. Computer programs are about equally split between the two representations and some offer the option of using either. Both methods will be used in this chapter to construct a network representation of the same small problem so that the reader may gain familiarity with both concepts.

A project which consists of 13 activities is described in Table 12.1. The logical ordering of the activities is defined by the immediately preceding activity or activities of each task. The activity durations are, for the moment, assumed to be known.

Table 12.1 – Simple project definition.

Activity	Immediate predecessors	Duration (days)
A	- - -	12
B	- - -	10
C	- - -	15
D	B	9
E	C	6
F	C	12
G	D,E	14
H	A	21
I	H	5
J	I	10
K	B	12
L	G,F	7
M	F,G,H,K	3

12.1.1 Activity-on-arrow representation

As activities A, B and C have no predecessors, they constitute the start of our project. Diagrammatically this may be represented as in Fig. 12.1. Note that the activities are represented by the arrows, and the start and end of each activity by the nodes. Working through our list of activities we see that activity D follows B, activities E and F follow C and activity G follows both D and E, i.e. activity G emanates from a node representing the completion of both activity D and activity E. The representation of this logic in our network is shown in Fig. 12.2.

Continuing the development of the network we see that H follows A, I follows H, J follows I, and K follows B. These simple extensions to our network are shown in Fig. 12.3.

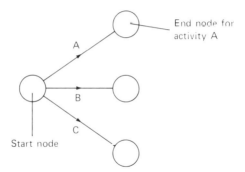

Fig. 12.1 – Activity-or-arrow representation.

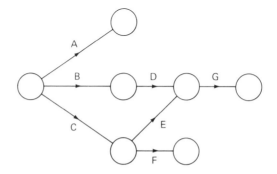

Fig. 12.2 – Developing the network.

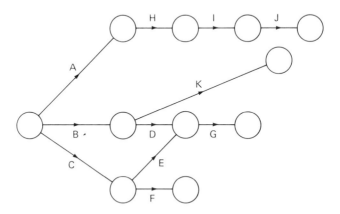

Fig. 12.3 – Further network development.

Activity L follows both F and G so as in the case of D and E we must use the same node to represent the completion of both F and G. However, we should note here that, if some activity had only F (or only G) as an immediate predecessor, we would not be able to combine the nodes representing the completion of F and G. There is no activity following either activity L or activity J; thus the nodes representing the completion of these activities may be combined to represent the completion of the project. These developments are shown in Fig. 12.4.

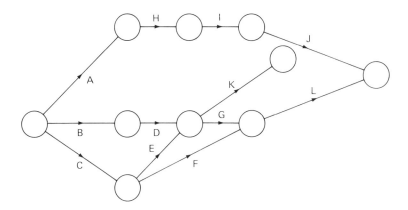

Fig. 12.4 – Further developments to the network.

Activity M now poses a problem, as we see that this activity has immediate predecessors F, G, H and K, i.e. activity M should start from the node which represents the completion of these four activities. This clearly is not possible as, for instance, activity I need only follow activity H, but, if the node representing the completion of activity H also represented the completion of F, G and K, then I would be forced to follow F, G and K in addition to H. This clearly does not conform to the required logical ordering of the activities.

To overcome this difficulty we must introduce the concept of **dummy activities**. These activities have a zero duration and their introduction to the network is only required to make the network a correct logical representation of the project. In this particular network the introduction of two dummy activities is shown in Fig. 12.5.

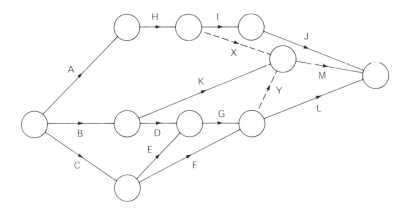

Fig. 12.5 – Final network representation of the project.

Note that the dummy activities X and Y (in Fig. 12.5) impose the logic that M cannot begin before F, G, H and K have been completed while I depends only on H and L depends only on F and G.

The completed network is shown in Fig. 12.5. The next step will, normally, be the computer analysis of the network to determine project duration, critical activities, etc. In order for the network to be translated into a form suitable for input to a computer, it is first necessary to number the nodes. To a large extent the number allocated to a particular node is arbitrary as long as it is unique. It is normal practice however, to begin numbering the nodes at the start node and to number sequentially working from left to right. An example of the numbering which may be adopted is shown in Fig. 12.6.

Activity A, for example, may now be identified as the activity between nodes 1 and 2 and computer input for this activity would take the form of the three numbers 1, 2, 12, i.e. start node, end node and activity duration.

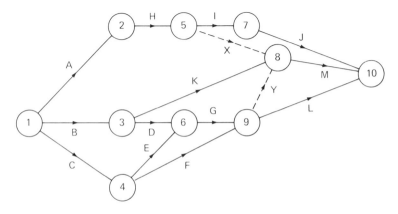

Fig. 12.6 – Numbering the network nodes.

12.2.2 Activity-on-node representation

To construct the activity-on-node network we simply connect each node (activity) with its immediate predecessor or predecessors by an arrow, the direction of which defines the precedence of the activities. The network derived by following this simple procedure is shown in Fig. 12.7.

Construction of the activity-on-node network is simpler than its rival and does not require the introduction of dummy activities. Advocates of this representation also assert that it is easier for the layman to understand. This being so, why not standardize on this representation? One reason is the advantage of the activity-on-arrow representation that allows the arrow length to be proportionate to the duration of an activity. The physical position of nodes in the network may then be related to a time scale. However, this is a fairly weak argument and the personal feelings of the author are that, whichever representation one becomes familiar with, the results will be perfectly satisfactory.

The data input required for computer analysis of the activity-on-node representation is usually a two-stage process. The first stage is a definition of the activities and their durations, e.g. A, 12. The second stage defines the precedence links between activities, e.g. A, H. In this way the network represented in Fig. 12.7 may be entered into a computer.

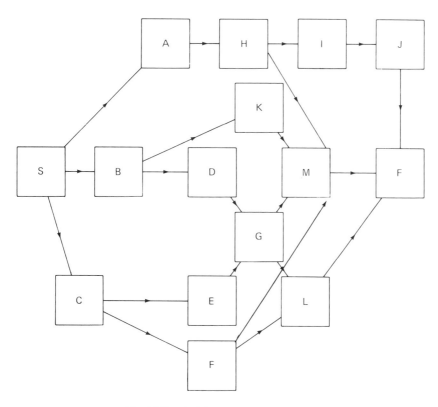

Fig. 12.7 – Activity-on-node representation.

12.2.3 The critical path

The duration of a project is the time taken to complete the longest path through the network. The longest path is called the **critical path** and the activities which make up this path are termed **critical activities**. Those activities which do not lie on the critical path need not necessarily commence at the earliest possible time, thus giving planners flexibility in scheduling the activities, and yet complete the project in the shortest possible time. Identification of the critical path (or paths) is therefore the next step in our time analysis. This task is carried out by calculating the earliest possible time at which each activity may begin. This process identifies the earliest possible completion time for the project. The latest time at which each activity may end (based on the earliest possible completion time) is then calculated. Those activities for which the earliest start time and latest finish time differ only by the duration of the activity form the critical path. These calculations would be carried out by computer in real-life applications, but to demonstrate the method we shall determine the critical path for our small example. To facilitate this, each node is partitioned as in Fig. 12.8.

In the first instance, consider the activity-on-arrow network reproduced in Fig. 12.9.

Activity H cannot begin until activity A has been completed. Activity A has a duration of 12 days; so, on the assumption that activity A begins at time 0 the earliest start time for activity H is 12. Similarly, the earliest start times for nodes 3, 4 and 5 may be calculated (10, 15 and 33 respectively). Node 6 has two entering arrows; so the earliest

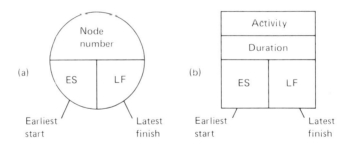

Fig. 12.8 – Node partitioning: (a) activity-on-arrow representation; (b) activity-on-node representation.

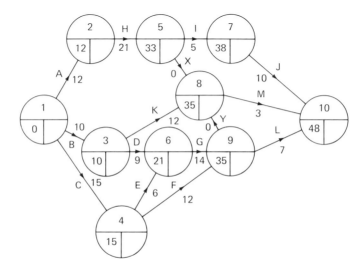

Fig. 12.9 – Earliest start times: activity-on-arrow network.

time at this node is the later of $10 + 9 = 19$ or $15 + 6 = 21$, i.e. 21. The earliest time at node 7 is simply $33 + 5 = 38$. Node 8 has three entering arrows, the earliest time at this node is, therefore, the latest of $10 + 12 = 22$, $33 + 0$ (duration of dummy activity) $= 33$ and $35 + 0 = 35$, i.e. 35. Node 9 has the earliest time $21 + 14 = 35$ or $15 + 12 = 27$, i.e. 35. Node 10 has the earliest time, i.e. earliest project completion time, of $38 + 10 = 48$, $35 + 7 = 42$ or $35 + 3 = 38$, i.e. 48.

The process of sequential calculations to find the earliest completion time for the project is called a **forward pass**.

The calculation of the latest time at each node begins at the final node, i.e. node 10. In order to reach this node at the earliest possible time (48), node 8 must be reached by time $48 - 5 = 43$, i.e. the latest allowable time at node 8 is 43. Similarly the latest time at nodes 7 is 38. Node 5 has two arrows leading from it; the latest time at this node, therefore, is the earlier of $38 - 5 = 33$ and $45 - 0 = 45$, i.e. 33. Continuing to work backwards through the network, i.e. performing a **backward pass**, the latest time at each node is calculated. These times are shown in Fig. 12.10.

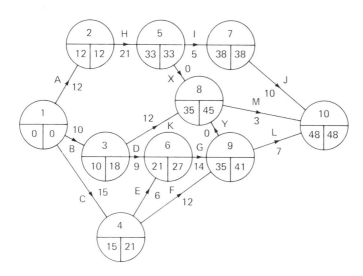

Fig. 12.10 – Completed activity-on-arrow network.

The nodes at which the earliest start time and latest finish time are equal define the critical path. In the example above, the critical path is defined by nodes 1, 2, 5, 7 and 10, i.e. activities A, H, I and J. Any delay in these activities will delay the project.

Consider now the activity-on-node representation of the project produced in Fig. 12.11.

Again we assume the project begins at time 0, i.e. that the earliest start time for node 1 is 0. The first node simply represents the start of the project and therefore has zero duration. The earliest start times for activities A, B and C are, therefore, also zero. Activities H, D, E and F all have only one entering arrow, i.e. one immediately preceding activity. Therefore, the earliest start times of these activities are simply the earliest start time plus duration of the preceding activity. Other activities, e.g. M, have more than one immediately preceding activity. In this case the earliest start time of an activity is the latest of the earliest finish times of all immediately preceding activities. In the case of M, the earliest start time is the earliest of $12 + 21 = 33$, $10 + 12 = 22$, $21 + 14 = 35$ and $15 + 12 = 27$, i.e. 35. Similar calculations for the remaining activities are required to complete the forward pass and to identify the shortest project duration as 48 days.

The backward pass through the network gives the latest finish time of each activity. For example, activity E has only one link emanating from it; so the latest finish time for this activity is simply the latest finish time of the succeeding activity (G) minus the duration of G, i.e. $41 - 14 = 27$. Activity C, however, has two succeeding activities (E and F). In order that E is not delayed, C must be completed by time $27 - 6$ (latest finish of E − duration of E). In order that F is not delayed, C must be completed by time $41 - 12 = 29$. The limiting or latest finish time for activity C is, therefore, 21. The completed time analysis for the activity on node representation is shown in Fig. 12.11. The critical path is the path (or paths), along which all activities have durations equal to the difference between the latest finish time and earliest start time, i.e. A, H, I and J.

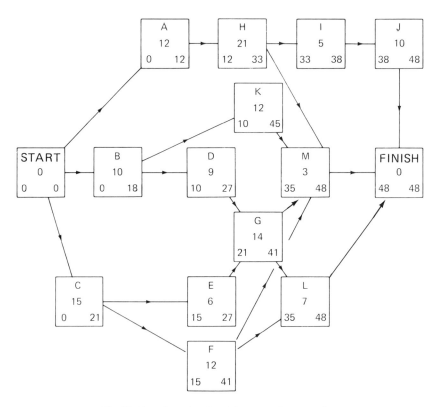

Fig. 12.11 – Completed activity-on-node network.

12.2.4 Non-critical activities

If the project is to be completed in the minimum overall time, every critical activity must begin at its earliest start time and be completed by its latest finish time. Other activities, however, are not so constrained and may be delayed by a certain length of time, termed the **activity slack**, without affecting the duration of the project. Clearly the allowable slack for each activity is of vital importance when the scheduling of individual activities is considered.

Total slack
The **total slack** TS of an activity is defined as

$$TS = \text{latest finish time LF} - (\text{earliest start time ES} + \text{duration } T).$$

Clearly $ES + T$ is in fact the earliest finish time EF, giving the alternative definition of total slack as

$$TS = LF - EF.$$

By the same token the latest finish time minus duration is clearly the latest start time LS of an activity, giving a second alternative definition of total slack as

$$TS = LS - ES.$$

Using the above definitions the total slack for non-critical activities may easily be calculated, e.g. for activity E, $LF = 27$, $ES = 15$, $T = 6$ and, therefore, $TS = 27 - (15 + 6) = 6$. For activity C, $LF = 21$, $ES = 0$, $T = 15$ and, therefore, $TS = 21 - (0 + 15) = 6$.

Free slack

This calculation of total slack may, however, be misleading as, in the example, whilst the total slack for activities C and E is 6 days it is not possible to delay C by 6 days and then activity E by a further 6 days without delaying the project. In other words the total slack of 6 days on activities C and E is in fact the same 6 days. Therefore, we may only delay activity C *or* activity E by 6 days. To avoid this confusion the concept of **free slack** is introduced to aid activity scheduling. The free slack of an activity is defined as the difference between the earliest finish time of an activity and the earliest of the earliest start times of all succeeding activities. This definition avoids any interference between slacks allocated to different activities.

Using this definition, the free slack FS (C) for activity C is calculated as

$$FS(C) = ES(E) - EF(C) = 15 - 15 = 0.$$

Considering the path CEGL, the total slack for each activity is 6 and any *one* of these activities may be delayed by 6 days without delaying the project.

The free slack for activity L may be calculated as 6 and the free slack for C, E and G is 0, i.e. the slack for the path CEGL has been allocated to activity L under the definition of free slack. The implication is that *only* activity L may be delayed which is as misleading as the implication that *all* activities (C, E, G and L) may be delayed. For scheduling purposes, therefore, total- and free-slack calculations are required if all options are to be considered.

The complete table of results of the time analysis is given in Table 12.2.

Table 12.2 – Table of time analysis results. [*]

Activity	Duration	Earliest start time ES	Earliest finish time EF	Latest start time LS	Latest finish time LF	Total slack TS	Free slack FS
A	12	0	12	0	12	0	0
B	10	0	10	8	18	8	0
C	15	0	15	6	21	6	0
D	9	10	19	18	27	8	2
E	6	15	21	21	27	6	0
F	12	15	27	29	41	14	8
G	14	21	35	27	41	6	0
H	21	12	33	12	33	0	0
I	5	33	38	33	38	0	0
J	10	38	48	38	48	0	0
K	12	10	22	33	45	23	13
L	7	35	42	41	48	6	6
M	3	35	38	45	48	10	10

[*] This problem is reworked in Appendix 12A using a program which the authors can make available.

12.3 UNCERTAIN ACTIVITY DURATIONS

The foregoing analysis assumed that each activity duration is known and fixed in advance. Clearly this assumption is not valid in real-life projects. On the other hand, using best estimates of durations based on experienced judgement will, hopefully, be close enough to reality to provide the basis of a meaningful plan. However, the project management method known as the **project evaluation-and-review technique** (PERT) introduces the concept of probabilistic activity durations, which allows an assessment of the confidence that may be placed in project duration calculations.

The method requires three parameters to define the probabilistic duration of an activity.

(1)   Optimistic forecast T_o.
(2)   Most likely forecast T_m.
(3)   Pessimistic forecast T_p.

In this way, the fact that some activity durations may be more accurately forecast than others may be reflected in the PERT time analysis. From the three time estimates, the expected activity duration T_e is calculated using the PERT formula:

$$T_e = \tfrac{1}{6}(T_o + 4T_m + T_p).$$

The optimistic and pessimistic forecasts are considered to be extreme values of the distribution of possible activity durations. $T_p - T_o$ therefore represents the range of the distribution which is, typically, six times the standard deviation (a statistical measure of the dispersion of the distribution). Thus the standard deviation of activity duration is $S = \tfrac{1}{6}(T_p - T_o)$ and the variance of activity duration is

$$S^2 = V = \tfrac{1}{36}(T_p - T_o)^2.$$

The variance of an activity duration, therefore, increases as the difference between T_p and T_o, i.e. the uncertainty increases. If the durations of activities A and B have variances V_A and V_B respectively, then the time to complete both A and B has variance $V_A + V_B$. It is this additive property of the variance which is utilized to calculate the variance or uncertainty in the duration of any path through a network and, in particular, the critical path.

Consider the example in Table 12.3 which has, clearly, been constructed so that the expected activity durations are identical with the fixed known durations used previously. The PERT time analysis proceeds in the manner described in the critical path method analysis section, with activity durations defined by their expected times T_e. The critical path, therefore, is AHIJ (as previously calculated) with expected project duration of 48 days. The PERT analysis now proceeds with an assessment of the uncertainty surrounding this expected project duration, as follows. The variance of the time to complete A, H, I and J equals $V_A + V_H + V_I + V_J = 11.1 + 5.4 + 0.1 + 7.1 = 23.7$. The standard deviation of this duration is, therefore, $\sqrt{23.7} = 4.87$. For ease of calculation and very little loss of accuracy, this figure is rounded up to 5.

Thus the critical path has an expected duration of 48 days with a standard deviation of 5 days. The expected duration of the critical path is calculated by summing the expected activity durations of the activities which make up the critical path. This sum of expected values allows the assumption that the duration of the critical path is normally distributed with mean 48 and standard deviation 5. This distribution is depicted in Fig. 12.12.

Table 12.3 — PERT example.

Activity	Immediate predecessors	T_o	T_m	T_p	T_e	V
A	—	6	10	26	12	11.1
B	—	4	11	12	10	1.8
C	—	12	14	22	15	2.8
D	B	6	8	16	9	2.8
E	C	4	6	8	6	0.4
F	C	7	12	17	12	2.8
G	D, E	8	15	16	14	1.8
H	A	12	22	26	21	5.4
I	H	4	5	6	5	0.1
J	I	6	8	22	10	7.1
K	B	8	12	16	12	1.8
L	G, F	1	8	9	7	1.8
M	H, K, F, G	2	3	4	3	0.1

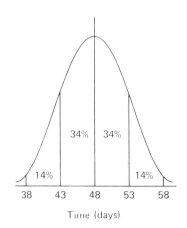

Fig. 12.12 — Normal distribution for duration of critical path

From Fig. 12.12 we obtain a picture of the probabilities involved in the duration of the critical path. For example, the probability that the critical path will be completed within 58 days is 0.98 and within 53 days is 0.84. It is usual, in fact, to assert that the duration of the critical path is also the duration of the project. However, having introduced the concept of probability it is now possible, or even quite likely, that some other near-critical path will have an actual duration greater than the originally perceived critical path. For this reason, the duration of the critical path and its associated probabilities provide an underestimate of the duration of the project and an overestimate of the probabilities of completion within a certain time. This is particularly true when a network has a large number of near-critical paths. In this situation, a more accurate forecast of project duration is achieved by means of simulation.

12.4 TRADE-OFF BETWEEN TIME AND COST

Consideration has been given to both fixed and probabilistic activity durations, but the duration of an activity may well be influenced by the resources allocated to it. If extra resources are allocated to an activity which lies on the critical path, the duration of the project will be reduced, which may well realize a cost saving. This saving must, however, be weighed or traded off against the cost of the extra resources. The more usual real-life situation arises when action has to be taken to reduce the remaining duration of an ongoing project, in order to meet contractual obligations. The problem then is to determine the most effective deployment and minimum cost of extra resources.

Some activity durations will be unaffected by the allocation of extra resources, and all activities will have a minimum duration, which it is impossible to reduce, irrespective of the resources allocated to it. In order to analyse the situation, activity durations are defined by three parameters.

(1)   Normal activity duration N.
(2)   Minimum activity duration M.
(3)   Cost function for the normal, minimum and intermediate activity durations.

The relationship between cost of extra resources and activity duration is shown in Fig. 12.13. The cost function depicted in Fig.12.13 reflects the common-sense view that, to reduce or crash an activity duration by one time unit will become progressively more expensive. However, for the purposes of a manual analysis, a linear cost function, i.e. a constant cost unit-time reduction, will be assumed. Consider the simple example in Table 12.4. Every day that the project is ongoing, it incurs a cost of £200. Calculate the duration of the project which minimizes cost.

Using the activity-on-arrow representation, we obtain the network shown in Fig. 12.14.

Table 12.4 – Time–cost trade-off example

Activity	Preceding activities	Normal duration (days)	Minimum duration (days)	Cost per day reduction (£)
A	–	5	3	30
B	–	7	5	40
C	A	6	4	60
D	B	8	2	80
E	–	14	10	100

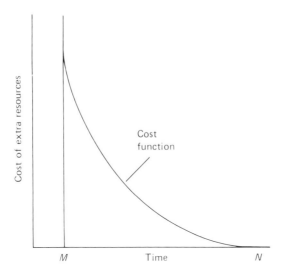

Fig. 12.13 – Relationship between cost and activity duration.

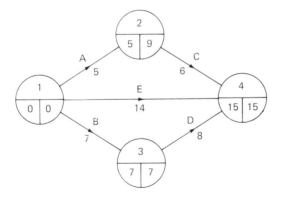

Fig. 12.14 – Network based on normal-activity durations.

The normal duration of the project is defined by the critical path BD of length 15 days. The cost of the project, at £200 per day is, therefore, £3000.

Examination of the critical path BD shows that the duration of both activities may be reduced. It is cheaper to reduce the duration of B and the cost of reduction is less than the saving of £200 which will result. Therefore, the duration of activity B is reduced by 1 day to 6 days giving the network shown in Fig. 12.15.

The critical paths are now BD and E of duration 14 days. The cost of the project is now £2800 + cost of reducing B by 1 day (£40) = £2840. This represents a saving of £160 Further reduction in the project duration involves the two critical paths BD and E, i.e. we must reduce activity E *and* either activity B or activity D in order to reduce the project duration. The cost of reducing E and B by 1 day is £140, which is still less than the saving. Therefore, the duration of E is reduced to 13 days and B to 5 days. This step gives the network shown in Fig. 12.16.

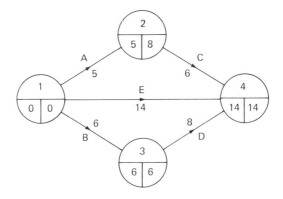

Fig. 12.15 — Network after reduction of activity B duration.

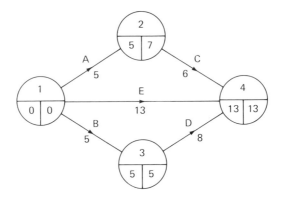

Fig. 12.16 — Network after reducing the duration of E and B.

The critical paths are still E and BD but now of duration 13 days. The cost is £2840 + £140 − £200 = £2780.

If the duration of the project is to be further reduced, then E and D must be reduced, as B has reached its minimum duration. The cost of reducing E and D is £180 per day, which is still less than the saving. In fact, E and D may be reduced by 2 days before another path becomes critical. This step gives the network shown in Fig. 12.17.

The critical paths are now BD, E and AC of duration 11 days. The cost of the project is £2780 + 2 × £180 − 2 × £200 = £2740.

Further reduction in the project duration may only be achieved if activity A or C is reduced as well as E and D. The minimum cost of reducing all three paths is £210, which would exceed the saving. At this point, therefore, the minimum project cost has been been reached. The time–cost trade-off curve for this simple example is shown in Fig. 12.18.

Note that, in this particular example, the minimization process terminated when the cost of further project duration reduction exceeded the resultant saving. The process may also terminate once all activities on a particular critical path have reached their minimum duration, making further crashing impossible regardless of cost implications.

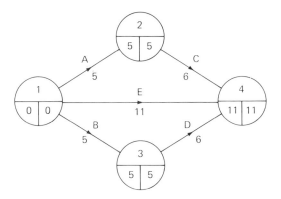

Fig. 12.17 — Network after reduction of E and D by 2 days.

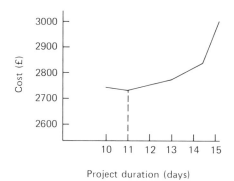

Fig. 12.18 — Time—cost trade-off curve.

12.5 RESOURCE AGGREGATION AND SCHEDULING

The resources required to carry out a project, e.g. manning, materials and capital, will vary over the life of the project. This variation may be reduced dramatically by the scheduling of activities and hence the resources used. There are two distinct problems associated with resource scheduling.

(1) To schedule the activities so that the resource usages are always within specified limits and the duration of the project is minimized.
(2) To schedule the activities so that the duration of the project is within a specified time limit and the peak resource requirements are minimized.

Problem (1), therefore, is to minimize project duration subject to a constraint on peak resource requirements whilst problem (2) is to minimize the peak resource requirements subject to a constraint on project duration.

Neither problem is trivial and heuristics used to obtain good solutions may be extremely complex. This, of course, does not need to concern most readers as these heuristics are computerized and resource scheduling or levelling can, realistically, only be tackled by computer. However, the first example used in this chapter may be modified to demonstrate the calculation of resource requirements during the life of a project, i.e. resource aggregation. A resource requirement has been defined for each activity and Table 12.5 shows the modified example. The resource may be considered to be the daily labour requirement to carry out the activity concerned.

Table 12.5 − Example including resource requirements.

Activity	Immediately preceding activities	Duration (days)	Resource requirement
A	−	12	6
B	−	10	5
C	−	15	4
D	B	9	8
E	C	6	3
F	C	12	2
G	D, E	14	6
H	A	21	4
I	H	5	2
J	I	10	3
K	B	12	5
L	F, G	7	4
M	F, G, H, K	3	6

Table 12.2 gives the time analysis results for the above project. These results may be represented diagrammatically as shown in Fig. 12.19. The diagram is known as a **Gantt chart**.

The Gantt chart allows the planner to see, at a glance, those activities which are planned to be active on a particular day and also the flexibility for scheduling individual activities within their earliest start times and latest finish times. The resource aggregation for the above project is given below in Fig. 12.20. The aggregation uses the assumption that all activities begin at their earliest start times.

The resource aggregation over the project duration shows a peak resource requirement of 23, on days 10 and 11, when activities A, C, D and K are active. Of these activities, only A is critical; so rescheduling C, D or K would reduce this peak requirement, i.e. level the resource requirement and yet maintain the project duration of 48 days. Alternatively, a limit of say 11 men may be placed on the resource availability. In this case, the duration of the project would have to be extended. Normally, activity K would be the first activity chosen for rescheduling, as it has the greatest slack. Most resource-scheduling heuristics use the criterion of greatest slack, when selecting an activity to be delayed, in order to meet resource availability constraints. In this way, the effect upon project duration is kept to a minimum.

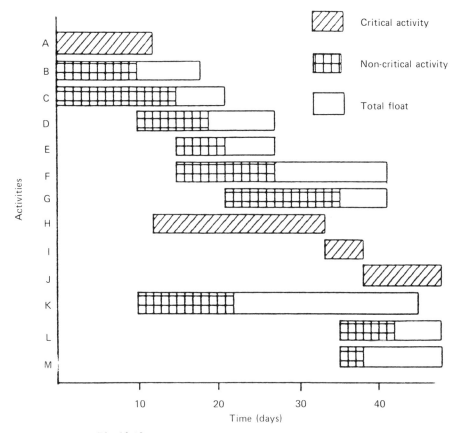

Fig. 12.19 – Gantt chart representation of time analysis results.

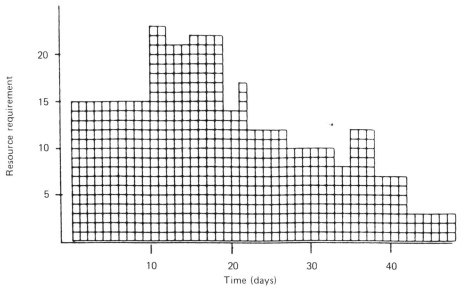

Fig. 12.20 – Resource aggregation for earliest start times.

APPENDIX 12A: COMPUTERIZED PROJECT MANAGEMENT

The authors have written a critical path analysis program, which can be made available. This program may be used to illustrate critical path methods and resource aggregation on small projects. With the development of the microcomputer, many project management packages have come onto the market. These packages perform most, if not all, the analyses illustrated in this chapter. The facility to use probabilistic activity times is, however, rare. Resource aggregation is available with virtually every project management package but resource scheduling is not so commonly available. It is important, therefore to examine carefully the facilities available, before selecting a project management package.

To use the package, proceed as follows.

(1)   'Boot up' the machine. This usually means switching on the machine with a 'DOS' system disc in one of the disc drives (drive 'A' in the simpler machines).
(2)   When the prompt A⟩ is shown on the screen, type BASIC (or whatever version of BASIC is available within the operating system) and then strike the return key.
(3)   When the prompt OK is shown on the screen, remove the system disc and replace it with the authors' disc.
(4)   Type LOAD "CPA" and then strike the return key.
(5)   When the prompt OK is shown on the screen, type RUN and then strike the return key.

You should then see the screen thus:

DEPARTMENT OF MANAGEMENT SCIENCE AND STATISTICS

UNIVERSITY COLLEGE OF SWANSEA

ENTER THE NUMBER OF ACTIVITIES IN THE PROJECT?   15

ENTER THE NUMBER OF NODES IN THE PROJECT NETWORK?   10

You can proceed by simply answering the questions which appear on the screen. If we repeat the example that has already been described in Table 12.1 and Fig. 12.6 (and solved manually), we answer 15 to the first question (remembering that there were 13 activities originally but two dummy activities had to be added) and 10 to the second. When we enter a response to a question, we must follow by striking the return key.

When the information on the first 15 activities has been entered, the screen should appear thus:

ACT. NO.		ACTIVITY DESCRIPTION	START NODE	END NODE	ACTIVITY DURATION
1	A		1	2	12
2	B		1	3	10
3	C		1	4	15
4	D		3	6	9
5	E		4	6	6

ACT. NO.	ACTIVITY DESCRIPTION	START NODE	END NODE	ACTIVITY DURATION
6	F	4	9	12
7	G	6	9	14
8	H	2	5	21
9	I	5	7	5
10	J	7	10	10
11	K	3	8	12
12	L	9	10	7
13	M	8	10	3
14	X	5	8	0
15	Y	9	8	0

ENTER 0 TO CONTINUE OR ACTIVITY NUMBER TO AMEND?

Do not forget the dummy activities (X and Y in this case).

It is easy to make a mistake when entering data. It is as well to check each line when you enter it; when all the data have been entered, the table may be corrected. Corrections are made to each line as desired when the table is complete, but as early lines have been recorded and possibly removed from the screen, it is as well to note errors as the table is compiled. A further opportunity will be offered to modify the data when the first time analysis has been completed; at this point, errors may be rectified or the effects of possible changes in input studied.

When all the data have been inserted, the program calculates and shows the following table, which is the same as Table 12.12 (except for a slight difference in the column order and that the computer table shows information on dummy activities):

ACTIVITY	BN	EN	DURATION	ES	LF	LS	EF	TS	FS
A	1	2	12	0	12	0	12	0	0
B	1	3	10	0	18	8	10	8	0
C	1	4	15	0	21	6	15	6	0
D	3	6	9	10	27	18	19	8	2
E	4	6	6	15	27	21	21	6	0
F	4	9	12	15	41	29	27	14	8
G	6	9	14	21	41	27	35	6	0
H	2	5	21	12	33	12	33	0	0
I	5	7	5	33	38	33	38	0	0
J	7	10	10	38	48	38	48	0	0
K	3	8	12	10	45	33	22	23	13
L	9	10	7	35	48	41	42	6	6
M	8	10	3	35	48	45	38	10	10
X	5	8	0	33	45	45	33	12	2
Y	9	8	0	35	45	45	35	10	0

PRESS ANY KEY TO CONTINUE

The computer asks whether you wish to determine resource usage. If you do, you will be asked the types of resource and the number of each type required for each activity. In this case, we input the information from Table 12.5, noting that there is only one type of resource.

When we have entered the resource information, the screen will display

DO YOU WISH TO PERFORM RESOURCE ANALYSIS (Y/N) ? Y

ENTER NUMBER OF TYPES OF RESOURCE (and press ⟨RET⟩) : 1

ENTER AMOUNT OF RESOURCE   1   ASSIGNED TO ACTIVITIES:

A? 6
B? 5
C? 4
D? 8
E? 3
F? 2
G? 6
H? 4
I? 2
J? 3
K? 5
L? 4
M? 6
X? 0
Y? 0

When the resource requirements have been recorded, the program will ask whether the resource use should be based on each activity starting on its early start or on its late start thus:

ENTER NO. OF RESOURCE TO AGGREGATE (1 to 1)? 1
Aggregate by early start and finish or late start and finish (ES/LS) ?ES

On being given an answer to this question (ES in this case), the program immediately calculates the number of resources used on each day of the project. Note that the resources used are shown each day, accumulated from activity to activity (thus 15 resources are used on day 1). The first 7 days of the calculation and the last 8 days are as follows:

DAY	ACTIVITY	RES. QTY	TOTAL RES.
1	1	6	6
1	2	5	11
1	3	4	15
2	1	6	6
2	2	5	11
2	3	4	15
3	1	6	6
3	2	5	11
3	3	4	15

4	1	6	6
4	2	5	11
4	3	4	15
5	1	6	6
5	2	5	11
5	3	4	15
6	1	6	6
6	2	5	11
6	3	4	15
7	1	6	6
7	2	5	11
7	3	4	15

Press 〈RETURN〉 to continue

Press 〈RETURN〉 to continue

41	10	3	3
41	12	4	7
42	10	3	3
42	12	4	7
43	10	3	3
44	10	3	3
45	10	3	3
46	10	3	3
47	10	3	3
48	10	3	3

Press 〈RETURN〉 to continue

Without further prompting the program will produce a histogram of the resource usage over the life of the project. This is shown in Fig. 12.21.

It is interesting to repeat the resource allocation with each activity starting on its late start. We obtain the histogram of Fig. 12.22 showing that the use of resources is much smoother (this smoother use of resources is gained, however, at the cost of using up all the available slack before starting an activity):

The resource histograms are the last of the information provided by the program. The user is then asked 'Do you want to exit or amend?'. a question which provides the opportunity to exit the system, if work is complete, or to rework the calculations with modified data. This opportunity to amend the data is important because it permits the user to check the network for sensitivity to changes in input data; it also allows mistakes to be corrected at a time when the whole of the previously input data are displayed.

AGGREGATE ANOTHER RESOURCE TYPE (Y/N)? ? N
DO YOU WISH TO AMEND RESOURCE DATA (Y/N) ? N
DO YOU WISH TO EXIT OR AMEND CURRENT PROJECT (E/A) ?

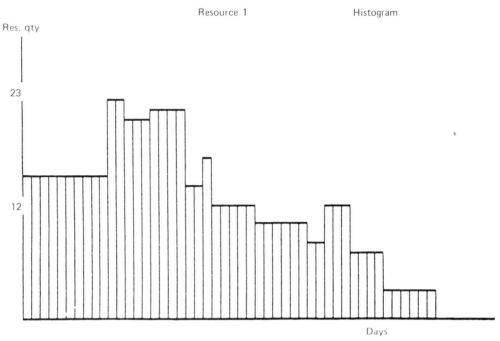

Press < RETURN > to continue

Fig. 12.21

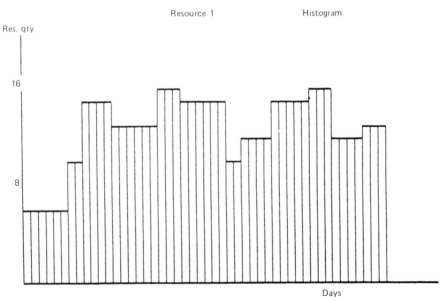

Press <RETURN> to continue

Fig. 12.22

13

Reporting and project meetings

13.1 PROJECT COMMUNICATION

All engineering work requires communication; indeed communication has to do with every mode of living and operating. In project work this is particularly true for both vertical and lateral communication is required in-house and extensive communication is required with outside bodies such as agents, subcontractors, consultants, research organizations, suppliers and of course the customer. Vital communication, or main stream communication, must be clear, free from errors and unambiguous for it is really the oil which lubricates the project's motion towards its target.

The main and secondary streams of communication can be represented as a ripple analogue as shown in Fig. 13.1. From this it will be appreciated just how many different types of communication media are used to get project work done—build standards, schedules, work sheets, report forms, drawings, process specifications, etc. In fact a good 'yardstick' for companies to develop is to set up a deliberate count of the paper used per project. In some cases this has clearly revealed undercommunication or over-communication in the written form.

The human difficulties and limitations in communication show up in their starkest form in advanced technology, where failure is usually very expensive and obvious. Inevitably, project managers are involved deeply with people and communication. In technology there is a tendency to allow insufficient time to overcome the difficulties in communication, for a great deal of time and effort is necessary to communicate well in the technical realm.

There are many barriers that prevent good communication taking place and the project manager must learn to overcome these. Some of the barriers are shown in Fig. 13.2.

There are three main areas of particular communication concern.

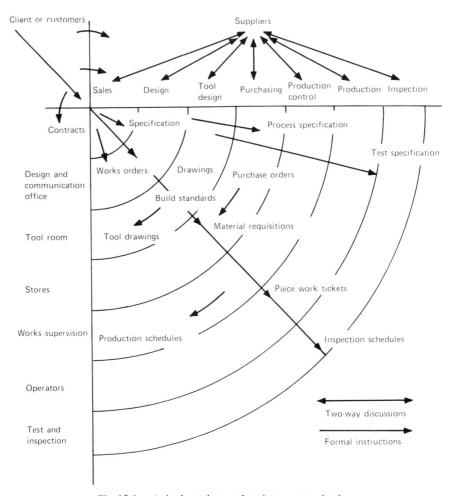

Fig. 13.1 – A ripple analogue of project communications.

— Firstly between the customer and the supplier, concerning his exact requirements, i.e. the specification of a project.
— Secondly, between design departments and development units, i.e. between those who propose possible solutions and those who validate them.
— Thirdly, between the designers who prescribe how the requirement is to be met and the producers.

The first might be called the specification communication problem, the second the design–development interface communication problem, while the last is the design–production communication problem.

13.2 THE COMMUNICATION PROCESS

All communication systems terminate ultimately in human beings. Man perceives the world around him by means of his five senses but mostly employs two in communicating.

Fig. 13.2 – Barriers to communication.

Hearing and seeing supply most of his input information. Upon receipt, this information undergoes a process of storage, collation and selection in the brain and nervous system before it is used.

However carefully the emission of a message is purified, there is no certainty that it will be understood in the way intended. The reason for this is that, behind the eye and the ear, a complex control system operates on the brain before the recipient can incorporate the message. Moreover, the degree of receptivity depends upon a number of subjective factors which can affect the way in which the message is interpreted.

The process, in its simplest form, can be visualized as depicted in Fig. 13.3. Here, communication is seen to comprise a number of identifiable parts. These are an information source, a message, a transmitter, a signal, a receiver and a destination. These terms may be appreciated better when they are related to the transference of design instructions.

In this case, the information source is a designer–draughtsman, who embodies in a drawing the message that he intends to tell the production foreman. When transmitted through the company's postal system (the communication channel), this message becomes a signal, which—when received—is converted back into a message by the foreman. The message that the foreman receives is what he understands from the drawing.

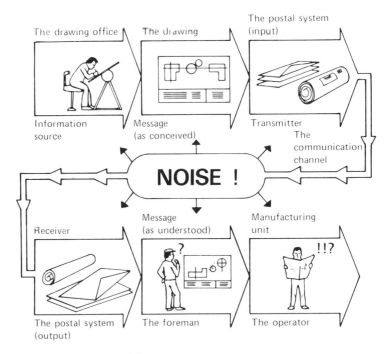

Fig. 13.3 – The communication process.

He then passes his understanding of the message to its ultimate destination—the manufacturing or construction unit.

Any communication can be depicted in this way and always the signal is conveyed via a communication channel.

Unfortunately, during this part of the process, it is subject to 'noise'. This 'noise' can be defined as anything that causes the message out of the receiver to be at all different from that which went into the transmitter, e.g. a smudged line, illegible writing or a creased print.

Very often redundancy in the form of word repitition or extra cross-sections is added into the message as a kind of insurance to overcome the effect of 'noise'. However, this alone will not ensure clearer communication. Poor reception can be caused by inappropriateness of the signal (say, a wrong cross-section or an incorrect projection) as well as by lack of redundancy with clarity of message.

Project managers will inevitably use various types of format to present their information; some may be in tabular or graphical form and others may be mostly written notes.

Graphics produced either by a computer or on a drawing board are used for presenting the bulk of design information. It has become, in fact, a universal language which is highly conventionalized, having its own syntax and grammar. Indeed, engineering organizations have been driven, in the interests of economy, to compiling a dictionary of their own drawing practices and standards. These are highly stylized to suit particular types of industries. All project engineers must be familiar with these.

13.2.1 Communicating the design aim: the project specification

Specification writing may be looked upon as part of technical writing. The relaying of intention from a customer to a producer demands considerable precision of statement. Such a statement has to be complete, relevant and unambiguous and it is worth remembering that specifications only have to be adequate to meet the true needs. Indeed the design which follows such a written intent is really the art of the adequate. The design must just meet the specification and no more. The central difficulty of reducing a firm requirement to a specification is the problem of translating an inexact expression of preference into numerical terms.

The customer talks of a 'smooth' control, a 'portable' load and, a 'reliable' performance. The customer may quote some of these in quantitative terms, thus feeling that he is safeguarding his interests by being more precise, but not every facet can be quantified anyway. In such cases, ranking of preferences may be the best approach. It is essential, however, to be as definitive as possible—to tie everything down. If loose ends are left, or a bit of slack to play with, this can well become the rope that hangs the project.

Such a document sets in train a paper work system whereby the requirement is passed on by the project engineer to the design team and from thence through to the manufacturing organization. The original document will by this time have passed through various stages of amplification and refinement which will all stem from the design aim. Thus eventually a specification hierarchy is formulated, see Fig. 13.4, where the main problems stem from the different languages used. These must be consistent and adequate so that no misunderstanding occurs.

Precise specifications are important if adequate production is eventually to take place and designers are to be assisted so that market requirements are satisfied without excessive cost. In these days there is an increasing tendency for national and international regulatory bodies to introduce specification restraints for safety and compatability reasons. Also, in certain cases, specifications may be mandatory and therefore must be unambiguous so that interpretations are the same between suppliers and customers.

Of even greater significance is the fact that many products interact in an intricate manner with the environment in which they operate. This interaction is often complex and difficult to describe.

Project managers have often to operate as interpreters and liaise with the customer and his representatives so that the best solutions are devised. In doing this he will often have to exercise skill in obtaining the best trade-off between cost, time and performance.

13.2.2 Communicating between design and development

Design may be seen as an interactive process, whether it be for a product or a project. Development of a product is usually a gradual evolutionary process but, for a project, development becomes an essential phase in the process of going from ideas to hardware. It might be looked upon as design carried out by other means.

For one reason or another the design when realized in prototype or 'lash-up' form does not perform as expected. This may be occasioned by faulty arithmetic or lack of imagination on the part of the design team. Alternatively it may be due to lack of design method or data.

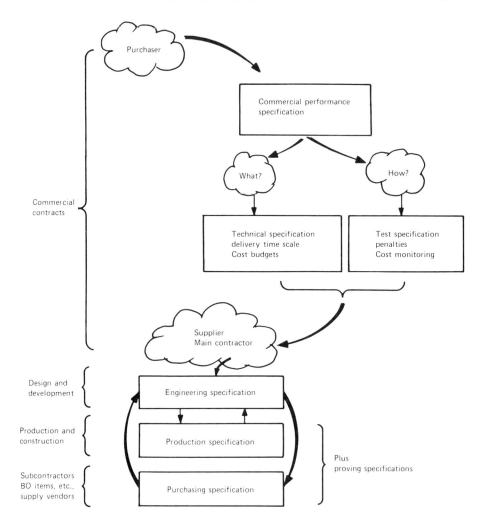

Fig. 13.4 – Specification hierarchy for a project.

Inevitably, design and development demands a close collaboration between the two parties concerned who, while they usually reside in the same culture, nevertheless generally have totally different outlooks and methods of approach.

A development team is constantly measuring, analysing and stating why a certain piece of equipment will not work or will break, but a design team is constantly synthesizing to devise a suitable solution. The project manager must constantly seek to reconcile these differing views. If conflict arises, he may need to step in and to decide on a course of action. Failure to do this often means that little forward progress is made on the project and, while design perfectionism must be avoided, so too must overdevelopment. The situation may be depicted as in Fig. 13.5, where the project manager sits, uneasily sometimes, between these two separate groups of people with their different attitudes. In some engineering work this design—development syndrome is not too noticeable but it often occurs in complex mechanical engineering work.

Here the project manager must be able to influence and direct both sides so that,
where necessary, appropriate trade-offs are obtained.

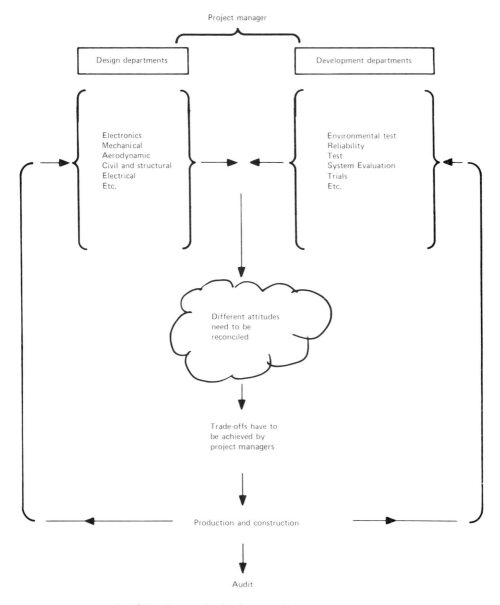

Fig. 13.5 − Communicating between design and development.

13.2.3 Communicating the design intent to production or construction
The interface between production and design is perhaps one of the greatest problems
associated with project work today. Here the project manager finds himself
communicating with many different parties, all of whom have their own axes to grind.
Often there are numerous specialist groups such as reliability engineers, value analysis

experts, inspection and quality control personnel, manufacturing engineers, assemblers, subcontractors and suppliers. He may have to take decisions which upset one or more of the people representing these groups.

There has to be an integrated approach to problem solving, and time will often not permit a sequential approach of design, delineation, production control, manufacture, etc. Often it boils down to a matter of just being sensible by recognizing what are the real aims that must be achieved if the project is to succeed.

One area of great concern to project managers is the cost of change for, inevitably, change of some sort will be necessary. The customer may change his mind, there may be design and drawing office errors, and production improvements may well lead to changes. Creeping 'improvement sickness' can often occur; modifications are introduced under the guise of cost reduction only to turn out to be cost raisers when implemented. The main difficulty that project managers encounter is generally how to estimate the impact of any change. In one firm the cost impact of change was analysed from historical cost records and found to be as high as 30% of the basic costs. In the light of such figures, management must seek to minimize design errors and the impact of corrective action and to quantify the effect of potential change prior to its implementation.

Direct links between design and production, right from the start of a project, are absolutely essential and here again project managers should play a major role. Joint decision making may be necessary as, for example, with the use of computer-aided design and manufacture which may be used to expedite drawings and to ensure that they reach production, subcontractors and specialist suppliers in the right order. Equally important is the need to ensure that the design is arranged to aid production to achieve, consistently, the required quality.

Clearly a project manager has a major contribution to make in the realm of technical communication between the various disciplines and functions concerned. He must be able to resolve interpersonal conflicts and to achieve the best trade-off solutions to the various problems that inevitably arise. This is particularly true in the areas of specification writing, design and development testing, and across the design–production interface. In these three important areas the project manager has to be able to overcome compatability problems between the purely technical facets of his project and the managerial requirements of time, cost and adequate performance.

Project managers must therefore be good communicators and co-ordinators to ensure that the specification performance is attained, that the delivery dates are met and that the project is completed within the budget set, for only then will customer satisfaction be achieved. However, in addition to these three areas of difficulty, project managers must communicate by means of meetings and reports.

13.3 MEETINGS

The very nature of project management makes it inevitable that certain meetings will have to be called in the day-to-day running of the project. There may also be standing committees where the customer and other agents are present. There are usually six-monthly or quarterly progress meetings and in the case of military projects the procedure is often stipulated in the contract. In effect these are part of an ongoing reporting system giving the current state of the project's progress in terms of time, cost and performance.

There are many definitions of committees, not all of them very kind, such as the following.

— 'A committee is a noun signifying many but not much.'
— 'A committee is a group of the unwilling called together by the ignorant to do the unnecessary.'
— 'A committee passes minutes but wastes hours.'

More seriously a committee has been said to be 'a body of people meeting round a table, to take decisions for joint action on behalf of some other (generally larger) body of which it is the committee'.

Presumably the process of decision making is by discussion and each committee has some terms of reference. Committees can be classified in various ways. There are, for example, official institutions' standing committees which meet at regular intervals to discuss various problems. There are also *ad hoc* committees or working parties called to study particular problems. Having solved the problem they are disbanded. Then there are executive committees, which have the power to make final decisions and enforce them, whereas advisory committees, as the name implies, merely have to advise and provide a platform for airing views. Usually, in project work the manager is more concerned with general meetings, although from time to time particular project engineers may be called on to serve on special government committees, or a professional institution committee. Such general meetings form important communication channels for projects.

A meeting may be said to be an assembly of three or more people whose objective is to achieve, by discussion and decision, something which cannot be achieved by the people acting in pairs or as individuals. It may be structured in a very formal way or by a casual meeting of interested people, convened on the spur of the moment, or anything in between. Whatever type of meeting it is, it is likely to achieve better results if it is guided skilfully towards its objective by the chairman or leader, and if the members of it are co-operating objectively.

Everyone taking part in a meeting must realize that the outcome depends upon the spirit in which they handle the problems before them as well as the skill and force with which they put their own point of view. Meetings will more easily find the best solution when all the knowledge available is pooled. Personal pride, prejudice, private squabbles, private distractions, shyness or self-agrandisement will hinder the meeting. In addition to mutual sharing and the interchange of information, meetings should serve to clarify, stimulate and sharpen participants' thinking.

13.3.1 Types of meeting
There are various types of meeting, such as the following.

(1) **The learning situation.** Here a manager or team leader may be trying to obtain feelings, attitudes and ideas from the group, or he may actually lecture to the group and invite questions or comments. The project manager will do this regularly with his team.
(2) **Getting a group decision, or making a plan of action.** In this kind of meeting, participation is the keynote. The group puts forward suggestions which are discussed and a possible plan of action drawn up. Differences are resolved and

a consensus obtained. Project managers use such meetings when some impasse occurs on their project work and a new course of action is required.

(3) **Problem solving**. A typical type of engineering meeting is one concerned with solving a problem. Various techniques such as brainstorming, synectics or value analysis may be used for working out possible solutions.

It is important for any project engineer to be clear as to which type of meeting he is attending or convening.

(4) **Reporting progress**. Every project has to be regularly reviewed to see how it is progressing and the project manager may need to give a presentation to top management of the current state of play. Such progress meetings are best conducted around a series of charts which will be discussed later.

Other types of progress meeting may be held with the customer, who may wish to have the necessary information presented in a certain way before the meeting takes place.

Before contemplating holding a meeting, project managers need to consider some initial factors which should be settled.

— What is the purpose of the meeting?
— What are the objectives?
— Who needs to be there?
— Would interviews be better?
— When is the best time to hold it?
— What factual information must be available before, or at, the meeting?

Remember that, in industry and certainly in government establishments, people like meetings. They are cosy; the speakers have a captive audience; they are not hard work (except for the chairman); the political intrigue is exciting; they can be very time consuming.

13.3.2 Some points to remember

(1)   Every meeting has two agendas.

(a) **The formal**. Known formal working agenda or objectives.
(b) **The informal**. Hidden objectives, motivated by interpersonal or inter-departmental struggles and misunderstandings.

Remember that the agenda is the route map for any meeting. It determines the subjects to be discussed and their order of consideration.

(2)   In an insecure environment, decisions are arrived at on the basis of avoiding open conflict. Sometimes people do not know what they are deciding or voting on. Often executive action is not specified.

(3)   Juniors may be inhibited by seniors. Contributions may therefore be unbalanced.

(4)   Time can be wasted by covering the same ground again and again.

(5)   The group can lose interest and stop working especially if the meeting starts late or goes on too long.

13.3.3 Behaviour at meetings
(a)   **The chairman or leader**

    (1)   defines the limits of the discussion,
    (2)   is impartial but gives some pros and cons to get people thinking,
    (3)   controls the discussion and speakers,
    (4)   makes frequent interim summaries,
    (5)   avoids arguing and throws controversies back to the meeting,
    (6)   draws conclusions, sums up at the end and states action to be taken, and
    (7)   thanks the members.

(b)   **The members**

    (1)   keep within the limits set by the chairman,
    (2)   discuss everything objectively,
    (3)   try to find solutions to problems, and
    (4)   must be simple, brief and clear.

13.3.4 Preparation for a meeting
Before the meeting,

    (1)   invitations must be given to the right people and the objective clearly stated,
    (2)   the agenda should be prepared and where possible sent to all who are to attend,
    (3)   notices, hand-outs, drawings, factual information must be collected and collated,
    (4)   briefing of members should take place where necessary,
    (5)   arrangements for minute taking should be made and
    (6)   physical comfort should be arranged—not too comfortable but good ventilation is essential.

13.3.5 Plan of the meeting
The project manager or chairman will have analysed the subject, seen what is the problem and divided the problem into manageable subsections, to be solved one at a time. He will have outlined the way that the meeting might go, but this plan must be flexible in the light of contributions from members.

To guide the meeting, and to provoke thinking, he will prepare

    (1)   general statements,
    (2)   specific statements,
    (3)   general questions and
    (4)   specific questions.

He will have considered his members' reactions and planned the approach—where to encourage and give credit, where the knowledge may lie, who to control, etc.

13.3.6 The minutes
The minutes are the only record that the meeting has taken place and decisions have been reached. They can be a launching pad or a diving board. They must, therefore,

(1)   be factual, impartial and balanced,
(2)   present a clear, concise and unambiguous record,
(3)   be brief and
(4)   be well set out to aid assimilation of contents.

Exactly how minutes are written depends upon the type of meeting. There are the so-called constitutional meetings where the minutes become an authoritative record of the proceedings. They, therefore, provide an accurate historical narrative of the committee's activities. There are also executive minutes where what has been decided upon has to be implemented. They are, therefore, the authoritative documents. Finally, they are the progressive minutes that provide a basis for evolving policy on the project concerned, and they are similar to the progress reports. A typical page from such a report is shown in Fig. 13.6.

Exactly how to structure minutes and other types of written project communication will now be considered.

TASK PROGRESS REGISTER	MAJOR TASK _ _ _ A₁ _ _ _ _	DOCUMENT CLASSIFICATION RESTRICTED	
DISTRIBUTION CODE C27		SHEET 1 OF 1 SHEET	
	TITLE	ORDER No	MANAGER	DEPT No
PROJECT	LT	15	J·WILKIE	APO
MAJOR TASK	ELECTRONIC PACK	0937	M·STEVENS	AW9

DATE	COMMENTS	ACTION
21.7.87	Start delayed pending revised aims. Ministry letter O/XYZ/4967 dated 4.7.87 refers	*AJMS.*
12.8.87	Instructions given to proceed now that Ministry decision on Aims is to hand	*C.Sharman*
8.9.87	Design Specification accepted by Committee	*L.Sharman*
4.10.87	Events 4270 and 4391 now slipping due to initial delays on Aim declarion. 4628 agreed adjustment to 4 June 1988. Ministry Memo O/XYZ/2631 dated 27.9.87 refers	*J.G.EJMS.*

Fig. 13.6 – A typical task progress register minute sheet.

13.4 REPORTS

There are a number of reports which have to be written for various purposes when carrying out project assignment.

13.4.1 Diary notes

In project work it is essential to record key decisions which may be taken at formal or informal meetings. A diary note for the file is a useful way of doing this. Its format should simply give the date, time and place and the people present when the decisions were taken. The heading of the subject should be chosen with care and should be followed by a simple but clear statement of the decision reached and, if necessary, any sketches or other data should be attached.

Project managers must remember that they automatically become the custodians of all project information and data of the 'what', 'when' and 'why'. The line managers have responsibility for the 'how'.

13.4.2 Visit reports

Project managers are constantly visiting firms, construction sites, manufacturing concerns, subcontractors, customers and other official bodies. It is again important to keep good records of such visits. Too often such reports are written in the time sequence in which they occurred; it is therefore difficult, on reading them quickly, to obtain the main ideas or even the purpose of the visit.

The rule is to put the 'what', 'where', 'when', 'who' and 'so what' first and then to follow this by the details expressing the 'why' and 'how'.

13.4.3 Monthly progress report

Of all writing jobs in project work (and, indeed, in technical work of any kind) the monthly progress report causes more grumbling than almost anything else except for having to attend so many meetings. Is such a report necessary? This can only be answered by top management and the project manager concerned, who must be clear why he needs such a report. Is it to inform, to guide or just to record progress? It is essential that such reports state problems fairly and do not strain to give results which are not yet achieved. A good deal of time can be saved if the format for 'ongoing' reports is clearly set out within wide margins to list the names of people who should take action on the various subjects. Also, a good clear diagram such as a bar chart or arrow network should be used to save writing.

Sometimes top management can be provided with progress against plans and with costs against budgets with appropriate forecasts of completion and current and foreseeable problem areas. One way of giving these is indicated in Fig. 13.7. Here cumulative planned expenditure and actual expenditure are plotted against time and the predicted performance after the review date is shown.

For top management a summary report may be provided showing manpower costs and direct costs for the major portions of a project together with a summary of major milestones of achievement (Fig. 13.8). This may be augmented by a cost–time slippage chart of the type shown in Fig. 13.9.

For individual work packages a slip chart may be used of the type indicated in Fig. 13.10.

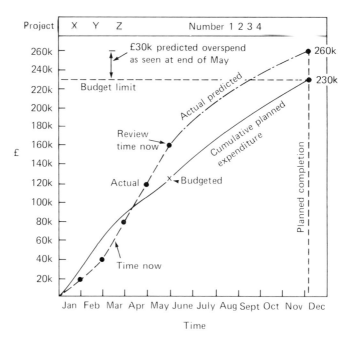

Fig. 13.7 — Plots of cumulative planned expenditure and actual expenditure against time and predicted performance.

The way such a chart is used can best be understood by following the plot of activity 2 in Fig. 13.10. The activity was planned to finish in mid-August and work started on it during the first week in March and continued steadily until the last week in April. All work then ceased on the activity owing to lack of material until the end of May when the material was delivered to site. Rescheduling the network gave a new finish date of mid-September but by the first week in June it became apparent that the labour for erection on this activity had been transferred to another portion of the project. This meant that the activity could not be finished until the end of October. A site meeting was called at the end of June and some replanning was undertaken. It was found that by delaying a non-critical portion of the project and reallocating labour it should be possible to complete the activity during the first week in September and thus hold the start-up date of the project.

A project manager when reporting to top management such as the managing director should concentrate upon identifying anomalies and upon the broader aspects of the project relationship with the company as a whole. Therefore, his main objectives should be to introduce a reporting method that

(1) informs him of the existence of any major problems likely to affect completion dates, costs or performance,
(2) describes what is being done to circumvent problems and how successful the action is likely to be,
(3) informs him of deviations from plans and why,
(4) assures him that nothing of importance has been overlooked and
(5) shows the relationship between the project, the company and the outside world.

Project system 'A,B,C' contract FG/100 Date 15 January 1976

Δ = scheduled completion
E = estimated completion
L = latest acceptable completion to meet period end date

S = slippage from schedule
O = cost overrun

Schedule no.	Item	Manpower costs (man hours 10,000)						Direct costs (£10k)						Schedule programme				Slack status (weeks)	Remarks
		Work performed to date		Overrun (underrun)	Total at completion			Commitments to date			Totals at completion			Year 1 JFMAMJJASOND	Year 2 JFMAMJJASOND	Year 3 JFMA	Day of month		
		Calculated value	Committed		Budget	Latest revised estimate	Overrun (underrun)	Commitment	Budget	Overrun (underrun)	Budget	Latest revised estimate	Overrun (underrun)						
	Overall system	320	360	40	1000	1090	90	105	117	(12)	300	325	25		E Δ	E	31 5 5	−3	Radar (O)
01	Radar	130	100	20	300	345	45	35	38	(3)	90	97	7	E L			26 1 5	−3	Stabilizer unit (SXO)
02	Auto follower	59	75	15	200	230	36	265	29	(2.5)	75	80	5	E L	Δ		3 7 10	+4	Auto giro (O)
03	Communication	24	26	(2)	70	75	5	16.5	18	(1.5)	40	43	3	E L	Δ		5 10 12	+12	
15	Computer	19	21	(2)	60	60	0	9	10	(1)	25	27	2				16 14 3	−4	Logis unit (S) (O)

Fig. 13.8 — Management project summary report.

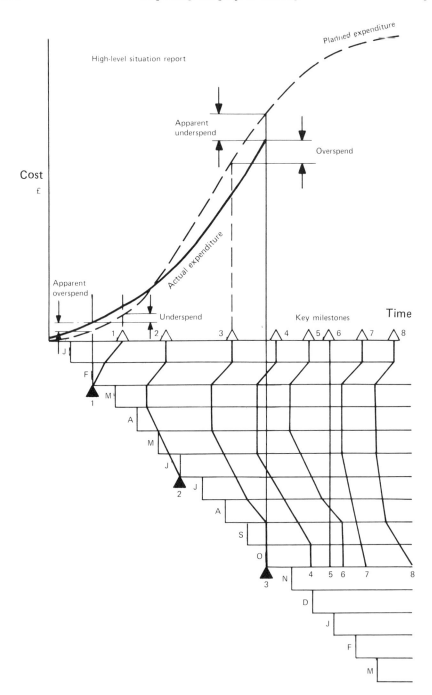

Fig. 13.9 – Cost–time slippage chart.

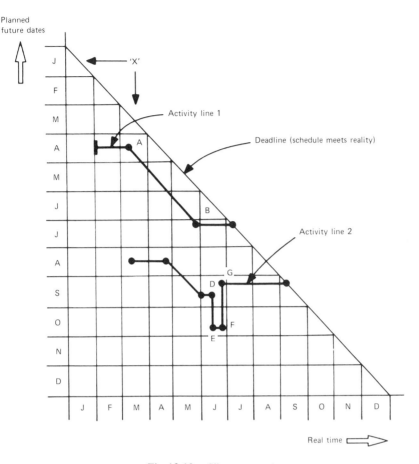

Fig. 13.10 — Slip-type graph.

The most satisfactory form of reporting should be brief, factual and at timely intervals. A short written report to a set format would be most helpful, both to present the information and to serve as a record for future reference. A monthly interval would be appropriate for this purpose.

The content of such a report is suggested in Appendix 13A.

13.4.4 Stop and release procedures

It is essential for all to know when work on activities must stop and for this purpose some firms have special notes which are signed by the project manager. With the 'apartheid' that so often exists between designing and manufacturing such notes are very important communication documents.

The correct circulation list must be used so that all understand when work is to stop or proceed, and this involves inspection, design, development, manufacture and construction.

13.4.5 Project critiques
These are special types of meeting at the operational end of the project to assess how performance servicing and general running of the project are going. They are particularly useful during the commissioning stage, allowing snags to be properly documented and special guides to be prepared to obviate such difficulties on future projects.

13.4.6 Project audit reports
Ultimately the project manage should write a complete 'overview' report of his completed project, setting down all successes as well as failures.

  For such work it is often necessary for project engineers to visit the actual sites and be resident for a period of time. Once again this emphasizes the mobility of project managers.

  The sort of questions which such a report will answer are as follows.

— What lessons can be learnt?
— What incidents are relevant to future project work?
— What steps have, or should be, taken to avoid similar mistakes?
— What better performance is now possible?
— How good was the planning?
— Was proper control exercised, on time, cost, quality etc?

  The project manager may need to have some time for reflection and to refer to his records before putting pen to paper.

13.4.7 Project design review reports
The design review technique and the project manager's involvement are given in Chapter 14. When conducting an in-house review it is essential to ensure that proper reports are issued, stating clearly the action to be taken. As an aid to this end it is useful to use an interrogation check-list of the type shown in Fig. 13.11 to comb through the various areas of the design and to use a final summary sheet similar to that in Fig. 13.12.

  It must always be remembered by the project manager that the review group is not a decision-making body; its prime function is to probe. It is the job of the chairman to record the prevailing view and to note any dissenting views. The final report must then state concisely whether the review group finds the response from the designers satisfactory or not. If the project manager is the chairman, then he must allocate considerable time to the running of such design reviews and make sure that all the necessary documentation and information is handed to the review group well ahead of the actual review date.

  Some further comments on the project manager's role in design reviews are given in Chapter 14.

13.4.8 Project action log and continuity file
The action log is an informal piece of documentation which the project manager needs to maintain. Essentially it is a jobs-to-do file. It is to list any unsolved problems or things that have to be completed on the project. A typical page from such a log is shown in Fig. 13.13 and it should be noted that, when an action has been completed, the date is entered in the last column. Not only does such a log become a historical record but also

		Check-list	Project definition		Design review no.

No.	Question	Answer		Chairman's comments (answer 'no' with your comment)
		Yes	No	
1	General requirements			
1.1	Are all requirements defined sufficiently to permit the design to be completed? Consider the following. 　Environment 　Mechanical and electrical performance 　Handling, weight, deployment 　Production aims 　Reliability requirements			
1.2	Has a test and repair policy been defined?			
1.3	Are all specified requirements considered capable of being met without exceptional difficulty (if 'no' identify areas of risk)?			
1.4	Are all proposed techniques and components proved through use in previous designs or applications?			
1.5	Have programmes been laid to product following, at least in draft before detail design commences? 　Design aims and technical requirements 　System specifications 　Design specifications 　Repair charts			
1.6	Has the customer agreed in writing to all (or any) proposed shortfalls in original requirements?			

Fig. 13.11 — Review report check-list.

No.	Actions requested by chairman	Answer		Chairmans' comments Indicates whether further arbitration is required	
		Yes	No		
				Signed Chairman . . . . Approved	Summary sheet Project definition Design review no.

Fig. 13.12 – Review report final summary sheet.

Date open	Action log		Date closed
	Action	Who?	
7/3	Get new estimate of machine time to check out REMOT routine	Wallis	9/3
9/3	See laboratory administrator chart transferring down time charges WE 3/18	Me	10/3
9/3	Find out whether customer wants output in metric units too	Me	14/3
10/3	Form 3630 due Monday	Me	13/3
15/3	Find out why report to W.V. 322 was not delivered on time	Luckwood	24/3
14/3	Verify plots of actuals for me in February	Smith	17/3
14/3	Check with Harwood (Lee's boss) to make sure Lee is going to stay on the project	Me	
17/3	Where is data from XYZ Corporation?	Luckwood	
20/3	Get copies of Wallis' memo to all project team	Cathy	21/3
24/3	See whether Klein can use our REMOT routine on his project	Lee	
27/3	What will late inputs on VW 322 do to our deliverables?	Smith	

Fig. 13.13 — Typical page from an action log.

it throws up patterns of problems that tend to occur on most projects. Once such a pattern is recognized, anticipatory action can often be taken.

The continuity file is to keep in date order copies of all the main project correspondence for quick-back-up reference. It is surprising how often it is impossible to locate a letter or instruction, etc., which is in some file somewhere. A continuity file will often prove very useful at site for this reason.

13.5 PROJECT PROCEDURE DOCUMENTATION FILE

Of great importance to good communication is formal documentation which will inevitably be generated throughout the life of any project. In addition to the above reports there will be specifications, drawings, standards, safety instructions, variations and modifications, instructions, etc. To be effective, all such documentation must be controlled for quality, standard and distribution. Certain standard reporting forms can be used and some of these are given in Appendix 13B.

13.6 INTEGRATING PROJECT INFORMATION BY USE OF PERSONAL COMPUTING

It is important, since project managers are busy people, that computer systems are user friendly. The project manager will then be prepared to use any system himself and thus to enhance its value. Standard software will enable project data to be stored, examined, changed or abstracted and manipulated. Networked systems make the data and procedures available to other workers on the project and provide a means of communication between users.

13.6.1 Software

As new software becomes available, so more use can be made of such a facility. Some typical project management software is given in the bibliography.

For very large projects the programme manager may well have an operations room where charts of various types are displayed and updated each week or month throughout the life of the project. Often it is necessary to communicate a summary of the results of tracking these data to produce a status report for the following purposes.

(1)   To inform a client of the project progress.
(2)   To inform top management of the project progress.
(3)   To persuade management to furnish needed resources.
(4)   To persuade management to terminate a project or to keep it going.
(5)   To document a request for progress payments.
(6)   To support an application for funding, loans or permits.

All project managers need to ensure that the programs which they use will produce the hard-copy output that they want.

13.6.2 Hardware for reports and graphics

The first thing that needs to be known about project management hardware is that there are two basic types of report formats: tabular reports and graphic or diagrammatic reports. Tabular reports do not impose any significant demands on hardware. These reports are generally pre-formatted for a 132-column presentation. All you need is a wide-carriage printer or a standard-width printer with a compressed-print capability.

Graphic or diagrammatic reports include resource and cost histograms, bar (Gantt) charts, network diagrams and project performance graphs; samples of these kinds of reports can be found in Chapter 10. For these types of report it may be necessary to have special equipment in order to obtain a presentable product.

The hardware options for report generation fall into three categories: non-graphics printers, graphics printers and pen plotters.

APPENDIX 13A: CONTENT OF A TYPICAL PROJECT MANAGER'S REPORT TO THE MANAGING DIRECTOR

Information should be presented in the form preferred by the managing director. This could be graphical, tabular or descriptive in nature. The structure of a typical report would be as follows.

(1) **Introduction.** A brief scenario should set the tone of the report, e.g. optimistic, pessimistic or crisis. This would help the managing director to decide where to put the report within his own programme of work.

(2) **Progress.** This action should describe the progress relative to

   – **initial plan** and
   – **last report.**

   A simple graphical presentation could be attached, if appropriate, and possibly a marked-up bar chart of the network. This should indicate the period to run on major activities. Key achievements should be listed and so should those whose finish is behind schedule.

(3) **Financial.**

   (a) **Overall programme.** The important facts reported should be
      – cost to date,
      – cost planned to this stage and
      – present cost prediction to end of phase and also to end of project.
         An attached 'S' curve should be used to summarize all this information and past history, if appropriate. A typical example of a cost–time slippage chart is given in Fig. 13.9.

   (b) **Major capital expenditure.** This should include major items purchased, sub-contractor payments and also intentions for the next period. A graphical portrayal of initial planned capital expenditure, expenditure to date and expenditure forecast could be used to summarize these data.

(4) **Labour and other resources.** This subdivision should detail changes in existing resources and those required for the future. Shortages and their consequences should be indicated. This enables the managing director to assess the project priorities compared with other demands within the company. The major headings should be

   – men and particular skills,
   – materials,
   – machines, including special types and justification for requirement,
   – facilities, including space, workshops, drawing office,
   – services, including gases and refrigerants, and
   – finance.

(5) **Major events.** The completion or delivery of critical items should be reported, together with those impending. Decisions which select single or monopoly suppliers and therefore could involve some risk should be communicated.

(6) **Specification changes.** Changes to specifications should be described, together with the possible implications on time, cost, quality, production and sales effects.

(7)   **Production and construction**. The project manager should report

— production cost estimates,
— production tooling required, status and cost,
— numbers produced to date and
— production problems.

(8)   **Sales** (if applicable). Information from the sales department should be continuously assessed and changes noted in

— expected sales price,
— forecasts of numbers to be sold,
— market requirements,
— competition and
— maintenance and servicing situation.

(9)   **Long-term plans**. Changes in the long-term plans should be recorded together with their effects under the previous headings.

APPENDIX 13B: SOME STANDARD FORMS FOR PROJECT REPORTING

Project objectives		
Project title	Project classification Product development Process development Other	
What are the commerical objectives of the project?		
What are the technical objectives of the project?		

Appraisal factors
 	
   Probability of achieving the commercial
     objectives   %
   Probability of achieving the technical
     objectives   %
	Prepared by:
	
	Name
	
	Company
	
	Date	

Development project	
Project title	Project application no.
Background (include major technical and commercial uncertainties and specific accomplishments necessary to the success of the project)	

Supported by:	Approved by:	Proposed by:
Divisional director	Head	Name
Date	Date	Company
Product planning manager		Date
Date		

Project supplement	
Project title	Project application no.

Amount of additional funding being requested	£
Total amount of present authorized budget	_____
Total amount of proposed amended budget	===========
Amount of additional funding to be supplied by company(ies)	£
Total amount of present recovery budget	_____
Total amount of proposed amended recovery budget	===========

Reasons for the request for additional funding

Effects on the finish date

Supported by:	Approved by:	Proposed by:
Division director		Name
Date		
Product planning manager	Head	Company
Date	Date	Date

Request for project cost transfer

Description and reason for transferring:

(N.B. If time transfer, operator name and month from which hours are to be transferred, must be stated)

Signed
_____

(Project leader)

Date
_____

Accounts department
_____

Actioned on journal voucher   No.

Signed
_____

Date
_____

Development programme				
Project title				
Project stage objectives	Timing	Man days	Materials (£)	Total costs (£)

At what stages should the project be reviewed?

Project stage	Date	Comment

Will additional staff be required (if possible specify approximate number and grades)?	Prepared by: Name Company Date

SUMMARY OF CHAPTER 13

(1)   Communication is essential in project management. Means of communication will include, for example, design specifications, build standards, schedules, work sheets, reports, drawings and process specifications. Precise documentation is essential but, however good it is, there will always be misunderstandings.

(2)   Major paths of communication are between the designer and the customer, between the designer and the development department and between the designer and the production department.

(3)   The project manager must ensure that communication is good and meetings are an essential means to this end. Meetings must be prepared for and properly managed, and there will be written inputs (general statements, specific statements, general questions and specific questions) and written outputs (minutes, and statements of what action is required and by whom).

(4)   Reports are an essential means of communication in project management, e.g. diary notes, visit reports, progress reports, instructions to start (or stop work), critiques, project audits, project design reviews and action logs.

(5)   Documentation must be standardized, and its quality and distribution monitored.

14

The project manager

14.1 INTRODUCTION

For large technical projects the project manager may need to have an engineering or science background. In systems or small projects, depending on their nature, a project manager may come from other spheres of activity such as commercial or sales. Whatever his initial experience and training may be, it is likely that he will need some exposure to additional areas of activity such as contract law, purchasing and site organization, etc., before he can be launched into full-time project work.

14.2 ENGINEERING MANAGEMENT

Engineers may climb up their organization to management positions in many ways, but it is important to realize that the criteria for choosing future managers in an engineering enterprise will generally be good present job performance—especially where the work extends over a number of disciplines. This factor inevitably means that the engineer concerned has had to take a wide view of his job and considers it in the light of business results. Other criteria may well be as follows.

(1) A demonstrated ability to work with equanimity under stress, and with fortitude and flexibility, so as to accept change if required.
(2) A time-and-cost consciousness to deliver on time within an agreed budget.
(3) An ability to work with varying types of people at all levels of the organization, revealing leadership qualities.
(4) An active interest in the function and role of management.

With these criteria in mind an engineer may be in any basic function of an enterprise—commercial, manufacturing, development, engineering, design or research—before he moves into a management position.

Each function has peculiarities of its own. In manufacturing, quick decision taking is required, often on minimum information. In research and development the time of response to a decision will generally be much longer and risk consequently much greater. In design, creative people have to be organized to produce useful ideas and to turn them into instructions but in all areas the basic planning, organizing and controlling functions of management have to be carried out.

Having successfully mastered departmental management a young ambitious manager might well try to move into project management, which is a special case of general management. Alternatively, he might move into product group management, running a number of sections looking after different engineering products.

Here the engineer's ability to organize, plan and control work over a range of products as opposed to one type of product will be tested. It is this factor which will make or break the would-be engineering manager. In project management, especially with large capital goods systems or military contracts, it is essential for the manager to have an overall view of the work. He must act as the custodian of the project's spending and be the keeper of its time scale. This work will require a manager to become conversant with contract law and internal accountancy, as well as engineering, production, and operating factors.

14.3 CHARACTERISTICS OF PROJECT MANAGERS AND THEIR TRAINING

The project manager is guardian of the time scale and custodian of project experience. It is, therefore, imperative that any would-be project manager should be able to see ahead; he cannot afford to dabble in technical details but needs to be able to programme those who do. He should be hardware orientated and keen to see ideas turned into working artefacts. He will consequently need to have some technical and commercial knowledge. In addition, the lessons learned from any project should be recorded, together with the project history, so that information is readily available in a relevant form for future additional projects. This sweep-up operation may well require a different type of person from those who started the project and for this reason some organizations have found it useful to appoint different project managers as the project progresses, employing a kind of rotating leadership.

Case histories have shown that successful project managers have come from various disciplines and departments in enterprises—from commercial departments to post-development services.

The role of the project manager is often given as that of a 'smoother'—smoothing out the path of a major innovation or new project from its conception through reduction to practice to a finally commercially viable project. In many companies the project manager can, if he is temperamentally suited, wind up in an executive role in connection with the new project. Sometimes, as the result of a successful project, product spin-off is obtained and a project manager may take charge of this new product line.

Invariably the project manager is strongly task orientated and derives his satisfaction from seeing something enter the market and make money, and he is not concerned with finer points of professionalism, and interdisciplinary rivalry, etc. Where he is called a co-ordinator, a manager, a leader, chaser or expeditor, it turns out that it is much more difficult to delineate his authority than it is to describe his responsibility, and it is at this point that conflict between the task organization and the functional or 'line' organization comes clearly into focus.

Sometimes companies have set up project teams or task force teams to try to drive the project through the conventional line pyramid organization. Too often such teams have become inefficient and meeting bound but nevertheless there are occasions when they can be a very potent mechanism for getting things done.

Looking at a variety of project managers the main common characteristics appear to be

(1)   strong, forceful but acceptable personality (diplomacy and advocacy should be strong traits),
(2)   intelligence with independence of mind,
(3)   proven ability in at least one branch of work essential to the project,
(4)   an appreciation of areas of work outside his experience (the ability to see things in the whole and to take a synoptic view of the task work),
(5)   a vital interest and concern to see a project completed,
(6)   an ability to direct and delegate technical work in a multidisiciplinary situation,
(7)   a certain amount of business acumen (an interest in financial procedures, contract law, etc., and an entrepreneurial dynamism) and
(8)   energy and resourcefulness.

The problem of how to develop project managers is one which has not been satisfied very well to date. The best project managers may well go into general management, but there are only a few such posts available; so the problem remains for the majority. It is unlikely that any enterprise will be able to take in projects so that complete continuity of project teams is preserved. More often, to keep a good project manager, he is pulled off his current project before it is finished, to manage a new project that the company has taken on. However, this poses additional problems such as who succeeds him on the current project and whether the transferred project manager will learn from the mistakes he may have made, not having been present to witness their impact in production and operation. An even worse problem is with those project managers who fail to make the grade. They cannot return to the specialist departments, having lost contact and their expertise being out of date. It would seem that electing to go into project management is very much a 'point-of-no-return' decision. Inevitably, some members of the project team will wish to stay in project work, and it may be significant that, since some projects have a production life span of 8–10 years, one project manager may only cover two or three projects in his working period, since engineers appear to be having a considerably reducing working life span, owing to technical and managerial obsolescence.

Having in mind the characteristics mentioned previously, it may well be found that successful extrovert designers can be developed and trained to become good project managers but, as already stated, project managers can be recruited from any part of a firm's organization provided that they have the correct personal qualities and background knowledge. The future of much of this country's engineering endeavour will increasingly become dependent upon having more competent project managers, and to this end adequate educational and training programmes must be organized.

14.4 THE PROJECT ENVIRONMENT

Managing a company, a function, department or section is usually a maintaining or holding operation which involves keeping things running to established patterns and criteria. Although, even at best, 'normal' management is concerned with managing confusion, contradiction and conflict, i.e. imperfection, there is nevertheless an implicit continuity and usually well-determined boundaries which give the process a measure of stability unknown in project management. Usually, familiar ground is being trodden for most of the time in conventional managerial situations, where there is comparatively little venturing into the unknown and where existing skill and knowledge are sufficient to cope with even the toughest problems. Change may be the one constant in normal management but the change is usually an evolutionary or planned process for most managers. Similarly, the very hierarchical nature of most organizations provides a structure which imposes some measure of formality, order and control over what people do, to whom they report and for what, and to whom they are responsible.

The very nature of most engineering projects suggests transcience and change—even turbulence—where formality and structure may be minimal, in order to permit maximum flexibility. Along with turbulence, there is the inevitable finite nature of the project and an accompanying lack of certainty about what will happen after completion. Finally, the norms and standards enshrined in company cultures, often hallowed by little more than the passage of time—but, nevertheless, 'sanctities' which characterize much of normal organization management—show up as anachronisms in projects where behaviour needs to be, above all, effective rather than normative.

Probably more than in any other managerial situation, the management of projects brings home the fact that managing is about moving consciously from a current situation A, to a requisite state of affairs B, by a given time. Moreover, in the management of projects much of B and even A (the start point) may be unknown quantities where the quality of a manager's 'hunch' and his preparedness to back it are more relevant attributes than the 100% application of IQ and logic.

Essentially a project manager is a co-ordinator of multidisciplinary work tasks and he has to take a 'helicopter' view of the whole project from a to z. The larger and more complex the project, the greater is the uncertainty involved—thus the greater the need for enterprise, innovation and courage (see Fig. 14.1).

It is the complexity of diversity of effort required which brings us up not so much against material limitations as against human characteristics and, therefore, the style of management required to direct, control and move them.

A project may, therefore, be regarded as an instrument of change where the project manager becomes the change agent. He acts as a catalyst, drawing the various specialist skills together and welding them into teams to accomplish work tasks.

Usually, the management and organization of projects—especially large and complex ones—involve the creation of new work groups and the reconciliation or synthesis of the talents of many people, from both within and outside the company.

14.5 THE PROJECT MANAGER AS A PERSON

Obviously, there is no one 'right' personality or universal style of managing which is ideal to run a project. Projects, themselves, vary in complexity, size, number and duration. The

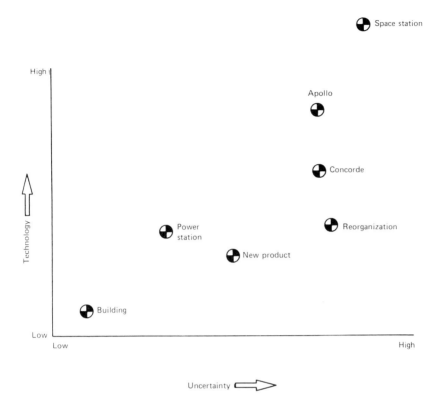

Fig. 14.1 – Projects in relation to technology and uncertainty.

project manager is constantly trying to maintain the agreed programme of work and consequently has to be good at planning and control. He must be responsible for the allocation of tasks and control of work progress and financial commitment, using the appropriate techniques. Experience, however, shows that 40% up on time estimates and 70% actual increase on budgeted costs are the slippage norms in project work.

Effective management is undoubtedly a major determinant of a project team's ability to keep to target. Both research and practical experience identify the following as vital elements in managerial effectiveness in project work.

14.5.1 Leadership
Leader roles (which may be performed alternately by several people) are vital to the successful management of a project and need to be undertaken and kept in balance.

These roles include the following.

(a) 'Inward' leader. Usually the project manager whose task is to continually review and initiate actions on the effectiveness of the project team (and individual members).

(b) 'Outward' leader. This again may be the official leader, whose primary task is to maintain boundaries between the project team and the world around, i.e. he works at such issues as:

  – interfaces with key individuals and functions external to the team,
  – securing resources, facilities and services for the team and
  – anticipating problems with the team's operational environment.

(c) **Exemplar.** This role aims to return the team periodically to

  – basic ground rules,
  – why the project team exists and what is its real task and
  – crucial theories, principles or concepts which are relevant. ('Let's get back to square one and move on from there'.)

(d) **'Eccentric'.** This role ensures that adequate innovation, novelty, new direction and change are injected into the group's thinking and work activity. While 80% of the eccentric's contributions may be inappropriate, the other 20% may produce results out of all proportion to their number.

(e) **Responsive follower.** This role is one which will be taken by many people. It involves recognizing which of the other leader roles are critical at any one time during crises or stagnations and then giving energetic committed support to that critical leader.

14.6 BOUNDARIES

The 'boundaries' of the project within which the project manager and his team work are normally set above the project manager's authority level, but he is responsible for managing them. These are illustrated in Fig. 14.2.

In the management of these boundaries he will be required to influence his superiors and peers as well as those who report to him.

The ability to get people of higher and equal status to do what needs doing, when it must be done, is probably the biggest test of the project leader's capacity as a manager. Equally, it is the area of biggest potential pay-off in his development both as a person and as a member of management.

14.7 MONITORING THE PROJECT

Rather like Clausewitz's description of war, management is an 'option of risks' and nowhere is this more evident than in the management of projects. Risks and problems are usually at their most daunting in the boundaries of the project and demand of the project manager that he both asks and finds answers to questions such as the following.

  – What are the real limits in this situation?
  – What would happen if . . .?
  – What alternatives do we have?
  – What else can we do?
  – We've never done it this way before—so what?
  – What are the consequences of doing this and how do we most effectively deal with them?
  – What are the consequences of *not* taking these risks?
  – Where are the critical relationships of blockages that will or could hold us up?

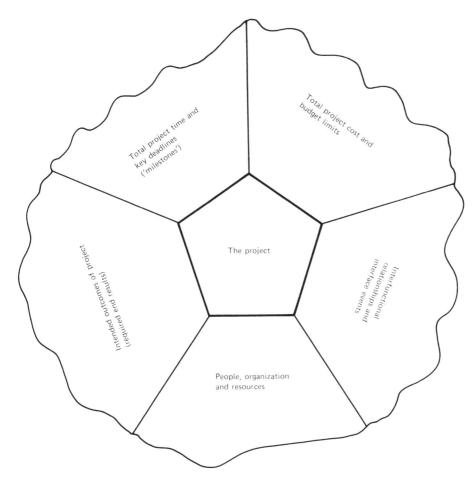

Fig. 14.2 – Boundaries of the project.

- Who is accountable for dealing with these issues?
- What is our power or access to power to deal with such problems?

The ability to predict potential crises, or problems, and a clear understanding of their likely impact upon the success of the project are vital in project management. Probably the most effective managerial element in this process is the more or less continuous monitoring of the situation, where potential risk and vulnerability analyses are the core activity. Similarly, opportunity analysis and continual awareness of strengths—and how these could be more effectively employed—are also vital to the practice of project management. The project manager must continually be in a position to exercise trade-offs for the overall benefit of the client. Consequently he must be always assessing risks, especially with respect to performance, time of completion and total costs.

A positive approach to managing, based on dynamic monitoring underpinned by thorough and appropriate planning, creates a sense of purpose and direction which are vital to sustain the motivations of the project team members. Being a thoroughly qualified engineer may be crucial as one aspect of project leadership but the authority of competence—which some see as the most influential form of authority—is also made up of managerial expertise and the capacity to make the right things happen when they are most needed. This is the very essence of project management.

14.8 ADDITIONAL SKILLS AND TECHNIQUES FOR PROJECT MANAGERS

Project managers should be engaged in the early stages of their project with the negotiations with the customers and later when any re-negotiations of the contract takes place. In-house negotiations may also be necessary especially where the project organization comes into conflict with the 'line' organization. Often a project manager will need to be engaged in the process of persuasion if he is to be successful.

14.8.1 Persuading others
The persuasion of another is all but impossible unless the persuader has esteem for his own opinions. He must be convinced that his position and opinions are sound and that they should be implemented.

There are many principles of persuasion but this short list may be helpful.

(1)   The opening and closing statements tend to be remembered longer.
(2)   Both sides of an issue should be presented but the most favoured position should be last.
(3)   Repetition aids learning and encourages acceptance.
(4)   The listener should be led to and through your very explicit conclusions.
(5)   Individuals tend to remember best that information which they need to know.
(6)   Within a quadrant of reasonableness or credulity, requests for large changes in opinion tend to produce large changes.
(7)   It is better to emphasize similarities rather than differences and to link differences on specific issues to prior agreements, if possible.
(8)   Statements from those who are deemed to have status and prestige are more readily accepted.

Anyone who attempts to apply automatically a set of guidelines or rules in a mechanical manner will encounter real problems. Such a deterministic view of man is not conducive to successful negotiation because it fails to comprehend the variability and the flair that is present in most men. Opinions are part of the total stock of personal possessions, and to challenge them borders on criticizing the person. The fragile and unique task of reinforcing or changing attitudes of each towards the other calls for consummate negotiating and interpersonal skills.

14.8.2 Controlling change
Reference has already been made to the fact that the role of the project manager becomes one of a change agent within his own enterprise. In the light of his tasks he is constantly trying to change attitudes and organizations. Perhaps Fig. 14.3 gives some indication of the possible steps required to achieve organizational change. Always the project manager

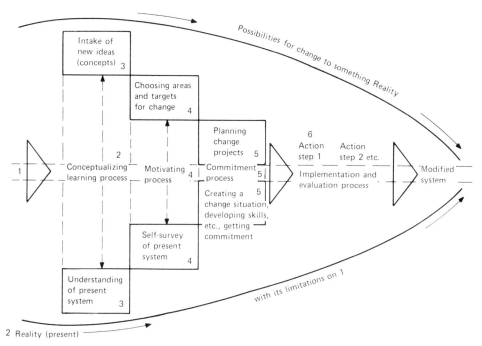

Fig. 14.3 – Organization change model.

must realize that many within his enterprise will view any anticipated change as threatening and for that reason reject it while others may view it as enhancing and embrace it. Change typically involves risk and consequently fear. The trust and support of the change agent during the period of greatest stress are vital to win success.

There are, moreover, value conflicts between the project manager as change agent and the normal line and staff personnel. The two different orientations lead to ambivalences, false starts, worries and concerns about how each will react and relationships often become strained.

14.8.3 Overcoming stress in the line organization

Clearly, conflict can emerge between the line of a vertically orientated management organization, with its clear-cut lines of authority and responsibility and the problem of getting the project task completed. Project management is an endeavour to provide a focus for all aspects of the specific task and another way of looking at a project manager is to think of him as a 'vest-pocket entrepreneur' whose main function is to co-ordinate activities in research, development, design and production or construction.

Where companies make a complete shift to a project management system from the traditional standard pyramidal structure, the resulting stress and strains can kill off the new managers and regression then sets in.

To a section head or department chief the introduction of a project manager can be viewed as a considerable threat. For one thing they see the possibility of losing control over their people at the operating level. They feel that the subordinates will become confused by serving two masters and they do not believe that it is possible for them to deal with the professional aspects of a subordinate's career because they may not be able to give a direct appraisal of how well he is doing. Furthermore, in a multiproject situation, competition between the various project managers may result in conflicting demands for priority and competition for scarce resources. The project manager is also seen as taking the kudos for a successful project away from the professional technical people.

The key to success lies in something more than having a winsome manner; really the skills of diplomacy and persuasion are needed to cultivate full participation by both parties so as to avoid trying situations where for example manufacturing people say 'If only I'd known, then we could have . . . .' In the engineering function, technical people have a lamentable tendency to believe that they are smart enough to second-guess the best course of action.

14.8.4 Understanding behavioural science in management
Some understanding of the findings of the behavioural scientists in connection with management situations are important in this respect.

Briefly, four main schools can be distinguished.

(1) **Scientific management** in which implicit assumption is that people avoid punishment and seek rewards by compliant behaviour. Greater effort—higher output—increased reward.
(2) **Human relations** in which the basic assumption is that people respond favourably and will therefore co-operate when their needs for recognition, status and dignity are satisfied. The approach here is characterized when a project manager considers individual and social needs rather than target achievement and task performance.
(3) **Participation** in which the basic belief is that man needs to create and shape his environment, rather than merely to react to it. Styles of participative management seek to relate individual effort to group task performance.
(4) **Human resource approach** in which the current evolving and converging theories of behavioural scientists emphasize the need for congruence between individual work objectives, organization structure and corporate goals. Project managers have to realise that the individual's needs (project team men or line men) for growth and self-fulfilment are seen as having their roots in achievement and job satisfaction.

14.9 HOW TO TRAIN, DEVELOP AND DEPLOY PROJECT PEOPLE

Where do project managers and engineers come from and go to? How can they be selected, placed and trained to give the best performance? In general terms a project man is one who has a broad technical interest as well as a feel for the business of engineering. They may come from any department in the company—design, production, commercial, etc.—or they may be recruited from outside.

Engineers who rise to management positions have generally turned in a track record in a department which shows

(1) technical ability,
(2) a time-and-cost consciousness,
(3) an ability to work with varying types of people,

(4)   both mental and physical activity and
(5)   an understanding of commercial and business factors.

For project management an engineer should, in addition, show that

(1)   he is keen to see end results,
(2)   he has well-developed analytical skills,
(3)   he has ability to lead a team of technical people and is flexible in style,
(4)   he shows an interest in project economics,
(5)   he has a strong forceful personality (diplomacy and advocacy should be strong traits),
(6)   he is energetic both physically and mentally and resourceful and has a clear recognition of realities,
(7)   he has business acumen and
(8)   he must be able to withstand adversity and conflict.

While this may sound a counsel of perfection, it is doubtful whether he will be successful if two or more of these factors are missing.

The above criteria for choosing effective project men may be useful but real development can prove a headache. On-the-job training is the best possible way but, unless carried out systematically with proper appraisal, it is unlikely to be entirely successful. Off-the-job training courses are few and far between but, where life case studies are used, they can help project people to understand and be sensitive to project situations. Certainly, many good courses giving engineers the rudiments of financial marketing and purchasing matters are available and have their uses.

Deployment of project people can also present problems for, although in theory it is possible to transfer people from one project task to another, in practice the two projects never seem to phase well. Project teams cannot be dismantled by moving people back into line functions again and it may mean that certain key project personnel have to be parked 'in orbit' for a period. Such a trip is to enable them to develop themselves, to review the past project that they have been engaged on and to help tendering people with possible new work.

Very successful project managers may be suitable material for general management appointments, but obviously there are a limited number of such positions that become vacant. It has to be confessed that entrance into project management is usually a one-way affair and therefore should not be taken on without careful consideration.

14.9.1 Self-development
Any project manager or engineer would be well advised to watch his own development as he takes up a new appointment and gradually wins acceptance. The situation is the same for any type of managerial job and can be divided into four main phases (Fig. 14.4).

—   **Phase I** is the initial installation period. Here the new manager is learning the job and his predecessor may be leading him gently into position, until he takes over the controls completely and goes solo.
—   **Phase II.** Here the real life challenges of the project work are met by the new manager. This is a 'make-or-break' period. He is still developing and, as time passes,

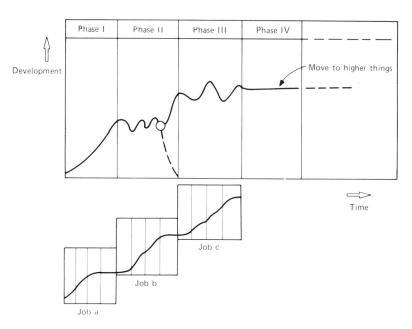

Fig. 14.4 — Four main phases in the development of a manager.

he overcomes difficulties and obstacles and learns to surmount many project problems. However, should he fall, he may well have a drooping curve which, if of sufficient negative slope, can lead to a mental breakdown.

— **Phase III**. At this stage he has the project system well under control and any violent external disturbance is tackled with considerable skill. The curve of his development is still rising, but not so strongly, and eventually it starts to flatten out. At this point the manager requires extra challenge, maybe by stimulus from his superiors or some outside agency, such as a management course. Alternatively he may have come to the end of the road and reached his maximum potential for this particular position.

— **Phase IV**. In this case he will require moving to some higher or equally challenging position elsewhere within the organization, or maybe outside the firm.

The slopes and degree of perturbation will, of course, vary from project man to project man but the general pattern will remain the same.

14.10 PARTICULAR PROBLEMS OF PROJECT MANAGEMENT

There are a number of special problems which are inimical to project management work. Many of these stem from the fact that project management is really a special case of general management but carrying only limited responsibility and authority.

There are a series of difficulties which can occur in the project design especially where research and development may be required. Another particularly difficult area concerns the handing over of design instructions to get prototypes, pre-production models and rigs, and full manufacture under way. This is even worse in the construction industry where too often there is complete divorce between design and construction.

Often steady-state manufacture takes considerable time to reach. Even then there are likely to be customer variations, additions and modifications which necessitate close project control.

14.10.1 Handing over design to production and construction
At this final stage where the actual hardware is produced, three departments are mainly concerned and the project manager may be viewed as balancing the sometimes conflicting interests of the design department, inspection department and manufacturing or constructing unit.

Necessarily there will be conflict which must be balanced by collaboration. Designers are interested primarily in performance and reliability while manufacturing organizations have, traditionally, been more concerned with time and cost.

Smooth transference of design intent only occurs when there is adequate communication which generally can be put into four distinct phases.

(1) **Preparation.** Wise project engineers will ensure that the works are brought into the design process as early as possible. Such aspects as machine capability and capacity can really only be given by the works concerned.

   Will semiskilled or unskilled labour have to be used? What jigs and fixtures will be necessary? Could this or that part best be made outside or purchased as standard items? These and other features may be classed as determining ease of manufacture.

   Another class of problems concerning handover are cost aspects and here the works are liable to ask for design alterations which can be disturbing to designers who are in the process of creating something new. It is worth remembering that it will nearly always be impossible to generate a new design with the lowest cost at a first attempt. Value analysis has indicated the 'gold in the mine' as far as old designs are concerned but the works can provide valuable help in design realization if they are allowed to contribute.

   An even more important aspect in the preparation for manufacture concerns the planned evolution of future designs. Joint plans must be to make a product whose performance, manufacturability and cost are intended to evolve progressively towards a level which is a significant improvement on current efforts. In electronics work this is a useful discipline to impose as designers are prevented from hampering manufacture by producing a large variety of packages for different circuit designs.

(2) **Actual handover.** Drawings need to be properly presented and a proper story built up as they are issued. Despite their preparation by a substantial number of engineers it needs to be remembered that most of the manufacturing and associated staff will be seeing the drawings and associated documents for the first time.

   For large projects the difficulty of handling, storing and distributing large numbers of prints and original drawings and modifications forces the use of microfilm as the best means of propagating design instructions.

   Again, very tight control must be exercised over any planned variations in design. Often, as with car production lines, successive models may have to possess special features and yet embody many unchanged parts. This calls for configuration management to be applied.

(3) **Development** The term development is used here in a limited sense. As successive models or units are produced from identical drawings, so a faster response is achieved which is quicker and nearer what is wanted.

In fact this is the learning curve being applied. It is an unfortunate fact of industrial life that the learning process in this development period tends to be 'teacher orientated' rather than 'learner orientated'. The design department is generally the source of new ideas and the works tend to feel inferior or hesitant of putting proposals forward. In good organizations there should be a mutual learning process as the works play their part in educating designers to understand how best to manipulate methods and what the man—machine system can do. It is extraordinary that most firms spend more money on machine tools and improved processes than on improving the means whereby design is carried out.

The key to obtaining a better performance lies in establishing an error free feedback system. By this means a gradual refinement takes place until the manufacturing reaches the requisite level required. There must be a true meeting of minds to achieve the right-quality hardware. It is in this area that project managers are particularly useful.

A cause of much regret is that so many works are full of social unrest and unprogressive ideas and our educational system has done little to redress the balance by guiding the best pupils into the design and instruction end of the business rather than where the real wealth is produced. Most graduates choose and are more suitable for research and development activities than for design and production. This leads to a false segregation of minds and can be damaging to performance.

As with construction, manufacturing has not always been well served by project managers and there is still need for improvement in this area.

(4) **Creating the design**. In this phase of the translation process the project team is generally more at home than when dealing with the works.

To understand the role played by a project manager or engineer, it is vital to appreciate the design process and the various aids that have become available to designers. It is important to realize that design is the heart of engineering and necessitates careful control of creative effort.

The design process can be represented as an iterative process in various ways and Fig. 14.5 depicts one of these. The penalties for failure in design increase with increasing size of the project, its complexity and its novelty. The constraints of time and money add further hazards.

Project people nearly always concentrate on obtaining an accurate authentic statement of the true requirements. What is the real vital engineering job to be accomplished? What are the criteria for success?

Indeed initial design decisions will have important end repercussions and the act of designing is really one of working through a good decision system.

The activity of designing

The activity of designing consists of a number of stages which may be described as follows.

(1) Setting and agreeing objectives which stem from an identified need.

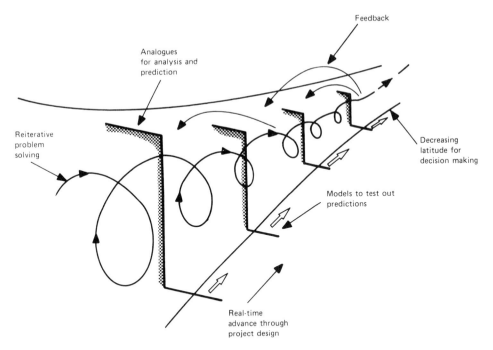

Fig. 14.5 – Schematic diagram of a design programme.

(2)　Establishing the conditions and properties required by the objective to be exhibited in the final hardware.

(3)　Determining the relationships between varying stages of the properties.

(4)　Ascertaining the limiting and ideal states of the properties.

(5)　Identifying any laws controlling the interdependencies of the properties.

(6)　Ensuring that feasibility studies leading the possible solutions do not conflict with (5) above and that they are acceptable by the criteria generated in step (1) above.

(7)　Selecting the optimum solution.

Thus the act of designing consists of three basic phases: problem formulation, generation of solutions, and deciding an optimum solution. These phases require creativity, evaluation and analysis and justification as indicated in Fig. 14.6.

For a design to be viable to a promotor, the project or product designed must command a value in exchange which is greater than its intrinsic value. In other words the hardware produced through engineering design must be worth more to a prospective user than the cost to the producer of the materials, labour and manipulative processes required for its production and construction. The margin between cost and value in exchange is a measure of the profitability of the design. Engineering designs are valued for their utility, i.e. their ability to fulfil some practical need. However, in addition to meeting a practical need there are often additional emotional and sensual needs to be satisfied. Thus projects have to appear aesthetically pleasing and their operation has to be safe and easy to handle. Against these factors it is also required to make the cost of manufacturing a minimum. For products which have to be sold rather than tendered for, marketing costs also have to be a minimum.

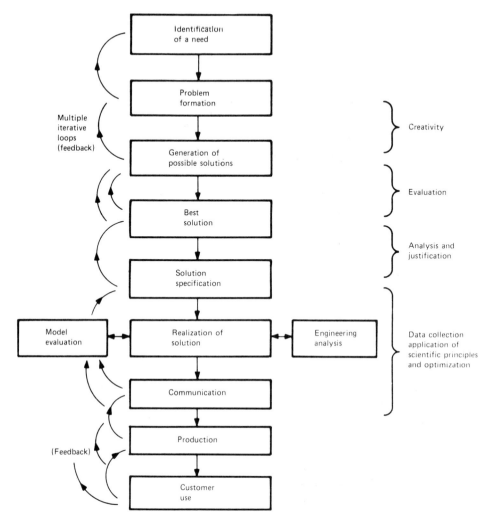

Fig. 14.6 – The design process.

14.10.2 The project manager's role in design

For project work, Fig. 14.7 sets out the various disciplines required to achieve the desired commercial viability to please both producer and customer.

Engineering design is not carried out on a solo basis but as a corporate effort requiring careful management. Care must be taken at all stages of the design process to avoid project engineers tampering with the process. Their function is not the 'how' but the 'when', 'where' and 'what'. Many project engineers have come from the design office and are often tempted to try to help with the designs. This must be resisted.

The project manager or engineer must play the role of the helper in achieving maximum co-operation and good attention of specialists. It is likely that much conflict will occur at this stage as other projects may demand and compete for specialist services.

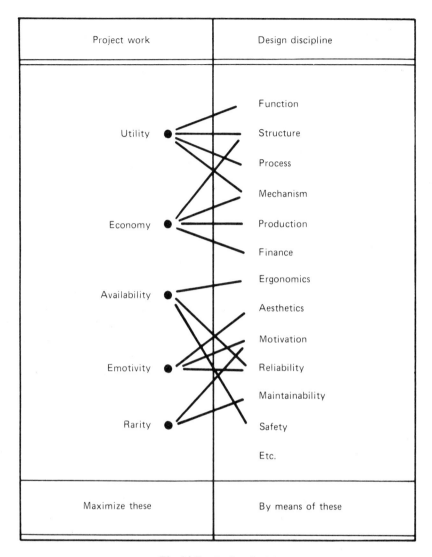

Project work	Design discipline
Utility	Function
	Structure
	Process
	Mechanism
Economy	Production
	Finance
	Ergonomics
Availability	Aesthetics
	Motivation
Emotivity	Reliability
	Maintainability
Rarity	Safety
	Etc.
Maximize these	By means of these

Fig. 14.7 – Design disciplines.

In addition, designers must be constantly warned against creating new designs when standard items could be used. Both standardization and reliability benefit from a strong organizational support and company policy. Unfortunately it is too often left to project groups to try to impose such requirements on design teams. Properly conducted design reviews can help in this area (see section 14.10.4).

14.10.3 The project engineer's role in research and development
Research can be fundamental and have little direct relevance to particular projects that the enterprise is engaged upon, but industry mostly carries out applied research to obtain better ways of doing things and to produce new ideas for projects. Fundamental research is generally carried out by universities, government establishments or very specialist

undertakings. Certainly, project people need to be aware of where various research work is being carried out and, if necessary, bring in special research knowledge for their contracts.

In-house applied research is likely to be supporting specialist functions, generally on a long-term basis. In emergencies, project managers may need to enlist the help of the company's research experts and in such situations they are likely to act as mediators helping to transfer useful relevant knowledge in a palatable form for the designers to use.

Development, on the contrary, may be looked upon as the hand-maiden to design. It is required to add design information in the early stages of the design process and to provide feedback later on. Development may be required—before design commences to confirm the feasibility of certain ideas, during design to demonstrate practibility of design work and after the design is complete to validate that performance and other factors are satisfactory. Fig. 13.5 indicates how a project management group man will have to mediate between the design departments and developing proving. Of course the amount of research and development undertaken will be primarily determined by the difficulty of the design. In the high-technology area, where there is little experience to guide in solutions, it may be extensive.

Development in the context of consumer durables is usually an evolutionary process whereby successive versions of the product have differed as the available material, skills and customer preferences changed. The differences were often quite small and the effect of changes were absorbed without shock, but in project activity there is generally an element of novelty because the present system does not answer the client's need.

Unfortunately, too often development is design carried out under another name and, instead of being a partnership, it turns out to be a confrontation. When analysing why any development is necessary the following four factors seem to occur.

(1) **Human error.** This may be due to inadequate mathematical models or faulty arithmetic or even lack of imagination in foreseeing a circumstance which is difficult to represent on paper. Some of these are all too familiar such as inaccessible fastenings or awkwardness in handling.

(2) **Lack of design method.** It may well be envisaged by designers that a certain type of construction may be realized but it may not be appreciated in advance how to proportion its constituent parts so as to obtain a correct overall total performance.

(3) **Lack of design data.** Certainly past experience and logged data accumulated from previous designs will be useful but there may be no past designs in the project area and the data may take considerable time to acquire; so intelligent guesses have to be made and development may prove these guesses to be wrong.

(4) **Lack of specification.** This is a dangerous reason for development and should not really be tolerated except for brand new designs. It is a golden rule that all specifications must be expressed in quantitative terms wherever possible.

At the final design validation phase it is necessary for development departments to take an objective look at the design from a number of differing vantage points such as reliability, systems operation and environmental tests.

Here again the project manager has often to act as mediator since design assurance departments (development) are often found in the sniping position. This is due not only to the nature of the work but also to the attitudes of those concerned. As previously mentioned, development departments are often staffed by graduate engineers who have not previously carried out design work. They therefore become self-appointed design critics who can be off-hand and even downright unsympathetic to those who have been responsible for a creative effort.

This brings up the need for formalized design reviews when an objective appraisal of the design at various stages of its realization is undertaken.

14.10.4 The project manager's role in design review

A design review is a formal documented and systematic study of a project providing an objective evaluation to ensure that a design will meet all of the specified requirements. It is not a post-mortem or a progress meeting.

While the appraisals are performed by specialists and practitioners as detailed studies, often in isolation from each other, they must be finally assessed within the overall project context at design review meetings. The project manager must ensure that this is done.

A design review will also seek to ensure that the proposed design can be produced, bearing in mind the production facilities, and that it can be tested against the requirements. It will also cover such aspects as scaling of spares and repair policy. If conducted properly, a review will reveal otherwise hidden snags and defects.

In view of the UK Health and Safety at Work Act the design review may be looked upon as a product liability preventer. There are, of course, other liability prevention tools, such as hazards analysis, failure mode and effects analysis as well as quality control and reliability methods, but the formal documentation and interrogation process involved in a design review ensures that companies maintain an accurate record of the design assumptions and criteria throughout the design process.

To achieve success, designs must be reviewed by engineering, finance, manufacturing, marketing, purchasing, quality and safety people, and other specialists, as a group and not in series. It must be stressed that a design review is not merely a 'design check' absolving the designers of all responsibility. A review is to ensure that the design is as soundly based as possible, but it must not become design by committee. It is now being accepted that some assurance is required to ensure that the new equipment or plant does not contain features that could lead to operational failure. Minimum life cycle costs are becoming vital for all customers.

Mechanics of conducting a design review

The exact procedure for conducting a review will vary according to the nature of the work undertaken for the project. However, there are some general steps which will be common to all design reviews. These concern the selection of a chairman, identification of project phase for review, schedule of meetings, and choosing participants.

The project manager is responsible for convening and scheduling the meetings, issuing an agenda, minutes and final report and, most important of all, ensuring that the recommendations are carried out. As chairman, he must seek to be impartial and his knowledge of a particular aspect of a project will come from the prior circulation of specified documents.

Design review participants

The types of people who will attend any design review will vary with the nature of the project, and with the type of review being undertaken. There will always be a core group whose responsibilities cover the administration and chairing of the meeting and the actual designers who prepare and substantiate their design decisions and methods. The preliminary design review will survey the concept or proposed design solution. This will be looked at by reliability and safety experts, etc.

Other members will be needed for the intermediate and final review meetings.

Dates for the reviews

Specified times for design reviews will need to be incorporated into the project design and development schedule. Such a schedule will depend upon the significance of the particular project under consideration, the complexity and the amount of previously proven components and subassemblies used in the design. Generally, reviews can be grouped into milestone categories applicable to any design and development efforts, such as

- preliminary design review, concept or proposal,
- intermediate design reviews, before the preparation of detail drawings,
- pre-release design review, before release for pilot production, and
- final design review, before the start of full production.

There may well need to be several intermediate design reviews depending upon the type of product or project under consideration. There may also need to be a final acceptance review before the delivery and handover to the customer. The project manager must be responsible for convening design review meetings and providing the participants with adequate information.

Information and data

As previously mentioned in section 13.4.7, at all review meetings the information and data should be distributed to all participants well before the meeting is convened. Such information, which depends on the milestone at which the review is being taken, describes any interfaces with other items. Such data might normally be thought of as layouts, drawings, specifications, anticipated customer needs, cost data, test reports, malfunction reports, relevant quality control analysis and any other pertinent data. A typical component review for a company-made part might include

- detail drawings (pictorial representation, description of materials, finishes, dimensions, tolerances, fabrication and assembly instructions),
- installation drawings (general configuration, any attaching hardware and spatial location of mountings, etc.),
- component specification (functional characteristics and test requirements),
- parts and materials lists (setting out specification and class of items),
- reliability analyses (failure mode and effect analyses) and
- stress analyses (any relevant calculations).

14.11 SOME FINAL THOUGHTS

Often in situations concerning design, development, and production and construction, project groups are engaged in creating an acceptable climate to proceed with the project concerned.

While project teams are there to drive their particular projects through the amorphous line organizations, they need to be diplomatic. Good relationship with the line managers is essential as is an ability to see both sides of any problem. When debacles occur in design or production, careful handling of the situation will be necessary if high stress conditions are to be avoided. The same applies to situations where work for a project is carried out by other parties such as subcontractors, vendors, consultants and specialist designers.

A good project manager will have a strong, forceful and assertive personality, but also energy and resourcefulness are essential. In desiring to achieve results he must realize that it is important to achieve harmonious relationships and good communications between technical departments both in house and out of house and between site engineers and designers as well as between customer and company.

Effective communication within the project group can be a problem and is generally a leading feature in improving performance. This is particularly true when modifications occur concerning the configuration of equipment, and it is essential to have proper procedures and documentation to acquaint all concerned.

14.12 VITAL CHARACTERISTICS

What then is required in the make-up of a good project manager? From the author's experience the following abilities are required.

(1) Ability to select and run a small team of people with varying knowledge skills.
(2) Ability to present cases well to top management and the customer.
(3) Strong motivation to see end results by given dates.
(4) Abilities to smooth out difficulties between specialist group heads and between specialists and his own team of project engineers.
(5) Ability to plan and control.
(6) Ability to avoid involvement in any detailed design or other technicalities, but an understanding of the nature of technical details and their problems. This requires wide technical experience.
(7) Ability to make good reports, to organize and to run meetings well.
(8) Knowledge of how to handle contract documents and to negotiate with the customer.
(9) Interest in project economics.
(10) A strong forceful but acceptable personality—diplomacy and advocacy should be strong traits.
(11) Business acumen—financial, administrative, and contract knowledge.
(12) Energy and resourcefulness.

From the above a project manager's job description should include the following.

(1) To initiate, review, approve and to submit, in good time, project proposals.
(2) To maintain surveillance over contract negotiations.
(3) To develop and maintain a programme (technical performance, time and cost).
(4) To establish and maintain a system of management control and reporting procedure (project status).
(5) To establish a balanced test programme.

(6)   To apply and administer modifications and changes.
(7)   To act as (primary) representative in dealing with the customer.
(8)   To compile all contract documentation.
(9)   To co-ordinate any support programmes, value engineering, quality and reliability and environmental engineering, configuration management, data control, design review, etc.

APPENDIX 14A: THREE PROJECT MANAGER JOB DESCRIPTIONS

Three project manager job descriptions are given in this appendix.

(1)   For a hospital and local university project.
(2)   For projects with an aerospace firm.
(3)   For projects with a civil engineering construction company.

Project manager job description 1

Employer

A hospital in partnership with a local university.

Function and responsibilities

—   To assist the Joint Policy Planning Committee in formulating policy for the project.
—   To manage all aspects of the project on behalf of the Joint Policy Planning Committee and in accordance with Joint Policy Planning Committee policy.
—   To identify and ensure the achievement of project objectives with particular reference to time and cost.
—   To act as the 'client's' formal channel of communication in dealings with the architects, contractors, consultants and similar bodies associated with the project.

Duties

—   To make recommendations on project management policy to the Joint Planning Committee.
—   To submit comprehensive and up-to-date reports to the Joint Policy Planning Committee on the status of the project.
—   To obtain comprehensive reports for the evaluation of project status from the appropriate parties on design, cost, time scales, etc.
—   To represent the interests of the hospital and university (as represented by the Joint Policy Planning Committee) in all negotiations.
—   To ensure that project interests are safeguarded in all contractual negotiations and to ensure that all contracts are designed to allow effective control of the work by the Hospitals Board and University Council.
—   To lead and co-ordinate the project group.

- To convene project progress and project review meetings.
- To define detailed responsibilities to all parties.
- To represent the project either directly or through nominated agents and in conjunction with such other officers as are appropriate in contacts with outside bodies such as University Grants Committee, Department of Health and Social Security and local government.

(Note. Formal communications with the Department of Health and Social Security and the University Grants Committee will be sent over the signature of the Director or Associate Director as appropriate.)

- To maintain overall supervision of design proposals to ensure compatibility with project objectives.
- To ensure the recruitment, training and administration of hospital and university project staff both for the conduct of the project and for subsequent operation of the New Medical Centre.
- To supervise tender procedures and formulation of contracts.
- To examine tender submissions with reference to the architect's advice, for compatibility with project objectives.
- To make recommendations, in consultation with the architects, to the Joint Policy Planning Committee for the placing of contracts.
- To interpret consultants' and contractors' contract responsibilities with respect to the Board of Hospitals and the Council of the University.
- To ensure recording of design approvals.
- To ensure the establishment and operation of fully defined procedures for design, progress and cost control and reporting, particularly in respect of variations.
- To investigate all proposed variations to contract and to reject, approve or pass recommendations to the Joint Policy Planning Committee for action as appropriate.
- To process interim certificates.
- To ensure the security of all hospitals and university property associated with the project.
- To signify client acceptance of contract to architect on completion.
- To oversee and co-ordinate the activities of the

    - planning
    - equipping
    - commissioning and
    - management services sections of the project group in respect of definition of objectives, provision of staff and resources, preparation of plans and programmes, operation of control and reporting procedures and obtaining funding approvals.

Project manager job description 2

Employer
An aerospace firm.

Responsibilities

(1) He is responsible for the initiation, review, approval and timely submission of project proposals.

(2) He exercises surveillance over contract negotiations with the customer to ensure that programme objectives can be met within the terms of resulting contracts.

(3) He is responsible for the development and maintenance of programme plans covering the technical, financial and schedule aspects of the project, for make or buy recommendations, for task assignments and for other instructions required to fulfil contractual requirements. He assures the development and maintenance of compatible implementation plans and programmes by all contributing organizations.

(4) He is responsible for the establishment and maintenance of the necessary system of management control and visibility on all aspects of project performance, such as conformance to contract terms and conditions, technical performance requirements and specifications, schedules, allocated funds, and post-delivery co-ordination.

(5) He is responsible for systems analysis and systems engineering, including

    (a) preparation of system specifications and functional requirements, and
    (b) systems integration.

(6) He is responsible for establishing a balanced test programme. Included is the responsibility for planning, scheduling, directing and controlling the programme, for assuring the timely availability of funds, manpower, facilities, equipment and other resources needed for testing, and for monitoring to assure that the programme is completed as planned.

(7) He is responsible for applying, establishing and administering configuration management.

(8) He is responsible for the allocation of funds necessary for performance of approved work and such reallocations as necessary owing to changing conditions. He recommends pre-contractual coverage as required.

(9) He is responsible for initiating corrective action when actual performance deviates or is predicted to deviate from established project plans.

(10) He co-ordinates the company position and serves as the primary representative in dealing with the customer and related contractors on project matters.

(11) He is responsible for contractual technical documentation. He determines data requirements, assigns responsibility and funding for the implementation and monitors to assure data are satisfactory and on schedule.

(12) He assures that properly co-ordinated and timely replies are provided to all correspondence received by the company in connection with the project.

(13) He assures the establishment, co-ordination and execution of support programmes to the extent required or permitted by the contract. In this context, support programmes include value engineering, quality control, reliability, maintainability, environmental engineering, configuration management, data control, design review, and components, materials and processes engineering.

(14) He regularly informs the division manager and other interested company management of project status and recommends management action as may be necessary for the expeditious conduct of the programme.

Project manager job description 3

Employer
A civil engineering construction company.

Responsible to
Director and Manager of . . . .

Objectives

To the client

— To relieve the client of the responsibility of providing an organization to deal with the design and construction of a project.
— For the overall planning, control and co-ordination of a project from inception to completion aimed at meeting a client's requirements and ensuring completion on time within cost and to required quality standards.

To the company

— To exhibit maturity, stability and integrity in his personal conduct of the company's business.
— To demonstrate determination and commitment to achieve objectives, and to exercise an adequate breadth of vision and a diplomatic managerial manner in the performance of his duties.
— To ensure that the company is seen to be implementing its stated business philosophy in satisfying the requirements of the client.

Responsibilities
To the client

Initial stages with the client

Client involvement

— To define the degree of involvement required from the client and define clearly a *modus operandi* between the client and the company.
— To set out clearly the approvals required by the client, indicating time constraints on approvals.

Communication and reporting

— To set out lines of communication and extent and frequence of meetings to be held between client and project manager.
— To establish the reporting required by the client and report on a regular basis on such subjects as

  (a) expenditure against budget and estimated cost to completion,

(b) actual progress compared with programme and definition of work still to be completed,
(c) regular update of schedules and budgets, and
(d) design changes and consequences.

Feasibility stage

Develop brief   To examine or assist in examining the client's basic proposals for the project and collect and examine all available existing data. To develop in conjunction with the client a firm clear brief for the project in qualitative and quantitative terms. Such a brief should clearly set out all management and technical functions and establish their boundaries. To develop the brief as necessary, including such means as flow lines and flow progress charts and to establish the best requirements for the client regarding plant, layout, selection of plant, handling, loading, storage of raw material and finished products, building type, environment, and labour force provisions. To investigate as instructed by the client new machinery and processes applicable to the development.

Project feasibility   As the brief is defined, to establish that the client has a viable proposition and that development is both technically and financially feasible.

Programme   To prepare a programme for the total project and establish a total time scale in conjunction with the client's requirements.

Design team   Where appropriate, to discuss and agree within . . . . and with the client on the selection of the design team. To select the team and confirm its appointment to . . . .

Site   To ensure that preliminary investigation of the site or sites is carried out and to examine alternative designs and layouts. To establish the optimum requirements regarding the basic layout and site requirements.
   To advise on the site location and suitability. To ensure that site possession will be available when required.

Government approval   To assist the client in obtaining basic approvals necessary from the goverment and local government.

Site investigation   To arrange when approved or considered appropriate for such site investigation including topographical surveys, soil reports, bore holes and such other geotechnical tests as necessary for the satisfactory design and construction of the project.

Preliminary drawings   To ensure that preliminary architectural and engineering drawings (and a preliminary material and equipment specification) are prepared for the purpose of planning approvals and establishment of budgets.

Budget   To see that a budget is prepared for the project (with investment proposals including cash flow projections as appropriate and required).

Outline planning approval   To define the basic building and structural requirements and to establish outline planning approval within the required time scale. To investigate and resolve any adjacent owner situations, preservation order situations, rights of way or easements. To ensure that the statutory authorities can provide the basic services required.

Feasibility report   To prepare a feasibility report outlining all aspects of the project for the client's approval.

Pre-construction stage

Contractor selection   To establish the general procedures for selection and appointment of domestic contractors, including the form of tendering, form of contract, terms of payment, degree of subcontracting required and labour relations policy.

Management structure   To set up a management structure for the project with clear procedures for communication to all participating parties and clear definition of inter-faces between contributing members. To define the responsibilities of all parties and manage them to carry out their tasks efficiently.

Communication   To set up procedures for clearly defining responsibilities of the team in respect of administration, accounting, purchasing, approvals, reports and meetings and to indicate documentation circulation. To hold such progress meetings as are necessary for satisfactory co-ordination of the works.

Programme   To produce a master programme for the design and construction phases and to communicate to all parties.

Design proposals   Following approval of the feasibility study, to obtain and develop firm design and structural requirements, plant layout, services and equipment. To check at all times that the design produced complies with the overall cost budget. To ensure that design consultants produce specifications for all aspects of the works and in preparation to consider such items as cost efficiency in operation and maintenance. To ensure that adequate provisions are made for the most effective form of heating, ventilation, air conditioning, recycling of heat and waste products, hoisting facilities, lifts, fire precautions, sprinklers, alarms, smoke detectors, security provisions, special storage requirements, means of escape, fire-fighting requirements, smoke control, refuse disposal and window cleaning and to note the effect of design decisions on such matters as future insurance requirements. To consider future maintenance and replacement of building fabric, finishes and services from the viewpoints of cost and practicality. To ensure that adequate access is provided to service installations for such maintenance and future replacement. To consider energy-saving measures.
    To ensure that the client is aware of developing design and specifications and that his approvals are obtained at the agreed stages of design and specification developments. To ensure at all times that all elements of design are properly co-ordinated and integrated within the master programme requirements and that the design fully takes into account the Offices, Shops, and Railway Premises Act, the Health, Safety and Welfare at Work,

etc., Act and other statutory requirements including Government circulars, Codes of Practice and relevant British Standards.

Monitoring of budget   Following completion of the initial conceptual design and master programme, to re-examine and revise the preliminary budget to produce a definitive budget for cost control purposes.

Costing   To establish costing systems to monitor the budget continuously in accordance with the feedback costs required by the client. To produce and update cash flow requirements.

Pre-ordering   To check on material availability and to initiate orders with the client's approval for long-delivery materials, plant and equipment in accordance with programming requirements. To monitor manufacturer's progress in design, fabrication and delivery.

Accounting   To establish accounting procedures and cost controls to cover the various stages of the project, i.e. planning and design, purchasing, construction costs, inspection and commissioning, and to co-ordinate contributions from all participants. At all times to monitor the project's viability on the client's behalf.

Planning permission and building regulations   To ensure that planning approval and building regulation approval is obtained in accordance with the programme requirements. To obtain building regulation waivers where necessary.

Contract documents   To compile all contract documents for the firm pricing and construction phase in accordance with the agreed policy regarding tendering and selection of contractors. To ensure that all quality control and testing requirements are clearly defined. To establish the client's requirements on such matters as liquidated damages, insurance requirements, performance or other bonds.

Contractor pre-qualification   If contractors are to pre-qualify, to obtain pre-qualification information from selected contractors well in advance of tender dates.

Selection   To produce a recommended list of contractors who will be invited to tender, and to send out tender documents to approved contractors.

Tender evaluation   To evaluate tenders received and to initiate the appointment of contractors. To see that the contract documents are properly executed before work starts on site. To ensure the contractor has complied with insurance and bonding requirements.

Site inspection   To ensure that adequate staff are available for the site management, inspection and quality control checking during the progress of works during the construction phase.

Construction phase

Monitoring of progress   To advise the contractor(s) of programme procedures and requirements. To arrange for all necessary feedback required and set out reporting procedures regarding progress. To ensure that potential delays are fully reported. To approve any subletting in accordance with the contract requirements. To monitor design information flow and client approvals and to ensure that programme requirements are being achieved.

Hoarding and existing site conditions   To ensure that the contractor erects hoardings and protection to other areas as specified and to record with the contractor the condition of adjacent buildings and surroundings, including pavings and roads.

Meetings   To set up regular progress meetings, with client, designers, contractors, sub-contractors and suppliers and to attend and chair such meetings as necessary.

Inspection of works   To co-ordinate, direct and inspect all construction work.

Certification of payment   To arrange for the work to be measured, valued and certified regularly and that payments are made to the contractor in accordance with contract requirements.

Safety   To ensure that site security and safety standards are maintained at all times.

Quality control and testing   To ensure that construction works are carried out in accordance with the specification and that quality control procedures, testing and other performance criteria are maintained, as set out in the contract document.

Anticipation   To identify problems with the contractor, to anticipate problems and to take such measures as are necessary to resolve these to the best advantage of the client.

Monitoring of budget and variation orders   To ensure that design information is produced in accordance with the master programme requirements and that variations are kept to a minimum. To establish procedures regarding the issuing of variations and their costing and feedback into the overall cost budget position, to produce costs-to-completion information on a regular basis and to ensure that the client is fully informed.

Training   If necessary, to arrange for the recruitment and training of personnel to operate the completed installation on behalf of the client.

Certification   To issue to the client's representative all certificates required under the conditions of contract.

Statutory undertakers   Where not the general contractor's responsibility, to place orders on behalf of the client and to ensure that all statutory undertakers carry out their works in accordance with master programme requirements.

Completion

Pre-commission   To ensure that all necessary pre-commissioning checks are carried out as necessary for the plant, equipment and buildings.

Final account   To ensure that all final accounts are dealt with in accordance with the contract conditions and that any claims are settled.

Commission   To assist the client in carrying out commissioning and to arrange for suppliers and contractors to put into operation such equipment and services necessary for the commissioning and any performance tests.

Manuals   To see that any necessary and agreed operating manuals, drawings and instructions are supplied to the client.

Defects liability period   To monitor the works during the defects liability period and to inspect at the expiration of this time. To release retentions on completion of any remedial works and to issue all necessary certificates in accordance with conditions of contract.

Feedback   Where appropriate, to advise the client of the final plant and machinery costs for grant and tax purposes and to assist in obtaining grants in accordance with the original brief.
    To supply final cost feedback information as required by the client.

Responsibilities
To the company in respect of the work

—   To determine and maintain clearly the objectives of the project as they relate to the individual contractor(s) and professional disciplines. To monitor achievement and to establish ongoing requirements that will satisfy the objectives of the project.
—   To ensure that the design development, whilst meeting the overall brief from the client, is undertaken in such a way that the work can be constructed as simply as possible and to set out to achieve an enhanced margin through this activity for the group.
—   To ensure that design information is obtained from the client and from the design team to enable proper evaluation of alternatives and proper quotations, when the method of product is finally agreed, so that there is no delay at any time to the effective progress on site and yet adequate time has been allowed to enable maximum economies to be effective.
—   To ensure that the quality of work and general control of the contractor(s) and professionals, and the project as a whole, is undertaken in such a way that the client has every confidence in recommending the group for subsequent work for that same client and to other clients to whom the company may refer to obtain a reference.
—   To ensure that the approach taken in design and construction produces a building

that offers integrity on completion and will not reappear as a cost burden on the client in remedial terms arising from short-term economic and building decisions.

- The project manager has full authority on behalf of the group for paying and controlling the performance of all professionals and contractor(s).

SUMMARY OF CHAPTER 14

(1) Project management is different from departmental management.

(2) The project manager must have an overall view of the work and fundamentally he is the guardian of the time scale and the expenditure. Nevertheless, with high-technology projects the project manager requires a technological background.

(3) The project manager is the custodian of project experience.

(4) The characteristics of a successful project manager include diplomacy, advocacy, proven ability in one aspect of the project, an appreciation of areas of work outside his specialist knowledge, an ability to direct and delegate in a multidisciplinary situation, and interest in financial, legal and entrepreneurial aspects of the project.

(5) The project manager must be able to implement and control change.

Bibliography

The following is a bibliography of books, articles and journals which have useful information for the project manager.

PRINCIPLES

Benningson, L.A. (1977) *Seeing beyond the blinding truths*, Booklet SIAR-E-39. Scandinavian Institute of Administrative Research.

Berger, M. (1969) If Noah build the ark today. *Management Review*, July, 2–8.

Boehm, B.W. (1988) *Software engineering economics*. Prentice-Hall, Englewood Cliffs, New Jersey.

Comparative project management (1969) *Proceedings of a Symposium on Large Projects, Proceedings, Institution of Mechanical Engineers, London,* **183**, Part 3K.

Cooper, D. and Chapman, C. (1987) *Risk analysis for large projects, models, methods and cases.* Wiley, Chichester, West Sussex.

Darnell, H, and Dale, M.W. (1983) *Total project management*. British Institute of Management.

Dunn, S.C. and Adams, F.J. (1967) Handing over design to the works. *Radio and Electronic Engineer,* **34** 209–216.

Gardner, J.B. (1973) Innovation through new ventures. *R & D Management,* **3**, 85–89.

Gehriger, H.. (1972) The ESTEC project control system. *Research Policy,* **1**, 274–295. (See also ESRO Reports SP-70 and SP-80.)

Hedger, E.F. (1968) Providing incentives for contractors. *Chartered Mechanical Engineer,* June, 251–253, 288.

Improving the time of construction of process plant, Proceedings of Conference (1973) Institution of Mechanical Engineers, London.

Kerzner, H. (1989) *Project management: a systems approach to planning, scheduling and controlling,* 3rd edn. Van Nostrand Reinhold, New York.

Knutton, H. (1972) The management of Army R & D project. *R & D Management,* **2,** 111–117.

Maieli, V. (1971) Management by hindsight, a diary of a project manager. *Management Review,* June, 5–14.

Morris, P.W.G. and Hugh, G.N. (1987) *The anatomy of major projects. A study of the reality of project management.* Wiley, Chichester, West Sussex.

Paton, T.A.L. (Chairman) (1970) *Large industrial construction sites,* Report of National Economic Development Office Working Party. HMSO, London.

Siddons, R.H. and Durnford, J. (1973) Engineering and construction of the British Steel Corporation's anchor project. *Journal of the Iron and Steel Institute,* April, 245–263.

Stone, R. (ed.) (1988) *Management of engineering projects.* Macmillan, Basingstoke.

Thompson, P.A. (1969) *The management of public works, Proceedings of Symposium.* University of Manchester Institute of Science and Technology, Manchester.

Thompson, P.A. (1983) Guidelines for project management. *Chartered Mechanical Engineer,* February, 37–38.

Turner, B.T. (1969) *Management training for engineers.* Business Books, pp. 280–303.

Turner, B.T. and Williams, M. (1983) *Management handbook for engineers and technologists.*

Walsh, M. and Wearne, S.H. (1981) Project management for R & D equipment. *R & D Management,* **11,** 123–125.

Wearne, S.H. (ed.) (1970) *Management and productivity of engineering site manpower, Proceedings of the MANPROD 70 Symposium* (also including summaries of 1967 symposium on cost control). University of Manchester Institute of Science and Technology, Manchester.

Wearne, S.H. and Cunningham, M.T. (eds) (1966) *Problems and efficiency in the management of engineering projects, Proceedings of a Joint Symposium.* University of Manchester Institute of Science and Technology, Manchester (out of print but available through interlibrary loan).

RESEARCH STUDIES

Allen, T.J. (1970) Communication networks. *R & D Management,* **1,** 14–21.

Burns, T. and Stalker, G.M. (1966) *The management of innovation,* 2nd edn. Tavistock Publications, London.

Gemmill, G.R., and Thamhain, H.J. (1973) The effectiveness of different power styles of project managers in gaining support. *IEEE Transactions on Engineering Management,* **EM-20,** 38–44.

Isenson, R.S. *et al.* (1969) *Project hindsight,* Final Report. Director of Defense Research and Engineering, Washington, DC.

Langrish, J., Gibbons, M., Evans, W.G., and Jevons, F.R. (1972) *Wealth from knowledge.* Macmillan, London.

Rubin, I.M., and Seelig, W. (1967) Experience as a factor in the selection and performance of project managers, *IEEE Transactions on Engineering Management,* **EM-14.**

Weltevreden, P.S. (1972) *Cost estimation and cost control of government sponsored nuclear and aerospace projects.* International Institute for the Management of Technology, Milan.

ORGANIZATION AND COMMUNICATIONS

Argyris, C. (1967) Today's problems with tomorrow's organisation. *Journal of Management Studies*, February, 48–55.

Da Vinci & Partners, Consulting Engineers – *An organization for discussion*, Report TMP 20 (1976). Technological Management, University of Bradford, Bradford.

Galbraith, J.R. (1971) Matrix organisation designs. *Business Horizons*, February, 29–40.

Johnson, J.K. (1984) Organization structures and the development project planning sequence. *Publication Administration and Development*, 4, 111–131.

Knight, K.W. (1977) *Matrix management*. Gower, London.

Miller, E.J. and Rice, A.K. (1967). *Systems of organisation*. Tavistock Publications, London.

Morris, P.W.G. (1979) Interface management. *Project Management Quarterly*, **10**, 27–37.

Organ, D.W. and Greene, C.N. (1973) The boundary relevance of the project manager's job. *R & D Management*, **3**, 7–11.

Turner, B.T. (1983) Project engineering and the need for good communication. *Chartered Mechanical Engineer*, June, 36–38.

Wearne, S.H. (1973) *Principles of engineering organisation*. Arnold. (With further references.)

Wilemon, D.L., and Cicero, J.P. (1970) The project manager—anomalies and ambiguities. *Academy of Management Journal*, September, 269–282.

TECHNIQUES

Block, E.B. (1971) Accomplishment/cost: better project control. *Harvard Business Review*, May–June, 110–124.

Howell, R.A. (1968) Multiproject control. *Harvard Business Review*, March–April, 63–70.

Holden, E., and McIlroy, P.K. (1970) *Network planning in management control systems*. Hutchinson, London.

Leech, D.J., and Turner, B.T. (1985) *Engineering design for profit*, Ellis Horwood, Chichester, West Sussex.

Lowe, G.W. (1973) *Project control by critical path analysis*, Business Books.

McLaren, K.G., and Buesnel, E.S. (1969) *Network analysis in project management*. Cassell, London (An introductory manual based upon Unilever experience.)

Mulvaney, J. (1969) *Analysis bar charting*. World Bank.

Operational Research Society and Institute of Cost & Works Accountants (1969) *Project control using networks*. Operational Research Society.

Peart, A.T. (1971) *Design of project management systems and records*. Gower, London.

Royal Navy (1973) *The new guide to development documentation system*, 3rd edn. H.M.S. Collingwood, Fareham, Hampshire.

Ruskin, A.M., and Estes, W.E. (1984) The project management audit. *Engineering Management International*, **2**, 279–286.

Staffurth, C. (1980) *Project control using networks*, 2nd edn. Institute of Cost and Management Accountants.

Turner, B.T. (1973) *Managing design*. Manlec.

Turner, B.T. (1973) Creativity in engineering—an overview of some methodologies of engineering design work. *CEI Paper*, No. 4.

Turner, W.S. (1980) *Project auditing methodology*. North-Holland, Amsterdam.

GENERAL TEXTBOOKS

Brech, E.F.L. (ed.) (1971) *Construction management in principle and practice.* Longmars, Harlow, Essex.

Brichta, A.M., and Sharp, P.E.M. (1970) *From project to production.* Pergamon, Oxford.

Cleland, D.I., and King, W.R. (1968) *Systems analysis and project management.* McGraw-Hill, New York.

Harrison, F.L. (1981) *Advanced project management.* Gower, London.

Horgan, M.O'C, and Roulston, F.R. (1988) *Project control of engineering contracts.* E. & F.N. Spon, London.

Kharbanda, O.P. *et al.* (1980) *Project cost control in action.* Gower, London.

Lock, D. (1977) *Project management*, 2nd edn. Gower, London.

Pilcher, R. (1982) *Appraisal and control of project costs*, 2nd edn. Waveland Press.

Rayner Committee (1970) *Government organisation for defence procurement and civil aerospace.* HMSO, London.

Silverman, M. (1967) *The technical program manager's guide to survival.* Wiley, Chichester, West Sussex.

Snowden, M. (1977) *Management of engineering projects.* Newnes, London.

Taylor, W.J., and Watling, T.F. (1970) *Successful project management.* Business Books.

Twiss, B.C. (1980) *Managing technological innovation*, 2nd edn. Longmans, Harlow, Essex.

CONTRACTS

Boyce, T. (1990) *The Commercial Engineer*, Hawksmere.

Horgan, M.O'C (1989) *Competitive tendering for engineering contracts.* E. & F.N. Spon, London.

Johnston, K.F.A. (1971) *Electrical and mechanical engineering contracts.* Gower, London.

Marsh, P.D.V. (1969) *Contracting for engineering and construction projects.* Gower, London.

Marsh, P.D.V. (1984) *Contract negotiation handbook*, 2nd edn. Gower, London.

Scott, P. (1974) *The commercial management of engineering contracts.* Gower, London.

Scott, W.P. (1981) *The skill of negotiating.* Gower, London.

Wearne, S.H. (1984) Contractual responsibilities for the design of engineering plants: a survey of practice and problems. *Proceedings, Institution of Mechanical Engineers, London*, **198B**, 97–108.

TEACHING

Lawrence, J.K. (1972) Project management, a relevant option in business schools. *Management Education and Development*, 3, Part 1, 63–73.

Remma Ltd (1971) *Project management course* (Rediffusion education tape and manual course.)

Wearne, S.H. (1965) Towards a science of project management. *New Scientist*, 15 July 162–163.

THE ROLES OF PROJECT MANAGERS

Gemmill, G.R., and Thamhain, H.J. (1973) The effectiveness of different power styles of project managers in gaining support. *IEEE Transactions on Engineering Management*, **EM-20**, 38–44.

Maeli, V. (1971) A diary of a project manager. *Management Review*, June, 5–14.

Management of an urgent public works project, Report TMR 4 (1975). Technological Management, University of Bradford, Bradford.

Organ, D.W., and Greene, C.N. (1973) The boundary relevance of the project manager's job. *R & D Management*, **3**, 7–11.

Owen, L. (1960) Management in engineering. *Proceedings of the Institution of Civil Engineers*, **17**, 219–225.

Rubin, I.M., and Seelig, W. (1967) Experience as a factor in the selection and performance of project managers. *IEEE Transactions on Engineering Management*, **EM-14**, 131–135.

Thamhain, H.J., and Wilemon, D.L. (1977) Leadership effectiveness in project management. *IEEE Transactions on Engineering Management*, **EM-24**, 102–108.

Wearne, S.H. (1984) The project doctor. *International Journal of Project Management*, **2**, 89–90.

RELATED BIBLIOGRAPHY

Management, a continuing literature survey with indexes, Special Publication NASA-SP-7500. National Aeronautics and Space Administration. (Series from March 1968.) (Available in UK on loan from the National Lending Library, Boston Spa.)

INTERNATIONAL CONTRACTS

Guide to using and placing turnkey contracts. UNIDO.

Kolrud, H.J. *et al.* (1979) *North Sea offshore construction contracts.* Federation of Norwegian Industries.

Sawyer, J.G., and Gilbert, C.A. (1981) *The FIDIC conditions; digest of contractual relationships and responsibilities.* Thomas Telford.

STANDARDS

Leader of major projects, administrative policy manual. Treasury Board, Canada, Chapter 141.

Terms used in project network techniques, British Standard 4335 (1987).

Use of network techniques in project management, British Standard 6046, Part 1 (1984), Part 2 (1981), Part 3 (1981), Part 4 (1984).

JOURNALS

Engineering Economist. Institute of Industrial Engineers, 25 Technology Park, Nercross, GA 30092, USA.

IEEE Transactions on Engineering Management. IEEE Publishing Services, 345 East 47th Street, New York, NY 10017, USA.

The International Journal of Project Management. (Quarterly.)

PM network. Project Management Institute, P.O. Box 43, Drescel Hill, PA 19026, USA.

Project. The bulletin of the Association of Project Managers.

Project Appraisal, Cost Benefit, Impact Assessment, Risk Analysis, Technology Assessment. Beech Tree Publishing, 10 Watford Close, Guildford, GU1 2EP, Surrey, UK.

Project Management Journal. Project Management Institute, P.O. Box 43, Drescel Hill, Pennsylvania 19026, USA.

Project Management Today. P.O. Box 55, Wokingham, RG11 4XN, Berkshire, UK.

ADDITIONAL ENTRIES

Baumgartner, J.S. (1963) *Project management.* Irwin.

Davies, D. (1967) *An introduction to technological economics.* Wiley, Chichester, West Sussex.

Groueff, S. (1967) *Manhattan project.* Collins, London.

Hajek, V.G. (1965) *Project engineering.* McGraw-Hill, New York.

Jonason, P. (1971) Project management Swedish style. *Harvard Business Review*, November–December, 104–109.

Pilcher, R. (1973) *Appraisal and control of project costs.* McGraw-Hill, New York.

Pilcher, R. (1985) *Project cost control in construction.* Collins, London.

Report of the steering group on development cost estimating, Vols I and II (1969). HMSO, London.

Staffurth, C. (1969) *Project cost control using networks.* Operational Research Society.

Steiner, G.A. (1968) *Industrial project management.* Macmillan, London.

Symposium on Project Management and Incentive Contracting Procedures, Management Study Group of Royal Aeronautical Society (January 1969).

Walker, A. (1985) *Project management in construction.* Collins, London.

PROJECT MANAGEMENT SOFTWARE

Over 60 project management software packages are available. For an exhaustive list of these refer to the following.

(1) *PC Yearbook.* VNU Business Publications, VNU House, 32–34 Broadwick Street, London, W1A 2HG.

(2) *The Software Users Year Book.* VNU Business Publications, VNU House, 32–34 Broadwick Street, London, W1A 2HG.

It should be noted that there is a wide range of facilities which are available in different packages. The most basic allow for planning single projects only; others allow for planning and monitoring single projects, and the most comprehensive allows for planning and monitoring multiple projects. Some include a database for recording costs; most do not. Some use the activity-on node convention, and others the activity-on-arrow conventions in the critical path method. A few use the acronym PERT in their names as a reference to the fact that they use the activity-on-node convention, although they may not apply the true PERT approach of requiring three estimates for duration. A package which is easy to learn because of step-by-step guidance through menus may become irritating to use when the user becomes familiar with it, because of the need to follow through every step. Great care must, therefore, be exercised when choosing a project management package.

The following packages have been used by the authors.

(1) Harvard Total Project Managment.
(2) Superproject.
(3) Pertmaster Advance.
(4) Project Planner.
(5) Hornet.

It is, however, difficult to comment on their qualities, except in the general terms used above, because designers continually improve their programs and improvements are incorporated into later editions.

Index